The Church in the Long Eighteenth Century

THE I.B.TAURIS HISTORY OF THE CHRISTIAN CHURCH
GENERAL EDITOR: G.R. EVANS

The Early Church
Morwenna Ludlow, University of Exeter

The Church in the Early Middle Ages
G.R. Evans, University of Cambridge

The Church in the Later Middle Ages
Norman Tanner, Gregorian University, Rome

Early Modern Christianity
to be confirmed

The Church in the Long Eighteenth Century
David Hempton, Harvard University

The Church in the Nineteenth Century
Frances Knight, University of Wales, Lampeter

The Church in the Modern Age
Jeremy Morris, University of Cambridge

The Church in the Long Eighteenth Century

David Hempton

I.B. TAURIS
LONDON · NEW YORK

Published in 2011 by I.B.Tauris & Co. Ltd
6 Salem Road, London W2 4BU
175 Fifth Avenue, New York, NY 10010
www.ibtauris.com

Distributed in the United States and Canada Exclusively by Palgrave Macmillan
175 Fifth Avenue, New York, NY 10010

Vol 1: *The Early Church*   978 1 84511 366 7
Vol 2: *The Church in the Early Middle Ages*   978 1 84511 150 2
Vol 3: *The Church in the Later Middle Ages*   978 1 84511 438 1
Vol 4: *Early Modern Christianity*   978 1 84511 439 8
Vol 5: *The Church in the Long Eighteenth Century*   978 1 84511 440 4
Vol 6: *The Church in the Nineteenth Century*   978 1 85043 899 1
Vol 7: *The Church in the Modern Age*   978 1 84511 317 9

A full CIP record for this book is available from the British Library
A full CIP record for this book is available from the Library of Congress
Library of Congress Catalog Card Number: available

Typeset in Adobe Caslon Pro by A. & D. Worthington, Newmarket, Suffolk
Printed and bound by CPI Group (UK) Ltd, Croydon, CR0 4YY

THE I.B.TAURIS HISTORY OF THE CHRISTIAN CHURCH

Since the first disciples were sent out by Jesus, Christianity has been of its essence a missionary religion. That religion has proved to be an ideology and a subversive one. Profoundly though it became 'inculturated' in the societies it converted, it was never syncretistic. It had, by the twentieth century, brought its own view of things to the ends of the earth. The Christian Church, first defined as a religion of love, has interacted with Judaism, Islam and other world religions in ways in which there has been as much warfare as charity. Some of the results are seen in the tensions of the modern world, tensions which are proving very hard to resolve – not least because of a lack of awareness of the history behind the thinking which has brought the Church to where it is now.

In the light of that lack, a new history of the Christian Church is badly needed. There is much to be said for restoring to the general reader a familiarity with the network of ideas about what the Church 'is' and what it should be 'doing' as a vessel of Christian life and thought. This series aims to be both fresh and traditional. It will be organized so that the boundary-dates between volumes fall in some unexpected places. It will attempt to look at its conventional subject matter from the critical perspective of the early twenty-first century, where the Church has a confusing myriad of faces. Behind all these manifestations is a rich history of thinking, effort and struggle. And within it, at the heart of matters, is the Church. *The I.B.Tauris History of the Christian Church* seeks to discover that innermost self through the layers of its multiple manifestations over twenty centuries.

SERIES EDITOR'S PREFACE

Against the background of global conflict involving interfaith resentments and misunderstandings, threatening 'religious wars' on a scale possibly unprecedented in history, Christians and the Christian Church are locked in internal disputes. On 2 November 2003, a practising homosexual was made a bishop in the Episcopal Church in the United States, America's 'province' of the Anglican Communion. This was done in defiance of the strong opinion in other parts of the 'Communion' that if it happened Anglicanism would fall apart into schism. A few years earlier there had been similar rumblings over the ordination of women to ministry in the same Church. A century before that period, the Roman Catholic Church had pronounced all Anglican ordination to the priestly or episcopal ministry to be utterly null and void because of an alleged breach of communion and continuity in the sixteenth century. And the Orthodox Churches watched all this in the secure conviction that Roman Catholic, Anglican and all other Christian communities were not communions at all because they had departed from the truth as it had been defined in the ecumenical Councils of the first few centuries. Orthodoxy alone was orthodox. Even the baptism of other Christians was of dubious validity.

Those heated by the consecration of a 'gay' bishop spoke on the one side of faithfulness to the teaching of the Bible and on the other of the leading of the Holy Spirit into a new world which knew no discrimination. Yet both the notion of faithfulness to Scripture and the idea that Jesus particularly wanted to draw the outcasts and disadvantaged to himself have a long and complex history which makes it impossible to make either statement in simple black-and-white terms.

One of the most significant factors in the frightening failures of communication and goodwill which make daily headlines is a loss of contact with the past on the part of those taking a stand on one side or another of such disagreements. The study of 'history' is fashionable as this series is launched, but the colourful narrative of past lives and episodes does not necessarily make familiar the patterns of thought and assumption in the minds of those involved. A modern history of the Church must embody that awareness in every sinew. Those embattled in disputes within the Church and disputes involving Christian and other-faith communities have tended to take their stand on principles they claim to be of eternal validity, and to represent the will of God. But as they appear in front of television cameras or speak to journalists the accounts they give – on either side – frequently reflect a lack of knowledge of the tradition they seek to protect or to challenge.

The creation of a new history of the Church at the beginning of the third millennium is an ambitious project, but it is needed. The cultural, social and political dominance of Christendom in what we now call 'the West' during the first two millennia made the Christian Church a shaper of the modern world in respects which go far beyond its strictly religious influence. Since the first disciples were sent out to preach the Gospel by Jesus, Christianity has been of its essence a missionary religion. It took the faith across the world in a style which has rightly been criticized as 'imperialist'. Christianity has proved to be an ideology and a subversive one. Profoundly though it became 'inculturated' in the societies converted, it was never syncretistic in the sense that it was willing to merge or compromise with other religions. It had, by the twentieth century, brought its own view of things to the ends of the earth. The Christian Church, first defined as a religion of love, has interacted with Judaism, Islam and the other world religions in ways in which there has been as much warfare as charity. We see some of the results in tensions in the modern world which are now proving very hard to resolve, not least because of the sheer failure of awareness of the history of the thinking which has brought the Church to where it is now.

Such a history has of course purposes more fundamental, more positive, more universal, but no less timely. There may not be a danger of the loss of the full picture while the libraries of the world and its historic buildings and pictures and music preserve the evidence. But the connecting thread in living minds is easily broken. There is much to be said for restoring as familiar to the general reader, whether Christian or not, a command of the sequence and network of ideas about what the Church *is* and what it should be *doing* as a vessel of Christian thought and life.

This new series aims, then, to be both new and traditional. It is organized so that the boundary-dates between volumes come in some unexpected places. It attempts to look at the conventional subject matter of histories of the Church from the vantage-point of the early twenty-first century, where the Church has confusingly many faces: from Vatican strictures on the use of birth-control and the indissolubility of marriage, and the condemnation of outspoken German academic theologians who challenge the Churches' authority to tell them what to think and write, to the enthusiasm of Black Baptist congregations in the USA joyously affirming a faith with few defining parameters. Behind all these variations is a history of thought and effort and struggle. And within, at the heart of matters, is the Church. It is to be discovered in its innermost self through the layers of its multiple manifestations over twenty centuries. That is the subject of this series.

Contents

In Memory of William Reginald Ward
(1925–2010)

With gratitude to
Alonzo L. McDonald

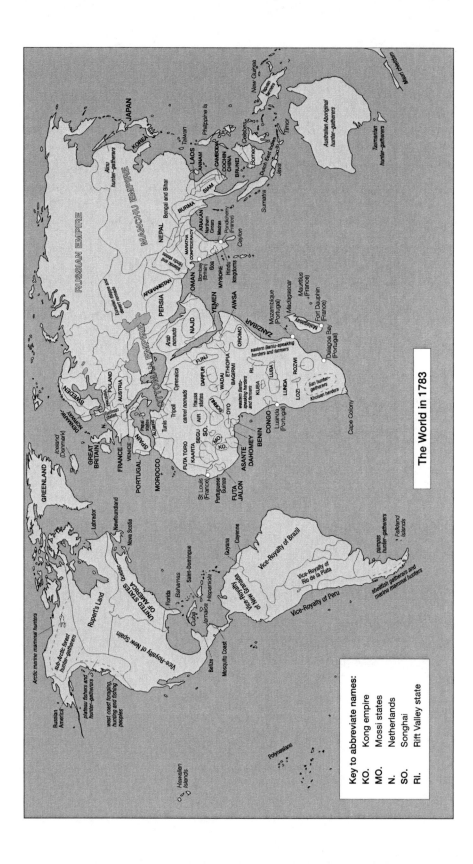

The World in 1783

Key to abbreviate names:
KO.   Kong empire
MO.   Mossi states
N.   Netherlands
SO.   Songhai
RI.   Rift Valley state

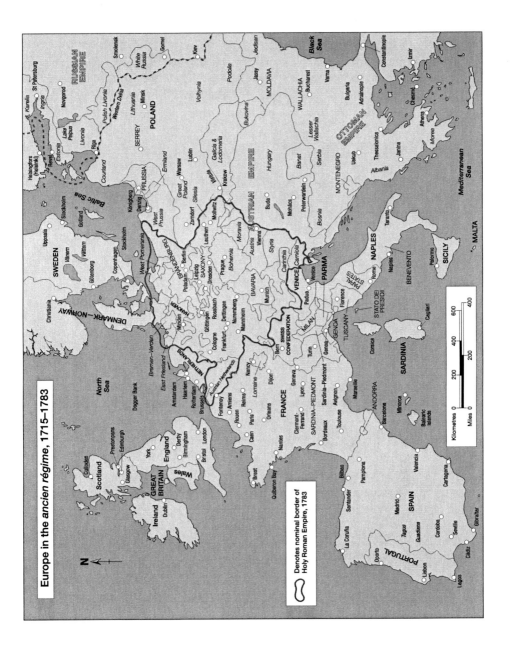

Europe in the *ancien régime*, 1715–1783

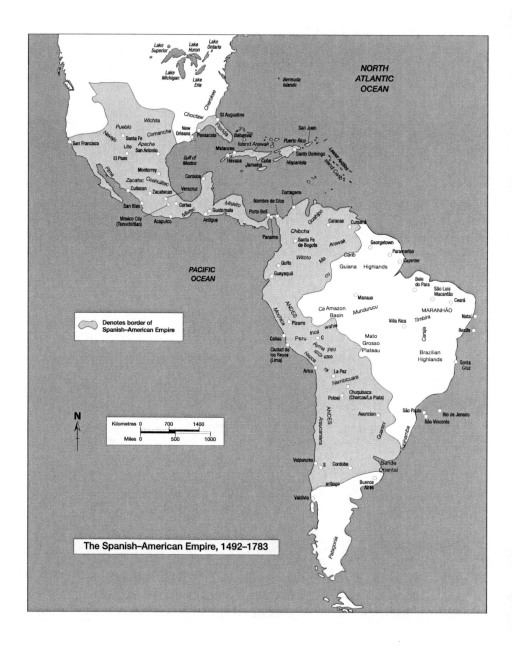

The Spanish–American Empire, 1492–1783

Preface

Writing a general history of worldwide Christianity in the long eighteenth century (*c.*1680–1820) is both a sacred responsibility and a fool's errand. Even a cursory list of some of the century's great themes and events is an indication of the foolhardiness of the project. These include the Enlightenment, Pietism, the Evangelical Revival, the growth of empires, the zenith (and the beginnings of the demise of) the transatlantic slave trade, the spring shoots of religious toleration, the beginning of the end of the great era of reforms of Catholic Christianity inspired by the Council of Trent, the Orthodox mission to extend Christianity throughout Russia and Asia, the religious implications of the American and French Revolutions, the grand era of baroque Catholicism in Latin America, the remarkable narrative of the rise of black Christianity in Africa, the Caribbean islands and North America, the demise of the Jesuits after two centuries of world-transforming Christian mission, the increasingly global religious competition between Christianity and Islam, the early imprints of secularization of land, thought, and states, and so on, and so on.

My first debt, therefore, is to those who have pioneered these manifold subjects and written about them with such distinction. In the interests of readability, I have tried to simplify very complicated debates and to limit endnotes to direct quotations and to places where unacknowledged reliance on the work of others would be simply unacceptable. I am grateful also to the editors of Yale University Press for permission to reproduce a short section from my book *Methodism: Empire of the Spirit.*

My second debt, more concretely, is to my colleagues and students at Boston University, Harvard, and beyond, whose profound insights are responsible for much of what follows. In terms of colleagues I am particularly grateful to the late Reginald Ward who first taught me to conceive of the world beyond the British Isles, to Dana Robert who gave me crash courses on Christian missions, and to the participants over many years in the North American Religions Colloquium at Harvard (Ann Braude, Marie Griffith, David Hall, Bill Hutchison, Dan McKanan, Bob Orsi, Jon

Roberts, Leigh Schmidt, and many others) whose expertise in the history of religion has rubbed off in incalculable ways. Similarly with Michelle Molina, who helped me understand the Catholic version of the 'religion of the heart' in the early modern period in fresh ways. In terms of students, I am particularly grateful to my graduate students at Boston University and Harvard, the early risers who took my course on 'Encountering the Other', and most importantly my three student research assistants – Matt Dougherty, Sonia Hazard and Dana Logan – who frequently outshone their teacher in the fine arts of historical research. In addition, David Hall, Brian Clark and Matt Dougherty generously read the manuscript and saved me from some inaccuracies and many infelicities. All remaining flaws are my responsibility alone.

My third debt is to the people and institutions that have facilitated the research for this book, including Alonzo L. McDonald for his generosity, Harvard Divinity School for granting me sabbatical leave, the Center for the Study of World Religions at Harvard for awarding me a timely research grant, and the National Endowment of the Humanities which believed enough in the project to award me an annual Fellowship. I am also grateful to the librarians and staff at Harvard's great libraries, the jewel in the crown of the university, especially those at the Andover, Widener, Yenching, Tozzer, Lamont and Fine Arts libraries. This book would be much more limited in scope but for all of these kindnesses. I am also very grateful, far more than mere conventions dictate, to the series editor Gillian Evans and Alex Wright at I.B.Tauris for asking me to write this book and for putting up with my extravagant requests for extensions.

Finally, I wish to thank again my longsuffering family, for their interest, sometimes genuine, in my latest writing fads, and especially to Stephen and Jonney for their sense of humour, and Louanne, who plays the roles of editor and intelligent general reader with remarkable patience and distinction.

David Hempton
Harvard Divinity School

Introduction

How should one go about writing a history of Christianity in the long eighteenth century, from about the 1680s to the 1820s? This deceptively simple question is really not very easy to answer. All the obvious caveats apply. The most basic problem concerns perspective. All historians, alas, come with a pre-existing ethnicity, language, gender, social class, religious tradition, scholarly expertise and, perhaps most significantly, acreages of ignorance and piles of unexamined assumptions. Where one stands and when one looks, for good and ill, largely determines what one sees. Moreover, the eighteenth century is a long time, the world is a big place and Christianity is a complex, fragmented and constantly changing religious tradition. One polymath historian who wisely confined himself to writing a mere survey of European Christianity in this period conceded that 'a God's-eye view or even a pan-continental perspective is out of reach' and that the basic historiographical and anthropological foundations for understanding the popular religious observances and lived-religious experiences of Europeans were simply not in place.[1]

Without the benefit of 'a God's-eye view', writing survey histories or even constructing course syllabi are dangerous occupations. Those teachers like me who tweak their syllabi from year to year in the light of new knowledge (both absolutely new and more often merely new to them), and who are foolish enough to keep records of the different editions, can testify how steep their learning curve has been and how fortunate they are that syllabi mostly do not get published. Survey histories do, but the same principles of provisionality, selectivity, incomplete knowledge, enforced reliance on the established literature and vulnerability to the fads of the discipline sadly apply.

One way of reducing the occupational danger of survey history is to survey the history of surveys, mostly so as not to repeat both what has already been accomplished and what has been neglected, but also to learn from the choices of others. One of the most distinguished and enduring surveys of the history of Christianity is the *Pelican History of the Church*, the eighteenth-century volume of which was written by Gerald R. Cragg, published in 1960, and revised in 1970. Taking as his starting point the Peace of Westphalia which brought to an end the Thirty Years' War, and ending with the French Revolution, Cragg's main theme was captured by his title, *The Church and the Age of Reason 1648–1789*. Of his 16 chapters, the great majority deal with the history of Christianity in Britain, France and Germany with particular emphases on the relationships between states and churches, and changes in the history of thought and culture. From this perspective, Cragg appropriately portrays the era as one of a crisis of authority for the churches as they confronted unprecedented challenges from rulers, intellectual elites and popular democratic forces. Cragg's survey still stands as an elegant tribute to how the history of eighteenth-century Christianity was conceptualized about half a century ago.[2]

Things have changed fast since then. Generic shifts in intellectual culture associated with post-colonialism, postmodernism and feminism have changed the assumptions and methods of historical discourse of all kinds. The maturing of religious studies as a discipline has opened up new approaches to the study of religious history, and the stunning shift in the centre of gravity of world Christianity in the twentieth century from the north and west to the south and east has made it impossible any longer to envision the history of Christianity as a purely, or even primarily, European phenomenon.[3] It is not surprising therefore, that *teams* of scholars have written many of the best recent surveys of the history of Christianity. Excellent examples include *The Oxford Illustrated History of Christianity*, *The Cambridge History of Christianity* and *A World History of Christianity*.[4] Paralleling this development has been the production of magisterial surveys of Christianity in precisely those parts of the world that have contributed most to the global shift in Christianity's centre of gravity over the past century. Good examples include Adrian Hastings, *The Church in Africa 1450–1950* (1994), Samuel Hugh Moffett, *A History of Christianity in Asia* (2005) and Ondina E. González and Justo L. González, *Christianity in Latin America: A History* (2008).

With these works in place it is paradoxically more difficult for any scholar to set out on a fresh survey history of Christianity for any period, but perhaps especially for the modern periods. Why not simply construct an encyclopaedia or an annotated bibliography and point readers in the right direction to publications already in existence? There have been many occasions in the writing of this book when that seemed a very appealing option. What kept me going were the ringing declarations in the editor's preface to this series that any new survey of the history of Christianity must be both new and traditional, familiar and unfamiliar; must accept that

Christianity has been both imperialist and subversive; must pay attention both to the past's complexities and to the ways that Christianity has shaped the present; and must recognize at the most profound level that Christianity is in its essence a missionary religion. I have learned over the years that all historians of Christianity must in some way become missiologists, of the kind that take seriously the restless energy in Christianity (often suffused with millennialism) to carry out its founder's instructions to carry the faith to all nations. These then have been the principles upon which I have gone about the most difficult intellectual challenge involved in the writing of survey history, namely making choices about what to include and exclude within the confines of a strict word limit. Of course, as someone has put it, all expansive histories are necessarily catalogues of omissions, both conscious and unconscious. Alas, that simply comes with the territory.

This history is organized around two major categories – Book One deals with the expansion of Christendom and Book Two with the transformation of Christendom. The first emphasizes growth and geographical extension beyond Europe to other parts of the world; the second emphasizes change, mostly within Europe, which had the highest density of Christians in the eighteenth century. The second book contains material that is more familiar and can be read independently (or even first if necessary).

The first chapter seeks to answer three questions. Suppose an interplanetary professor of religion visited the earth in the eighteenth century. What would she most notice about the shape and extent of world Christianity? Second, given that Europe was still the continent in which most of the world's Christians lived in the eighteenth century how did Europeans 'map' other civilizations and how did they think about the non-Christian religious traditions of the world? Third, given that Christian expansion in the early modern period was partly facilitated by the growth of European empires, both Catholic and Protestant, what was the relationship between Christianity and empire?

The second chapter, 'Heart Religion and the Rise of Global Christianity: New Selves and New Places', is in the nature of an experiment. The pioneers of Christian missions in the early modern world were, generally speaking, the members of the great Roman Catholic orders, especially the Jesuits, and German Pietists and early Evangelicals who blazed the trail of Protestant missions. Why and how did they do it? What spiritual disciplines and modes of thought persuaded them to launch out into new social spaces to convert new (to them) peoples? What views of themselves and of self-transformation, both for themselves and of the 'others' they were seeking to change, did they hold, and how successful were they in propagating those views?

The third chapter, 'Encountering the Other', is an attempt to come to grips with the history of the expansion of Christendom through the telling of stories about seminal events and people, chosen because they illustrate the most important themes about the spread of Christianity in the eighteenth century. My chosen events happened in China, India and Latin America; the people were situated in the Caribbean islands, North America and West Africa. The themes they highlight are: the power dynamics involved in the encounters between European Christians and native peoples; the kinds of Christian hybridities that emerged from such encounters; the difficulties involved in determining what was the essence of Christianity as it was exposed to different cultural contexts; the importance of population mobility, especially that associated with the execrable slave trade which carried millions of Africans to the New World on the ships of the Christian empires; the significance of changing political, ecclesiastical and intellectual currents in Europe on the kind of Christianity that was exported overseas; and the ways in which native peoples appropriated, modified, subverted, converted to and resisted the Christianities that were brought to them.

Book Two is a deliberate shift of gear away from the *expansion* of Christendom to its *transformation* in Europe and beyond. Chapter 4 deals with the array of intellectual and cultural shifts we have designated with the hotly contested term 'Enlightenment'. What was being enlightened and what were the consequences for current and future expressions of Christianity? I wish to be clear that I am not advocating here any meta-narrative of progress or decline or anything else; rather, in a case by case way, I seek to explain the convoluted and haphazard roots of some of the most important changes associated with Christianity's dance with modernity such as the growth of religious toleration and the abolition of slavery, as well as saying something about the respective impacts of the rise of science, the alleged beginnings of secularization and the challenges posed to traditional Christian theology by new knowledge. These are of course controversial issues and my modest aim is to attempt some ground clearing and some elementary construction of possibilities. Those looking for a linear or teleological approach to these issues had better start somewhere else.

Chapter 5 seeks to explain that other great shaper of Christianity in the eighteenth century, namely the remarkable surge in religious revivalism and Evangelicalism from the Urals in the East to the Appalachians in the West, which helped transform the ecclesiastical landscape of the British Isles and North America, and which laid the foundation for the remarkable growth of Anglo-American overseas missions from the eighteenth century onwards. From where did revivalism emanate, and why did it transcend state boundaries to become such a widespread phenomenon? This chapter also seeks to come to terms with the rise of the most significant new religious movement birthed by the Evangelical Revival, Methodism. Who were the Methodists, what did they believe, and why were they more successful than countless other Pietist and revivalist religious movements in the eighteenth century?

Chapter 6 seeks to highlight and explain different patterns of relations between church and state in the eighteenth century which came to have immense influence on the future shape of Christianity. It will look at how traditional pockets of Catholic strength in countries like Ireland and Poland came to be established; it will explore how reforming monarchs and enlightened absolutists tried to subject churches to state control and ordering; it will seek to explain how Russian tsars, beginning with Peter I, tried to subordinate the Orthodox Church's political power and exploit its material wealth; it will look at how the United States of America broke free from the traditional pattern of Christianizing the people by means of established churches and experimented with the separation of church and state; and it will investigate the forces that were undermining religious establishments, albeit with different consequences, in France and Britain in the era of the French Revolution. It will conclude with an assessment of the impact of revolutions, primarily the American and the French – the great shock events of the eighteenth century – on Christianity in the modern era.

As you will see from these choices, this book is not ordered around specific religious traditions – Protestant, Catholic or Orthodox – nor does it employ a strictly chronological or regional approach. Still less has it adopted an encyclopaedic method with potted accounts of the most important things that happened in the eighteenth century. Part of the reason for not going down those roads is the blessed assurance that fine examples of such work already exist and I saw no realistic prospect of improving upon them. What follows then is a combination of story, analysis and interpretation, which seeks to penetrate to the heart of some of the most important themes in world Christianity in *the long eighteenth century*. Expressing chronology in such imprecise ways is also a risky business. When I used a similar phrase in a previous book one witty reviewer responded by stating that I had a Salvador Dalí propensity to melt time. Surreal and melting clocks notwithstanding, the reason for adopting this way of thinking about chronology is not only an act of obedience to my editors, but also a sober recognition that when 20 centuries of Christianity are condensed into seven volumes the arithmetic necessarily produces untidy results.

BOOK ONE

THE EXPANSION OF
CHRISTENDOM

CHAPTER I

Surveying the Contours:
Maps, Travels and Empires

Conceptualizing the scope and extent of global Christianity in the eighteenth century is no easy matter. As we saw in the introduction, the 'God's eye view' is, alas, not available to mere mortals. Perhaps the next best thing is to imagine a long-living, scholarly space visitor – a Professor of Comparative Interplanetary Religions perhaps – who is able to get grants to visit different parts of the world over the course of the entire century to carry out a research project on world Christianity.[1] What would have been the most striking aspects of the history of Christianity from around 1680 to 1820 for someone with no established presuppositions and no previous engagement with the debates about the fate of Christianity in the age of Enlightenment and revolutions? Such an exercise will test our customary assumptions that Christianity is a Western, even a Western European, religion. If not in the earliest and the most recent centuries of the Common Era, when all agree that Christianity is anything but a predominantly Western religious tradition, we take for granted that, in between these two periods, Christianity was rooted and minted in Europe. Therefore, for most Europeans it represents something of a stretch to view early modern Christianity even in a transatlantic, never mind a global perspective. Yet perhaps the most striking aspect of early modern Christianity is its geographical reach to surprisingly large parts of the world.

What then would our visiting professor be expected to find if she were able to make multiple site visits to Christian spaces in the decades from the 1680s to the 1820s? We might expect her to begin in Europe with some of the better-known and most influential places in the evolution of the Christian tradition. She would notice immediately that the rupture caused by the sixteenth-century Protestant Reformation was far from healed and that Europe was deeply divided by religious geography and religious tradition. Various forms of Reformation Protestantism were dominant in the countries of Northern and Western Europe, including England, Scotland, Wales,

Denmark, Sweden, the Netherlands, Switzerland and the various states and principalities of northern Germany. Roman Catholicism remained in the ascendancy in much of Southern and Eastern Europe, including Portugal, Spain, France, Italy, most of southern Germany, the Habsburg Empire and Poland. But she would soon have discovered that the religious map of Europe was much more complicated than this bald summary indicates. Europe contained a bewildering cluster of small states and principalities many of which changed confessional allegiance in the eighteenth century and had substantial religious minorities within their borders. To the east lay Russia, which was largely Orthodox, but had substantial Catholic and Muslim minorities. To the south-east lay the largely Muslim and, after 1683, shrinking Ottoman Empire, which also had substantial Catholic and Orthodox minorities.

If our professor was researching Protestantism at the start of our period, she might begin with constructing an ethnographic study of the French Huguenot refugees who were forced out of France by the revocation of the Edict of Nantes in 1685 when Louis XIV, the Sun King, brought in some dark clouds of confessional cleansing. A decade later she might show up in London when England apparently forsook Stuart Catholic absolutism, or so the Protestant narrative goes, and Parliament passed an Act of Toleration (1689) conferring a measure of religious toleration for Trinitarian Protestant dissenters. Roman Catholics and non-Trinitarians were nevertheless excluded, showing that religious toleration, one of the apparent benefits of modernity, was a limited possibility only under certain defined conditions in some parts of Europe, but was still almost non-existent in most of early modern Europe.

If she had an eye for the future shapers of Protestant Christianity our professor might have found herself in one of Philipp Jakob Spener's (1635–1705) classes (the original small groups of Protestant spirituality) in Frankfurt or reading his *Pia Desideria* (1675), which set the tone for the 'religion of the heart' that later so much infused the spirituality of Pietism, Methodism, American Evangelicalism and global Pentecostalism. She might also have made her way to the University of Halle where August Hermann Francke (1663–1727), one of Spener's avid admirers, set about creating a set of institutions in the spirit of his *Great Project for a Universal Improvement in all Social Orders* (1704). In support of this scarcely modest vision, Francke established at Halle an Orphan House, a dispensary, schools and teacher-training institutions and a Bible Institute. Orphanage houses became ubiquitous institutions in the global spread of Protestantism and Francke's dispensary was the world's first producer of standardized branded medicaments on a commercial scale. Through his formidable correspondence and network of contacts, Francke's influence extended into the emergent Prussian state of Frederick the Great (1712–86) and spread internationally through German migrations and through the formation of the first organized Protestant overseas missions in Tranquebar in India.[2]

Still with an eye to the future development of Protestant forms of Christianity our professor might have taken an interest in the Oxford 'Holy Club' organized in the late 1720s and early 1730s around Charles (1707–88) and John Wesley (1703–91), which became the genesis of the Methodist movement, the largest religious tradition to emerge from the Evangelical religious revivals of the eighteenth century. Also in Methodist vein, she might have attended one of George Whitefield's (1714–70) great outdoor sermons in London and Bristol or across the Atlantic in Boston and Philadelphia, which were among the largest gatherings of assembled people in the early modern world. She would also have noted that these great outdoor events ran counter to the prevailing method of Christianizing European populations in the eighteenth century by means of territorial parishes, resident clergymen and parish churches. This spatial move into the fields and beyond parish boundaries was an outward and visible symbol of a profound transformation in European Christendom associated with the Evangelical Revival. Things would never be quite the same again.

If our interplanetary professor moved on to research Roman Catholicism she would have had a manifestly different set of experiences. She might have been swept up in what has been called a golden age of religious revivals in the rural hinterlands of Catholic states in Southern and Eastern Europe. Pilgrimages, confraternities, theatrical missions conducted by members of the religious orders, Marian devotion, saints' cults, holy sites, healing miracles and renewed devotion in rural parish churches all combined to produce a major shift in the strength of early modern Catholicism. At the beginning of our period Catholicism was a religion of the towns with the countryside relatively neglected, while at the end of our period many of the rural areas were areas of faith, even fervour, while the towns were slipping away. In that sense the French Revolution merely confirmed what was already obvious, namely that urban elites had lost interest in Tridentine Catholicism even as the Church was still useful for rites of passage and requiem Masses.[3]

It is equally possible that our professor would have detected signs of unease and discord throughout Catholic Europe as the militancy and zeal of Tridentine Catholicism began to wane. Marian sodalities declined in significance, anti-papal sentiment grew among educated elites, the Jesuits were first suspected and then repressed, enthusiasm for overseas missions dimmed, Catholic rulers asserted their agenda above, and sometimes against, those of the Church, and the Protestant seaborne empires seemed poised to overthrow Catholic supremacy overseas. Although there were unmistakable signs of vibrancy in eighteenth-century Catholicism as evidenced by the founders of new missionary orders such as Alphonsus Liguori (1696–1787) (Redemptorists) and St Paul of the Cross (1694–1775) (Passionists), the world of Counter Reformation Catholic renewal was already in trouble long before the storming of the Bastille in 1789.

If our visiting professor became interested in religious art, architecture and music she might have found herself at the first performance of Johann Sebastian Bach's (1685–1750) *St John Passion* in the St Nicholas church in Leipzig (1724) or at the opening night in Dublin of George Frideric Handel's (1685–1759) much beloved oratorio *Messiah* (1742), or at a performance of António Teixeira's (1707– after 1769) magnificent *Te Deum* in Lisbon Cathedral. She might have developed an interest in hymn-singing, which became one of the greatest legacies of eighteenth-century Protestant spirituality, most notably perhaps the hymns of Isaac Watts (1674–1748) ('When I Survey the Wondrous Cross'), Charles Wesley ('Hark the Herald Angels Sing') and John Newton (1725–1807) ('Amazing Grace'). She would have been there for the completion of St Paul's Cathedral in London (1675–1710), Christopher Wren's (1632–1723) late Renaissance style masterpiece, with its giant dome inspired by St Peter's Basilica in Rome. She might have toured the remarkable examples of church building and renovation in baroque and rococo styles in the cities and even the smaller towns of Europe, and she would have found some fine examples of decorative religious art especially in the work of the great Venetians Sebastiano Ricci (1659–1734), Giovanni Piazetta (1682–1754) and Giambattista Tiepolo (1696–1770). However, she would also have noticed the growing dominance of classical themes, idealized landscapes and aristocratic portraits among some of Europe's most famous artists, along with wit, satire and nightmare in the paintings of William Hogarth (1697–1764) and Francisco Goya (1746–1828).

Above all she would have been impressed by the sheer pervasiveness of religious art throughout Europe, especially in Catholic countries where monarchs, aristocrats, popes, bishops, clergy, monasteries, confraternities, hospitals and educational institutions all commissioned art with religious themes for religious purposes. The Roman Catholic Church remained the most important institutional patron of religious art throughout the eighteenth century as well as having the largest treasure trove to conserve and protect. From parish churches to gravestones and mausoleums, and from elaborate family chapels to popular trinkets, religious art was simply ubiquitous. It is true that religious commissions declined after mid-century and that the Church as purveyor of art suffered some tough blows at the hands of Jansenist austerity and Revolutionary iconoclasm, but even after the French Revolution and Napoleonic celebrations of military heroism, Catholic art remained remarkably resilient.

If our interplanetary researcher were to measure the strength of European religiosity by the sheer prevalence of religious art and architecture, she would not have concluded that the eighteenth century showed clear signs of incipient secularization. Even in Protestant countries, where the relationship between art and religion was more uneasy, Protestants became less iconophobic and less resistant to visual representation of religious themes over the course of the eighteenth century. In England High Church enthusiasm for religious images, widespread Gothic revivalism, Thomas Gainsborough's (1727–88) nature canvases with their religious allusions, William Blake's (1757–1827) religious (albeit heterodox) images, and John Constable's (1776–1837) altarpieces all indicated that both Anglican and dissenting Protestants were willing to embrace art as a vehicle for inspiring devotion. All of this has persuaded one scholar to conclude that in the eighteenth century it is possible that visualization may have driven theology more than the reverse, and that secularist Enlightenment propaganda notwithstanding, the eighteenth century was a remarkably productive era of religious art and music.[4]

If our professor wanted to step beyond the Protestant environs of Northern Europe and Catholic lands to the south in order to catch a glimpse of the many traditions of Orthodox religion to the east she might have read the remarkable travel journal of Vasyl Hryhorovyc-Bars'kyj (1701–47), whose epic 24-year pilgrimage is recorded in one of the great Christian manuscripts of the eighteenth century. Beginning in his native Kiev in 1723, Bars'kyj's travels took him through Eastern Europe to Italy, Greece, Asia Minor and the Holy Land. He wrote as an Orthodox traveller who sought out Orthodox communities and monasteries wherever he went. His copiously illustrated journal is a mine of information about the customs, churches, architecture, liturgies, worship and traditions of scholarship of many of the great centres of Orthodoxy in South Eastern Europe and Asia Minor. He visited outposts in Italy, stayed with Serbian and Greek communities, studied in 20 of the great Orthodox monasteries, mastered many languages, copied Egyptian hieroglyphs and researched liturgies and architecture with painstaking attention to detail. His journal is also a sustained defence of the Holy Orthodox tradition against the perceived oppressions of Roman Catholics, Muslims and hostile states and principalities. Bars'kyj began his travels as a mendicant Slav pilgrim begging for alms as his sole means of financial support and ended his life as a celebrated scholar of the Orthodox churches. He died in Kiev in 1747, a month after returning from his grand tour of the Orthodox early modern world. His autograph manuscript of the state of the Orthodox tradition in the early eighteenth century is as good a starting point as any to investigate the elaborate liturgies and monastic disciplines at the centre of Orthodox spirituality about which Western scholars still know very little.[5]

Our visiting professor would undoubtedly have spent time in Constantinople, which was not only the capital city of the Ottoman Empire but also the seat of the Ecumenical Patriarch, first in honour of all the Eastern Orthodox bishops. Although theoretically the four eastern patriarchs were equal, over the course of the eighteenth century the Constantinople Patriarchate extended its control over other Orthodox communions in the Balkans, and increasingly spoke for the Orthodox. The patriarchate was solidly in Greek hands. Two other autocephalous churches, in Ohrid for the Bulgars and in Pec for the Serbs, were abolished in 1766–67, giving the Constantinople Patriarchate jurisdiction over the entire Balkan peninsula and the Aegean and Ionian islands. Our professor might have been particularly interested in how the Christian Orthodox Church survived under the imperial control of a Muslim sultan. She would have discovered that the Ottoman Turks on the whole put up with other monotheistic religious traditions (as 'people of the book') and organized them into communities, known as millets, which had a great deal of autonomy in terms of faith, law and practice. Of course, religious conversions and intermarriage between different faith traditions were forbidden, intermingling was actively discouraged, non-Muslims paid extra taxes and knew they were regarded as decidedly inferior in status. In short, conquered people of another religion were accorded a second-class status under the direction of their own ecclesiastical authorities, were forbidden to make converts and were sometimes actively persecuted or subjected to coercive violence. Moreover, the Balkans were on the front line of almost permanent conflict between the European Christian empires and the Ottoman Turks, which cast an inevitable sense of violent instability over the whole region throughout the eighteenth century. Additionally, tensions were not just between Muslims and Christians, but within different expressions of Christianity. Orthodox believers in Catholic states such as Transylvania fared no better, possibly even worse, than they did in the Ottoman Empire. Nevertheless, life on the ground among Orthodox Balkan peasants was as much regulated by the rhythms and practices of Orthodoxy as it was in territories outside the Ottoman Empire.[6] Popular forms of religious belief and practice survived beyond the gazes of rulers and elites.

So far, our interplanetary professor has spent her time largely in Christian Europe among its three great faith traditions – Roman Catholic, Protestant and Orthodox – but what would she have discovered about the geography of early modern Christianity if she had sailed on one of the boats carrying imperial trade, African slaves, European migrants and Catholic and Protestant missionaries to the Americas, Africa or Asia? She would soon have realized that the geographical expansion of Christianity from Europe to other parts of the world had proceeded rapidly, if haphazardly, in the two centuries before her own arrival. European Christendom was remorselessly extending its geographical reach, with profound consequences for all aspects of global civilization.

If she were looking for the heart of this expansion on the continent of Africa, she might have fetched up in the kingdom of the Kongo, which had come under Portuguese influence since the late fifteenth century. Underpinning the early growth of Catholic Christianity in the Kongo were four features: the more or less steady adherence of the Kongolese monarchy to Christianity for over 200 years; the support of a ruling elite which took on many of the trappings of the Catholicism of the Portuguese nobility; the establishment of a Catholicized capital city and cathedral in São Salvador; and the growth of a Portuguese immigrant community sustained by the slave trade. In the seventeenth century Kongolese Catholicism was further strengthened by the zeal of Jesuit and especially Capuchin missionaries, the important work of lay interpreter-catechists, the emotional power of the symbol of the cross and the growing acceptance of the Catholic sacraments of baptism and marriage. However, as with all encounters between European Christianity and the 'other', it would have been difficult for her accurately to estimate the extent of Catholic penetration of the Kongo, for many of the signs of Christian expansion were on a deeper level profoundly ambiguous.

No doubt our alien professor of religions would have been particularly intrigued by the story of a young Kongolese woman named Dona Beatriz Kimpa Vita (1684–1706), who in 1704 claimed that during an illness she had been possessed by St Anthony. Through her visions and experiences she brokered a distinctively Kongolese version of the Christian faith that had been brought to her by the Roman Catholic religious orders. According to her new vision, Jesus was born in São Salvador, was baptized in the river Zaïre, and he and Mary were Kongolese, as were many of the saints of the Christian tradition. Dona Beatriz not only constructed a new, indigenized history of Christianity, but also preached a radical, and for a time, hugely popular message around the authority of St Anthony, the need for purification and a revision of the traditional prayers of the Church, especially the Ave Maria and the Salve Regina. Dona Beatriz was aided in her efforts by an army of little Anthonys who took this message to the towns and villages of the rural hinterlands. Perhaps inevitably, all this came to a sticky end. Dona Beatriz became pregnant to her male assistant, João Barro (her Guardian Angel, St John), which was particularly problematic given her self-declared emphasis on chastity. She soon fell foul both of the ecclesiastical leadership of the Capuchins and the political leadership of the Kongolese elites and paid the ultimate price of being burned (along with Barro) as a witch and a heretic in 1706. In a moving denouement, her child was spared by a last-minute intervention by a Capuchin priest.[7]

Our professor would likely interpret this strange tale as partly a reflection of the social and political instability of the Kongo in the early eighteenth century, which was in a state of civil war, and as an example of a hybridized Christianity which blended traditional Kongolese beliefs and practices with a particular kind of European Catholicism. The remarkably popular Antonian Movement may be seen both as a sign of the success of Catholicism in the Kongo and of its slow demise throughout the eighteenth century. Many of the gains of the seventeenth century, when it seemed genuinely possible that Christianity in Central Africa could have achieved the same kind of lasting penetration as happened in Latin America, simply ebbed away in the eighteenth century. The reasons for this decline were not so much inhospitable climate, distance from Europe, the strength of indigenous traditions and native resistance, formidable though some of these were, as they were the systematic resistance of the Portuguese to missions of other nations, the baleful effects of the slave trade, the general decline of missionary enthusiasm in Catholic Europe and the increasing rigidities of canon law and missionary practice.[8] What this example from Central Africa illustrates is that trends in Europe, as much as the inherent difficulties of Christian transmission overseas, helped determine the scope and shape of world Christianity in the eighteenth century.

Suppose our professor had travelled to the other side of sub-Saharan Africa. She would have found in Ethiopia evidence of one of Christianity's ancient churches with roots deep in the Coptic Orthodox tradition coming out of Alexandria. If she was familiar with one of Christian Europe's most intriguing texts, Francisco Álvares' (c.1465–1541) *A True Relation of the Lands of Prester John of the Indies* (1540), an account of Ethiopian Christianity through the eyes of a Portuguese missionary and explorer, she would have had very high expectations. Here in a continent little known by Europeans until the arrival of the Portuguese was an account of a land of ubiquitous churches and monasteries displaying a vibrant Christianity sustained by the Ge'ez Bible and the Ge'ez musical traditions. Indeed, the legend of Prester John, a medieval European tradition devoted to the idea that there was in existence a luxuriant Oriental church hidden deep within the Muslim and pagan worlds, seemed to Álvares a perfect fit for what he encountered in Ethiopia in the early sixteenth century. However, if our professor had read Álvares, she would have been disappointed by what she found in her eighteenth-century tour. By then a combination of factors including weak ecclesiastical leadership (the Ethiopian Church was governed by a single Egyptian bishop), internecine theological disputes over the two natures of Christ, ruinous dynastic wars, apparently endless violent conflicts with Muslims, the decline of the once influential Jesuit and Franciscan missions and much else besides had produced a 'riches to rags' story. According to its historian, 'Christianity in Africa did, then, enter the nineteenth century weaker and more imperilled in its one traditional area of strength than it had been for centuries.'[9]

When taking leave of Africa, our professor might have travelled one of the slave-trading routes across the Atlantic to North America where she would have discovered an immense, almost bewildering diversity of Christian belief and practice across the continent. If she had arrived on the east coast, she might have thought that there had once been a land bridge to Western Europe. The remarkable religious variety opened up in the English-speaking world by the dislocations of the English Civil Wars in the 1640s was in full display along the eastern seaboard of North America. Anglicans were particularly numerous in Virginia and Maryland, Congregationalists were in the ascendancy in Massachusetts, Connecticut and New Hampshire, Presbyterians from Scotland and the north of Ireland were thick on the ground in New Jersey, Delaware, Pennsylvania and New York, Quakers fetched up along the Delaware Valley in New Jersey and Pennsylvania, Baptists pushed out from their base in Rhode Island to establish strong communities in North and South Carolina, and later in the century Methodists surged into Maryland and Virginia. Even her discovery of this scale of religious pluralism among predominantly English speakers was only scratching the surface of what was going on. If her linguistic and ethnographic skills were up to the task our professor would have discovered Reformed communities of Dutch and French origins, strong pockets of Swedish and German Lutherans (the most numerous of the non-English speakers), and smaller settlements of Mennonites, Amish and Moravians, most of whom settled in Pennsylvania. The great majority of people she would have encountered on the eastern seaboard were of European Protestant descent, but not all. She would have discovered small Jewish communities in many of the seaports and larger numbers of Roman Catholics mostly in Maryland, Pennsylvania and Nova Scotia. If our professor had scheduled her visit later in the century or in the early part of the nineteenth century, she might also have stumbled across some of the more unusual communal societies of Christians, such as those formed by the Shakers

(United Society of Believers in Christ's Second Coming) in New York and New England.

Perhaps the most perplexing aspect of our professor's field trip to the eastern part of North America would have been what to make of the religious encounters between European settlers and native peoples, and between the European Christians and the large numbers of African slaves who populated the southern part of the country. As it happens both were subjected to various types of Christian missionary influence over the course of the eighteenth century. Both populations responded with a combination of resistance, subversion, accommodation and acceptance, but whereas Native Americans were a diminishing population who mostly rejected the religions of the Europeans, a sizeable and expanding minority of African Americans, despite their enforced bondage, embraced Evangelical forms of Protestant Christianity brought to them mostly by Baptists and Methodists. Accounts of both of these patterns will be supplied in Chapter 3.

Suppose for a moment that our professor had not landed in North America in one of its Atlantic seaports, but had rather chosen another point of entry. One possibility would have been to travel with French Jesuit missionaries down the St Lawrence River to Quebec, Montreal and the Great Lakes, and on down the Mississippi Valley to Louisiana and New Orleans. Along the way she would have found small pockets of a hybridized kind of French Catholicism among some of the Native American peoples such as the Hurons, the Iroquois and, further south, the Choctaw, but she would also have found a stronger and more enduring representation of French Catholic culture among the descendants of French Catholics, many of whom were migrants from Nova Scotia, in Louisiana.

But what if our professor had decided to move in to North America not from the north and the east with the English, French and Germans, but from the west and the south with the Spanish? Starting in Mexico City at the heart of the Viceroyalty of New Spain she might have accompanied Franciscan and Jesuit missionaries in their efforts to establish missions in New Mexico's Rio Grande Valley (severely dented by the Pueblo Revolt of 1680), Sonora and Arizona (which met similar fates in the Pima Indian revolts of 1751 and 1781) and along the coasts of Baja California and Alta California. Between 1769 and 1823 the Franciscans established 21 missions as profitable agricultural communities in what is now California, from San Diego in the south to Sonoma (north of San Francisco) in the north. If our intrepid professor had the energy to continue travelling north she would eventually have stumbled across Russian Orthodox missions on the southern coast of Alaska. At the end of the eighteenth century, just at the point when the Spanish Empire had stretched to its outer limits in northern California, the Russian tsar, Paul I (1754–1801), founded the Russian American Company (1799) which had as one of its objectives the promotion of the Orthodox Church in North America. The expansion of world Christianity in the eighteenth century had thrown up yet another unlikely faith frontier.[10]

If our professor had travelled south rather than north from Mexico City into Latin America she would have discovered well-established traditions of Iberian Catholicism sinking deep institutional roots into American soil. The creation of dioceses and archdioceses, the growing numbers of secular clergy, the expansion of monastic life, especially female convents, the popularity of confraternities and brotherhoods, the increasing economic significance of the religious orders (including extensive landholdings) and the building of imposing baroque churches all testified to the fact that Roman Catholicism in Latin America, regardless of what would happen to its original imperial sponsors, was there to stay. Nevertheless, our professor of religion would have noticed that despite rigorous attempts to impose a distinctively European church on the Americas, a combination of racial mixtures, geographical diversity and cultural resilience ensured that a distinctively 'American church was being born with American saints and sinners in abundance both in and out of the institutional church'.[11] Even so, the church in Latin America could not escape the impact of events in Europe that changed its *modus operandi* in the eighteenth century. In Spain the new royal house of the Bourbons, especially in the reigns of Charles III (1716–88) and Charles IV (1759–1808), made a sustained effort to bring the church under royal control by appointing European-born clergymen to the highest positions in the colonial church, convening ecclesiastical councils (the first since the sixteenth century) in Mexico City, Lima, Charcas and Santa Fe de Bogota, reining in clerical privileges, seizing ecclesiastical resources, urging greater use of the Spanish language in church rituals, ordering the secularization of all parishes controlled by religious orders and expelling the Society of Jesus from the Spanish Empire in 1767. Squeezed from above by royal demands and treated with less deference by secular elites in the Americas, the eighteenth-century church in Latin America, whether in Spanish or Portuguese territories, was not short of challenges to its authority in the Americas.

Our professor of religion might have concluded that for all the sustained efforts of the Bourbon governments to bring the church under more efficient control, many of their policies were counter-productive and contributed to the alienation of diocesan priests who were in no mood to support their royal masters when independence movements gathered steam in the early nineteenth century. Yet it would be a mistake to paint a picture of the eighteenth-century church in Latin America as a fragmented and crumbling institution living on borrowed time, for there were unmistakable signs of life and vitality. Our professor would have noticed the huge popularity of the once condemned cult of the Virgin of Guadalupe, ubiquitous processions and celebrations on the great feast days of the Christian calendar, the rise of lay communal organizations for both men and women, and the resurgence of lay retreats and parish revivals, which all showed that despite the problems of coping with the sturdy survivals of native religion, Roman Catholicism by the eighteenth century had sunk deep roots into popular culture. The sustained efforts of generations of Catholic missionaries, who even by the late eighteenth century were pressing on into upper California, southern Chile, the Amazonian interior and the Chaco regions of Bolivia and Patagonia, had resulted in the establishment of a church which, although owing much to violent colonialism, could make legitimate claims to be genuinely a religion of the people.[12]

Perhaps what our professor of religion would have noticed most in her travels throughout the Americas would have been the large numbers of African slaves. She would have seen slaves in every colony from Canada and New England in the north all the way south to Spanish Peru and Chile. If she had also visited the Caribbean islands, the centre of the most lucrative trading routes of the eighteenth century, she would have visited some islands where the slaves constituted population majorities of 90 per cent or more.[13] For most eighteenth-century European minds, there seemed to be no apparent incompatibility between Christianity and slavery.

If our professor decided to travel east to Asia, rather than west to the Americas, she most likely would have found herself regaled with melancholic stories of opposition, persecution and decline. Unlike Christian missionaries to Asia up to 1500 who came mostly by land, she would have arrived by sea to find the assorted remnants of the Christian communities established during the pioneering era of Jesuit missions in the sixteenth and seventeenth centuries. In Japan, the mission begun by the great Jesuit Francis Xavier (1506–52) had long since been decapitated. The last Christian missionary to Japan in the early modern era, Giovanni Battista Sidotti (1668–1714), entered Japan in 1708 and died in prison six years later. The Tokugawa shoguns, fearful that Christian missionaries were merely the advance guard of European temporal conquest, showed little mercy to Japanese Christians, who nevertheless survived in small pockets of 'deep silence' in isolated places until the arrival of better days. Our professor would have found much stronger communities of Catholic Christians in China, Vietnam and the Philippines, but they too seemed past their peak. Estimates of numbers are notoriously unreliable, but it seems likely that in Tonkin and Annam (present-day Vietnam) the number of Christians may have declined by about a half (to around 250,000) from the 1650s to the 1750s. The subsequent expulsion of the Jesuits did not help matters, but conversely the rise of French colonial influence and the missionaries sent out by the Paris Society of Foreign Missions, along with the improved training of native catechists, may have stopped some of the haemorrhaging, albeit at the expense of laying the foundations for fresh colonial conflicts down the line. She would have discovered still smaller remnants of Catholic missions in Siam (Thailand), Laos and Burma.

If our professor had sailed on to the Philippines, she would have discovered a pattern a little more like the one she encountered in Latin America, that is a relatively strong Roman Catholicism borne on the wings of colonial conquest rather than being dependent solely on the missionary enthusiasm of the Catholic religious orders. Writing of the Philippines, one historian has stated that 'no comparable mass penetration of an Asiatic culture by the Christian faith had ever before been achieved outside the continent's Greco-Roman dominated western coast on the Mediterranean Sea'.[14] However, whereas in second- or third-century Europe the expansion of Christianity came from below without government support, Christian expansion in the Philippines came on the coat tails of Spanish colonial power. For all of its substantial achievements, Filipino Catholicism was hampered in the eighteenth century by the inadequate training of indigenous priests, the lack of a vernacular Bible and, inevitably, by the expulsion of the Jesuits. China presented an equally complicated picture. The glorious years of the great Jesuit missionaries Matteo Ricci (1552–1610), Adam Schall (1591–1666) and Ferdinand Verbiest (1623–88) at the Chinese court, seemed a thing of the past. The consequences of the Chinese Rites Controversy (see Chapter 3), imperial persecution and internal Catholic quarrels may have reduced the Christian population of China by as much as half over the course of the eighteenth century. There was nevertheless still in existence a thriving popular Chinese Catholicism which showed unmistakable signs of numerical recovery by the end of the eighteenth century.

In short our touring professor would no doubt have agreed with a recent assessment that the 'closing decades of the eighteenth century were sombre years for Catholic missions in Asia. Japan was still enveloped in the anguished silence that followed the great persecution. In China the missions were closed by an imperious, suspicious Qing dynasty, which regretted it had ever favoured them. The Dutch and English were sweeping Spanish and Portuguese shipping, the lifeline of the Catholic missions, out of South Pacific Seas and the Indian Ocean.' In addition, the Jesuits who had been the remarkable pioneers of Catholic missions, had been expelled by the monarchs and the papacy that had once relied upon them as the primary agents of Christianization in new worlds.[15]

Christianity in eighteenth-century India also seemed to be in numerical decline though there were strong pockets of Portuguese Catholicism in and around Goa, of St Thomas Christians along the Malabar Coast (split between Roman and Syrian jurisdictions), and the frail beginnings of Lutheran Pietist, Dutch Reformed and English missions along the coasts (see Chapter 3). Generally speaking, Christianity was more or less confined to the coastal regions of south-western and south-eastern India, having achieved little penetration of Mughal North India.

If our professor had abandoned travel by sea and attempted to return to Europe from India by land, she would have had to look hard for communities of Christians in the great Ottoman and Persian empires. She might have stumbled across small pockets of Nestorians in the Kurdish mountains, some Catholic Uniates in Iran, and larger numbers of Armenian Orthodox, one of the most divided and fragmented Christian churches in the world, who unfortunately found themselves repeatedly on the front lines of the conflicts between Persians and Ottoman Turks.[16] In the Middle East, once a far more important centre of Christianity than that ruled from Rome, she would have found diminished but still thriving Christian populations living under the unfriendly jurisdiction of the Ottoman Empire. The Eastern Syriac churches suffered most from Ottoman rule, but substantial numbers of Greek Orthodox, Armenian Orthodox and Copts (mostly in Egypt) were living uneasily within the Ottoman Empire. She would also have been struck by the sheer diversity of Christianity. As a result of earlier jurisdictional and doctrinal schisms the complex array of Eastern and Oriental Orthodox churches also had corresponding Catholic counterparts. There were Maronite (mostly concentrated in what is now Lebanon), Chaldean, Melkite, Syrian, Armenian, Coptic and Ethiopian Catholic churches. Complementing her earlier visit to Constantinople, our professor would certainly have visited Cairo, a city of comparable size to Paris in the eighteenth century, with perhaps as many as 40,000 Coptic Christians (Jesuit estimates), or around 10 per cent of the population. In Egypt as a whole there were around 200,000 Coptic Christians, but under Muslim rule the great Egyptian monasteries (only seven survived) and Cairo churches were not exactly thriving in the eighteenth century. As the more reliable figures of the early twentieth century show, when Christians comprised about 11 per cent of the total population of the Middle East, centuries of Ottoman rule did not extinguish a wildly diverse Christianity in the Middle East in the early modern period, but nor did Christianity flourish under a mixture of limited toleration at best and bouts of more active persecution at worst.[17]

As she meandered her way back to the heartlands of European Christianity, our professor might have paused to review her slide collection of the dominant images of Christian art and artefacts she encountered on the non-European leg of her global perambulation. Possibly her largest collection would have been examples of the glories of Latin American baroque which by the eighteenth century was no longer an extension or transposition of European continental baroque. By then the emergence of indigenous architects and local Amerindian, mestizo, mulatto and African artisans, built and decorated structures that departed in significant ways from European models. If she had to choose three representative, but stylistically rather different, examples of Latin American baroque for her end-of-tour slide presentation she might have chosen one each from Mexico, Peru and Brazil. A good candidate for the first would be the Jesuit Church of San Francisco Xavier in Teptzotlán, Mexico, with its Iniesta designed façade and tower and its visually stunning interior altar screens designed and constructed by the indigenous Zapotec painter Miguel Cabrera (1695–1768) and Criolla sculptor Higinio de Chávez. Among the finest extant examples of baroque religious art in Mexico, the altarpieces are riotous examples of Catholic iconography, replete with images of Francis Xavier, the Virgin of Guadalupe and the saints of the global church. For her second example, she might have chosen the Jesuit Church of Santiago in Arequipa, Peru, appropriately described as one of the masterpieces of colonial South American decoration. Completed in 1698 it inaugurated the Peruvian 'mestizo style' which exerted such influence over church building in the Viceroyalty of Peru in the eighteenth century. The iconography of the mestizo style blends European Christian symbols with pre-Christian Incan depictions of local flora and fauna with sacred significance. The interior sacristy, in particular, is a colourful, exotic and flamboyant tribute to the creative spirit of the mestizo style. For her third illustration, our professor might have chosen the Church of São Franciso de Assís in Ouro Prêto, Brazil. The first major commission of Antônio Francisco Lisboa (1730 or 1738–1814), otherwise called O Aleijadinho ('the little cripple'), who is widely regarded as the genius of Brazilian baroque, the church, with its undulating façade and sensuous bell towers, is one of the most visually stunning examples of the baroque (bordering on rococo) style in Portuguese Brazil. Inside, Manoel da Costa Ataíde (1762–1830) painted the nave's ceiling with iconography depicting the eclectic racial mixing of Latin American Catholicism.[18]

Outside of Latin America, our professor might have collected images of martyred Jesuits as reproduced in their published 'Relations', of Russian Orthodox icons with their fantastically intricate liturgical calendars, of

Chinese clocks either made by or inspired by Jesuit missionaries, of the great stone, grass-roofed cathedral church in São Salvador in Kongo, or of St Thomas' Anglican cathedral in Bombay. She would also have slides of the newly constructed baroque and rococo churches of St Petersburg, as unmistakable evidence of new Western European influence, as well as the traditional wooden churches in much of the rest of Russia. Comparing and contrasting the Domenico Trezzini (*c.*1670–1734) designed baroque cathedral of SS Peter and Paul in St Petersburg (1712–33) with the riotous 22 drums and cupolas of the wooden Church of the Transfiguration on Lake Onega (1714) would highlight the competing influences on Russian Christianity in the early eighteenth century. Our professor would already have come to the conclusion that a study of eighteenth-century Christian art and architecture outside Europe would reveal plenty of examples of Christian art with little or no influence from Europe (especially in the ancient eastern churches), plenty more deriving from European colonial influence (especially in the Americas), and yet more illustrating various kinds of hybridity and indigenization.

Aside from a slide collection, our interplanetary professor would have returned to the great capital cities of Western Europe with a number of strong impressions about the state of global Christianity in the eighteenth century. She would have sensed that the great era of Christian expansion associated with the Iberian sea-going empires and the Roman Catholic missionary orders was beginning to decline. Conflicts between the papacy and Catholic rulers and between the missionary orders themselves over power, jurisdiction and styles of mission helped undermine the Catholic cause from within, while the rise of the Protestant seaborne empires, especially the Dutch and the English, posed new threats from without. In addition, those parts of the globe which European states had neither conquered nor settled, namely most of Africa and Asia, exhibited unmistakable signs of Christian decline, mostly from a low base. On the other hand, despite native resistance and the survival of indigenous religious traditions in truncated forms, Christianity had arrived to stay in the Americas. A complex mixture of imperial power (and competition), apocalyptic zeal, missionary ardour and settler opportunism irrevocably transformed the religious geography of the Americas in the early modern period. All of this would have been obvious to her, but as she pored over her fieldwork notes a number of difficult questions would have occurred to her. How could one account for this expansion of Christianity into new spaces in the early modern period? What drove it? And how should one understand the nature of the encounters between Europeans and other peoples? These are the questions to which we must now turn.

European ascendancy and global mapping

On the eve of the Protestant Reformation in the early 1500s, Christianity was a religion more or less confined to Europe and the Orthodox (and Catholic) environs of the Middle East and Western Asia, with the exception of the Coptic and Ethiopian churches of Africa, a small Nubian residue also in Africa, the early beginnings of Portuguese Catholicism in Africa, the Thomas Christians of southern India and the scattered Nestorian churches of Asia. In contrast, by the end of the eighteenth century, 'Christianity girdled the globe from China to Peru' and had effectively become a global religion.[19] The factors promoting such a dramatic change included improvements in ship construction and navigation, inexhaustible searches for new trading routes and the rise of the European (principally Iberian) seaborne empires. In religious terms, although there were sporadic efforts at overseas missions by European Protestants, the driving force behind post-Reformation Christian expansion was largely an achievement of the Catholic religious orders. The pioneers were the Franciscans, Dominicans and Mercedarians, but they were quickly followed by the Capuchins and most importantly the Jesuits, who became the most potent Christian missioners of the early modern period. By the beginning of the eighteenth century Christianity had been established by force and persuasion in great tracts of the Americas in the West, and had achieved significant toeholds in the East, albeit with less force and more persuasion.

The story of the tangled causes and consequences of this Christian expansion, its manifold cruelties and acts of compassion, its achievements and limitations and its cultural subjugations and hybridities, has been told in the preceding volume of this series. Although its character changed in ways that this volume will seek to explain, the global expansion of Christianity continued apace in the eighteenth century, along with the growing European ascendancy from which it benefited. The roots of that ascendancy were primarily economic and military, but there were also social, political and cultural factors in play. In terms of economics, Europe enjoyed a huge hinterland of underexploited resources including timber for ship construction, coal that provided fuel for what has been called 'industrious revolutions', substantial food supplies including fish from the Atlantic Ocean and the produce from the slave plantation system, and better agricultural techniques. As a result, in this period the cities of North West Europe grew much faster than those in China, India, the Middle East and Africa. To these economic factors was added the competitive advantage accruing from relatively independent banking and commercial institutions such as the Bank of England and the British and Dutch East India companies, the world's first multinational corporations. Moreover wealthy elites in eighteenth-century Europe, whether based on land or capital, enjoyed considerable legal protection under Roman or common law against rulers, governments and marauders. Europe's growing ascendancy was also facilitated by a growing military capacity, which was itself a product of technological and financial superiority. European states needed large navies to patrol the routes of the slave trade and emerging empires and became more expert at raising the vast sums of money required for the world conflicts that broke out in the eighteenth century. Finally, Europe extended control over international trade, including the execrable slave trade, so that Europeans benefited most even from the produce of non-Europeans. In this way 'Europe connected, subjugated, and made tributary other people's industrious revolutions.'[20]

For European Christians, however, Europe's growing ascendancy was regarded less as a product of its economic advantage and military power than as a reflection of the superiority of its culture and civilization, especially its religion. The chief source of authority for thinking about other cultures and religions was of course the Bible (supplemented when necessary by classical texts), which remained the most influential lens through which to view 'others'. The medieval method of placing cultures and religions in the categories supplied by the biblical narratives remained potent well into the eighteenth century. For example, Asia was primarily the Asia of the children of Israel contending against its idolatrous peoples and false religions; or again the common idea that Moses had once travelled in Siberia and Mongolia; or that Africans were descended from the curse of Noah upon Ham; or that the lost tribes of Israel somehow made it to the Americas; or the notion that God specially favoured the populations living in the temperate climates of places like Europe. These categories allowed Europeans to experience an expanding world within the comfortable narratives of space and time embedded within their sacred texts. At the same time vast new quantities of information about extra-European cultures were becoming available through ubiquitous travel and adventure literature, detailed missionary reports from the Catholic religious orders and the direct encounters of traders, soldiers and settlers. Moreover this information circulated faster within Europe through the growth of libraries, newspapers and religious periodicals. As information spread about 'new' peoples and 'new' lands, older ways of knowing and interpreting the world increasingly had to account for the insights gleaned from first-hand experience, direct encounter and from what has been called cultural 'autopsy'.[21] Foreign cultures were being subject to personal inspection and critical dissection in a more detailed way than ever before.

Faced with the challenge of new information, European Christians did not abandon their reliance on ancient texts, but rather expanded from them. Refracted through the lenses of their sense of religious and cultural superiority, Europeans brought together biblical and Enlightenment classifications of the 'others' they were encountering. Biblical conceptions of space and time remained the standard. Hence, travelling to extra-European cultures was like travelling backwards in time to an era of primitive simplicity. In this way geographical travel became time travel, as non-Christian cultures were regarded as the same as those that existed in biblical or pre-biblical times. For example, in a memorandum written for Nicolas Baudin's (1754–1803) expedition to the South Pacific in 1800–03 the French scholar Joseph Marie Degérando (1772–1842) wrote that in observing the peoples of the Pacific 'we shall in a way be taken back to the first periods of our own history. ... The philosophical traveller, sailing to the ends of the earth, is in fact travelling in time; he is exploring the past; every step he makes is the passage of an age. Those unknown islands that he reaches are for him the passage of human society.' [22] Similarly, in the case of the Americas, native peoples were classified as young in the progress of civilization, having less advanced languages, customs and work habits than Europeans. They were part 'noble savages' and part barbarian wanderers, but crucially they were regarded as being of the same human stock and were therefore prime targets for Christian conversion and cultural uplift. To European Christians 'savage cultures' were literally 'decomposed cultures' based on instinct and intuition while European culture was characterized by artifice and deliberation.[23] Yet that very deliberation produced nuance and complexity as Europeans reflected on their impact on 'primitive' cultures. Some European Catholics and Protestants could see that Europeans exported cruelty and greed as much as they exported refinement and cultivation, and European Protestants came to believe that Catholic missionaries had both collaborated in *conquistadore* depredations and spread idolatry and superstition. In that sense the same argument made by Catholics for converting natives could be reapplied by Protestants to convert those 'ruined' by their encounters with European Catholics. Classifications of progress, as with beauty, were in the eyes of the beholder.

The same held for attitudes to race. There was no single view of racial differences in Enlightenment Europe, but the dominant view throughout the English-speaking world was the one most associated with the Scottish universities, namely that all humankind shared the same origins, as the Bible seemed to teach. This was not only a sustaining ideology for Christian missions but also helped justify the spreading of Christian 'civilization' to all peoples. There were, of course, influential polygenist advocates in the Anglophone world, and even more in France, which sometimes resulted in the kind of racial language that disfigured the writings of Hume and Voltaire. More common, however, was the assumption that the Bible and empirical observation of racial differences could be brought into scientific harmony, and that there was in existence a single humanity in need of Christian mission regardless of their racial and religious characteristics.[24]

When encountering other religious traditions, Europeans tended to apply assumptions based on their own constructions of Christianity. Thus other religions were thought to have fixed bodies of doctrines emanating from sacred texts and expounded by priests, who also controlled all rites and rituals. This approach at least supplied a basis for comparison, but whereas Christianity was regarded as a religion in which God worked through men, other religions were regarded as mere human inventions and therefore fatally flawed. Judaism and Islam, though monotheistic and sharing as Abrahamic faiths a similar sacred history, were in their different ways regarded as deviant and heretical. Islam was constructed not as a major religion in its own right requiring contemporary investigation, but as the regrettable creation of a seventh-century impostor named Mohammed. Although some eighteenth-century European writers found some beauty in the Koran and some admirable qualities in Mohammed, most regarded Islam as at best a religion suitable only for ancient Arabs and at worst a nefarious and potentially violent competitor. Completely absent is the notion that Islam was a dynamic and living faith tradition; rather it was seen as an ancient heresy, 'keeping its hold on an ignorant population by suppressing all questioning and intellectual endeavour. Its fate seemed to be bound up with that of the great empires who were thought to enforce it, the Ottomans, the Persians and the Mughals.'[25] In that sense European Christians encountered Islam not as an equal religious tradition but as the underpinning faith of real or potential enemies. There were of course many non-Western Christian churches within the Ottoman Empire, including Greek Orthodox, Armenian, Assyrian, Coptic and various iterations of Catholicism, but even there the emphasis was not as much on fruitful encounter as on the maintenance of separate communities under the umbrella of strictly limited toleration. European *philosophes* sometimes admired the tolerance, but they almost never admired the religion. As the eighteenth century developed, a combination of enlightened critique of all brands of enthusiastic religion and a heightened Evangelical sense of religious heresy combined to harden, not soften, European attitudes to Islam.[26]

A similar trajectory of hardening relations with other world religions holds for European Christian attitudes to Hinduism, Buddhism and Confucianism. As we shall see later, a combination of a greater drive for orthodoxy within Catholicism and a surge of Evangelical zeal among

Protestants undermined the adaptive flexibility in interfaith encounters pioneered by the Jesuits in the sixteenth and seventeenth centuries. In the case of Hinduism there was some respect accorded by English writers on account of its great antiquity (though this occasioned some dating problems for biblicist Christians) and its educated elites, but there was near universal contempt for Hindu conceptions of polytheism, the transmigration of souls and caste divisions, and for its riotous profusion of cults and images. Among the Chinese and East Asian religions, Jesuits made a distinction between Confucianism, which could be accommodated, and Buddhism, Taoism and the Japanese religions, which could not. As we shall see later, the Jesuit approach to Chinese Confucianism was reined in by papal enforced orthodoxy, and by the time Evangelical missionaries reached China and other parts of East Asia, Asian religions were emphatically regarded as pagan enemies of conversion, not as partial facilitators of common religious truths as some Jesuits had earlier thought.

Europe and the wider world: from the particular to the general

So far we have we have tried to conceptualize European Christians' encounters with the rest of the world through the devices of imaginary travelling and religious 'mapping'. We have explored some of the foundations of European power, its sense of religious superiority, and its civilizational chauvinism. But how did these attitudes play out in the minds and behaviours of Europeans in the eighteenth century? This is, of course, an impossibly large and difficult question, which will absorb many of the pages to follow, but let us start with a very particular and peculiar story and try to uncover its wider meaning and applicability.

In May 1713 Jean Pierre Purry (1675–1736), a native of the French-speaking Swiss canton of Neuchâtel, sailed aboard the *Prins Eugenius* from Amsterdam to Batavia (Jakarta) under the auspices of the Dutch East India Company. Along the way the ship made stops at the Cape Verde Islands and the company's Cape Colony in South Africa before arriving at its destination in February 1714. Purry also seems to have found his way to a group of islands, the Terre de Nuyts, located just off the south-central coast of Australia near the Eyre Peninsula. Purry brought to his travels some previous experience in the wine trade and a strong desire to make money. Based upon his travels to the southern hemisphere and his general reading of geography, climate and soil fertility, Purry constructed a general theory about the location of the world's most divinely blessed and most suitable lands for colonization. According to his theory the earth had 24 climate zones extending from the North to the South Poles, but it was the fifth climate zone around the latitude of 33 degrees north and south that had the best possible combination of sunlight, temperature, precipitation and soil fertility. On his return to Amsterdam in 1718 Purry published his theory in an attempt to enlist the support of the directors of the Dutch East India Company for commercial colonization ventures in the 'Country of Kaffraria' (South Africa) and the Terre de Nuyts (Australia).[27]

At the heart of Purry's theory was the idea that a traveller following the 33rd parallel north and south would come across the most productive land in the world. The northerly route would take one through Tunis and the Barbary Coast, Damascus in Syria, the divinely blessed land of Canaan and Nanking in China. The southern parallel goes through Chile, the Cape of South Africa and the Terre de Nuyts, the latter two being precisely the lands that Purry wanted the company to colonize. As it turned out, Purry's appeal to the Dutch East India Company failed, as did his second pitch to the French royal officials, but he had better luck with his third attempt, this time with the British who granted him land in South Carolina, also on the magic latitude, for his model colony. The British capitulated partly because it suited them to have a European Protestant buffer against the Indians, but Purry's colony, appropriately named Purrysburg Township, was not a success. Purry died there in 1736, having spent 'one third of his life bringing to fulfilment a vision grounded in empirical study and articulated to audiences around the world in three of the great empires of the eighteenth century'.[28]

More important than the peculiar and unique details of Purry's life are the common assumptions built in to his proposals to the colonial and commercial elites of Amsterdam, Paris and London in the early eighteenth century. His works are part biblical worldview, part theory of race, part travel narrative, part bourgeois aspiration, part business venture, part empirical observation, part justification for European colonialism, part product of imperial rivalry, part Enlightenment vision of fruitfulness and prosperity, part defence of land seizure and part justification for slavery. Purry's particular theories of climate and fertility may have commanded both fascination and ridicule, but many of the assumptions upon which they were based were widely shared among early modern Europeans.[29]

What strikes the modern reader most are the number of biblical allusions in his text. Not only does the 33rd parallel providentially run through the land of Canaan, but biblical characters are frequently appealed to for strategy, or as examples of wise stewardship of the earth's resources. Moreover, Purry's whole scheme of colonization and land seizure rested on a particular theology of justice. Countering the argument that colonization is fundamentally unjust to native peoples, Purry quotes God's injunction to the Israelites in the Bible, 'for the Earth is Mine; God said to the Jewish people, and you are alien and itinerant in my home' (Leviticus 24). Since in this view God owns the earth and all its peoples are merely aliens, there are no foundational rights to land based on longevity of occupancy; rather all have the right to cultivate the land 'as long as each one only takes what he needs'. How this limitation was to be determined or implemented is of course never discussed. Purry goes on to assert that 'uncivilized and simple people like a lazy life above all', and that 'the settling of a good European colony would bring all sorts of goods and advantages to them'. Purry thought that Protestant Christians would treat native peoples much better than the Catholic Iberian empires had done, but he also thought that slavery was justified. Carlo Ginzburg has observed that Purry's defence of slavery is, perhaps surprisingly, not based on the Bible. Presumably Purry could easily have extracted a biblical defence of slavery from precisely the same part of the Bible he quoted about God's ownership of the land (Leviticus 25:44 states 'it is from the nations around you that you may acquire male and female slaves'), but he chose instead to appeal to the classical civilization of the Romans who did not work their own soils. Purry nevertheless had an optimistic appreciation, gleaned from experience in Java, of what slaves could accomplish if they were properly instructed.

In short, Purry's story, however peculiar, is a biblically and classically grounded defence of the superiority of European civilization, its right to colonize others, its right to employ slave labour and its enlightened capacity to pursue fruitfulness and happiness in the most agreeable climate zones of the world. All this was declared not only to be somehow permissible or even justifiable, but also to be the very will of God. Purry told the directors of the Dutch East India Company that the pursuit of colonization, not merely colonial trade, would be 'founded upon charity toward others as upon the love of God':

> I mention charity toward others because you would not be doing anything in doing this that would be directly opposed to equity or justice. On the contrary, you would have the opportunity, without harming anyone, to assist a large number of your poor brethren who are overcome by misery and afflictions. I also mention the love of God because it would be a way to contribute something to the Rise of His Kingdom and you would then have the glory and the distinction not only to own one of the most beautiful and best countries in the universe, but mainly to have been one of the first to have carried the torch of the Gospel among a large number of poor people who do not yet have the honor of knowing His Divine Name.[30]

There could be no more ringing declaration of the merits of European empire and Christian mission, which is the subject to which we must now turn. As we shall see, Purry's propaganda is not exactly how it worked in practice.

Empire and mission

There was an undeniably close relationship between colonial expansion and missionary zeal in both the established Catholic empires and the emergent Protestant empires of the early modern period, but determining the nature of that relationship at different times and in different places is more difficult than it first appears. Of course the expansion of European empires, accompanied as they were by military force, colonial trade and the extension of cultural power, opened up fresh channels and opportunities for missionaries. Missionaries travelled to new places on board the ships of colonial trade, they sailed under the auspices of colonial rulers to whom they owed allegiance and they were often beneficiaries of the sinews of empire, including military protection, access to resources and slave labour. Moreover, the great majority of European missionaries, whether Protestant or Catholic, considered themselves 'the bearers not merely of a superior religion, but of a superior culture'.[31] Hence they were critical of native religious traditions and were generally slow to accept indigenous clergy.

In the Iberian empires the basic framework for the expansion of Christendom was supplied by the rights, privileges and duties conferred by the papacy on the Iberian monarchs, the *Padroado Real* in Portuguese jurisdictions and the *Patronato* in Spanish. Established by a series of papal bulls and briefs in the late fifteenth and early sixteenth centuries, these gave the Iberian monarchs substantial powers over the erection of ecclesiastical buildings, the presentation of suitable candidates for colonial church appointments and control over ecclesiastical jurisdictions and revenues. Hence, it was clear that 'cross and crown, throne and altar, and faith and empire' were to proceed together, and that Roman Catholic missionaries, whichever religious order they belonged to, were as much agents of colonial control in areas of Iberian conquest as they were emissaries of the Church Militant. Catholic missionaries, despite some notable exceptions, were also directly implicated in the colonial slave trade. Authorized by papal bulls, justified by economic necessity and implemented as a tool of European civilization, slavery was widely practised by the religious orders in Spanish and Portuguese America and in other parts of the world. There were of course some dissident religious figures who condemned the African slave trade as unchristian and immoral, and many more who tried to inject humanitarian imperatives into a cruel system, but on the whole the Church was a facilitator of the slave trade, not its nemesis. The same could be said of its role in sustaining a hierarchical classification of races, with white Europeans at the top and African slaves firmly at the bottom.

However closely associated Catholic missionaries were with instruments of colonial exploitation and control in the Iberian empires, the harmony of interests between cross and crown was never absolute or completely uncontested. The primacy of religious motivation, a desire for converts, a strong sense of vocation, and on occasions even an embrace of martyrdom, meant that the Catholic orders often disagreed with colonial officials about establishing priorities and devising strategies for the Christianization of native peoples. Conflicts were often sharpest either on colonial frontiers where missionaries had disagreements *among* themselves and *with* colonial officials about the appropriate level of military support for their mission, and in well-established pockets of clerical control where the regular clergy had no desire to see their influence over indigenous people weakened by crude displays of imperial hegemony or settler exploitation (see Chapter 3). Catholic missionaries in Iberian America were well aware that the church could not be built on gunpowder alone, but they also knew that the threat of gunpowder was part of the toolkit of their mission. Other tools included images and artefacts, art and architecture, rituals and festivals, services and sacraments, print and instruction, censorship and inquisition, celibacy and confession, millennialism and martyrdom, surveillance and prosecution, and punishment and persecution. Collectively, over time these instruments exercised a powerful and enduring influence. Hence, the sheer persistence of Roman Catholicism in the old empires of Spain and Portugal, right up to the present, was no mere product of imperial might, even if it could not have been accomplished without it.

The relationship between religion and empire in the emerging Protestant empires of Britain and the Netherlands in the seventeenth and eighteenth centuries was rather different from the Iberian pattern we have just discussed. Protestants, at least to begin with, did not so much conquer and rule as trade and settle, and generally speaking they did not have anything quite like the missionary religious orders of Roman Catholicism. A combination of a siege mentality in Protestant Europe in response to the gains of Counter Reformation Catholicism, a theology that emphasized divine sovereignty over human instrumentality, and the realities of naval and military power in the early modern period ensured that Protestantism was slower than Catholicism to expand outside Europe. There are of course well-known examples of English Puritan, Dutch Reformed and German and Swedish Lutheran forays into new worlds in the seventeenth century, but it was not until the eighteenth century that Protestantism emerged as a major competitor to Roman Catholicism outside Europe. Notwithstanding the importance of Dutch colonies in the West and East Indies, the most significant bearers of extra-European Protestantism were the British. What the British brought to the table were growing military and commercial power, a strongly providentialist anti-Catholicism, a remarkable diversity of Protestant religious traditions and the propensity of those traditions to migrate in search of better conditions. As they envisaged new worlds, British Protestants shared many characteristics with their Iberian Catholic competitors including European Christian chauvinism with respect to other cultures and religious traditions, deep involvement in the slave trade and a sense of millennial and providential empowerment. On the other hand they were critical of the brutality of the *conquistadores* and could not emulate the same pattern of ecclesiastical control that Iberian Catholics were able to promote in the Americas. The sheer diversity of British Protestantism, and the fact of growing pluralism and religious toleration, meant that the religious character of the emerging British Empire came to be strongly Protestant but weakly Anglican. In short, within colonial possessions, the Protestant principle was more widespread and commonly shared than the establishment principle.

It was not that the Church of England made no attempt to extend its control over the fledgling British Empire. In North America, for example, the Church made serious efforts to become a working colonial establishment. Under the auspices of the Society for Promoting Christian Knowledge (1698) and the Society for the Propagation of the Gospel in Foreign Parts (1701), print and people were sent across the Atlantic in considerable numbers. Before the American Revolution the SPG sent over 600 clergymen who established over 300 churches outside the Anglican heartlands of Virginia and Maryland. Although Anglicans had some success stories, notably their influence over Yale College and their forays into Puritan New England, the tides of empire were not moving in their direction. Competition from non-Anglican British Protestants (most notably Ulster-Scots Presbyterians), fast-growing religious pluralism in the American colonies and the primacy of trade in imperial policy all made it difficult for Anglicans to make their case as the rightful Established Church of the British Empire. In addition, although George Whitefield was an ordained Anglican clergyman, the impact of the Great Awakening on the American colonies did not work in favour of the Anglicans. Nervous of his unorthodox methods, suspicious of the religious enthusiasm he generated and critical of his overtures to dissenters, colonial Anglicans largely missed out on the religious transformation he helped promote. Anglicanism nevertheless maintained an important position in the American colonies, and over the course of the century became the officially recognized established church of the Canadian territories to the north which were ceded to Britain by the Treaty of Utrecht (1713) and the Treaty of Paris (1763). Anglicanism also took strong hold in some of the British Atlantic and Caribbean islands, including Barbados, Jamaica, Bermuda and the Bahamas.

Nevertheless, try as they might, eighteenth-century Anglican bishops could not muster sufficient political or religious capital to persuade the British political elite that British colonies should be organized as little mirror images of the English Established Church. Unable to establish colonial bishoprics, and forced to play second fiddle to the trading aspirations of colonial officials, colonial Anglicanism was in a parlous position even before the American Revolution wrought havoc on its not inconsiderable eighteenth-century achievements. As one historian has it, 'Free trade in commerce, and faith, was the new world order', at least in North America.[32]

Hence, the most significant developments in the spread of British Protestantism in the eighteenth and early nineteenth centuries were not so much orchestrated by an ecclesiastical establishment as they were by the consequences of population movements, the slave trade, the Evangelical Revival and the rise of the voluntaristic, Protestant missionary societies. Partly fuelled by a fast-moving circulation of print, people and ideas, and partly boosted by international trade and warfare, British Protestantism established a substantial bulkhead in North America in the eighteenth century and then in the wider world in the nineteenth century. As Protestantism spread, it too had to negotiate racial, cultural and religious differences, and it too had to face difficult questions about the relationship between religion and empire. The sheer circulation of people and ideas in the British Atlantic world in the eighteenth century produced an eclectic and messy set of encounters that make it difficult to talk with assurance about European, African and American characteristics. Rather, all of these identities were complex in themselves, quite apart from the results of their encounters with one another. There was nevertheless a distinctively Protestant milieu that emerged in the Anglophone world in the long eighteenth century that survived the depredations of wars and revolutions.[33]

Generally speaking, within eighteenth-century Protestantism the migration of people preceded the arrival of missionaries and the arrival of missionaries preceded the establishment of formal missionary societies. Those societies, partly based on Moravian precedents, nevertheless became ubiquitous in the early nineteenth century. Just as earlier Catholic missionaries sometimes anticipated and sometimes followed the trappings of empire, Protestant missionaries also had to negotiate their relationship with empire. How was this done, and what were the consequences?

The three most common charges brought against British Protestant missionaries are that they were agents of imperialism, destroyers of indigenous cultures and instigators of a new era of bad feelings between Protestant Christianity and other world faiths. With the Bible in one hand and the flag in the other, these zealous storm-troopers of the British Empire allegedly supplied much of the religious ideology, some of the manpower and not a little of the cultural chauvinism underpinning Britain's rise to globalism in the eighteenth and nineteenth centuries. But recent scholarship presents a much more ambiguous and complex relationship between religion and empire.[34] One of the difficulties of a subject like this is that one has to bring into conversation with one another three traditions of historical writing that are generally kept separate, namely, British imperial history, British domestic religious history and the local histories of overseas regions affected by colonialism. One also needs to pay close attention to the religious motivation and theological characteristics of Protestant missionaries before trying to grapple with both the intended and, perhaps even more important, the unintended consequences of their missionary zeal in an imperial context.

Trying to make sense of the encounters between multi-denominational Protestant missionaries and a wide variety of host cultures in multiple regions across the world over two centuries of British imperial expansion is obviously complicated work. Generally speaking, however, missionaries were not so much advocates of imperialism as they were genuine religious enthusiasts who could not avoid interacting with agencies of imperial control even if they had wanted to. To the extent that missionaries benefited from open doors, social stability and personal safety, they had a vested interest in empire, but they also had the capacity to subvert aspects of colonial governance, to work with fellow missionaries from other (sometimes competing) countries and to place their religious mission on a higher plane than mere political control or economic development. Naturally, emphases varied among denominations and over time. Generally speaking, Anglicans were more wedded to establishment models of Christianization, including the establishment of bishoprics and territorially organized churches, than dissenters, and missionary strategy ebbed and flowed according to resources, levels of optimism, theological characteristics, styles of colonial governance and individual personalities. Nevertheless, most missionaries at most times did not want to be imperial propagandists and had no interest in becoming colonial rulers. The kingdom they were attempting to build was not one that could be ruled from offices in London.

One of the most significant theological variables in the relationship between missions and empire is the Evangelical Protestant emphasis on eschatology. Millennialism was not only a major factor in stimulating missionary zeal, as in the explosion of Protestant missionary societies in the 1790s and early 1800s, but was also a source of ideological friction and strategic disagreement, as Protestants differed over the timing and circumstances of the promised Second Coming of Christ. To a modern audience all this may seem like trivial hair-splitting over the interpretation of opaque prophetical literature in the Bible, but to contemporaries it had immense implications for how missionaries should go about their business and how they should relate to indigenous cultures and other faith traditions. Of particular interest, in the light of subsequent history, is how Evangelical Protestants conceptualized their relationship to Islam. In the early nineteenth century many believed that through scholarship and persuasion it could be demonstrated that the Bible was a superior text to the Koran, and that as this truth was proclaimed Islam would simply crumble, but over the course of the nineteenth century substantial Islamic gains across the continent of Africa forced a major reappraisal of prophetical interpretation as well as operational strategy. Theology was important in other respects also. Theological changes such as the rise of Arminianism and the decline of rigid Calvinism, a renewed emphasis on providence (general and particular) and the growth of holiness traditions all led to different patterns of encounter between missionaries and indigenous peoples within the context of empire.

In short, it is an exaggeration to view all British Protestant missionaries as the mere foot soldiers of empire or to see Protestant missions as unalloyed cultural imperialism. In most categories of analysis from educational provision to the transmission of new concepts of time and ritual, mission is more about negotiative exchanges, albeit with significant inbuilt power differentials, than about unadulterated cultural imposition. In understanding missions, one needs to be as aware of diffusion, limitation, resistance, translation, subversion and liberation, as one is of repression, control and exploitation. There is also need for care in trawling through the vast acreage of missionary propaganda. For example, some missionaries developed arguments in support of their utility to empire because either they wanted to raise financial support for financially strapped missions or they saw a competitive advantage in presenting their case that way. In the interests of appealing to a wider public, some also argued that far from missions depending on empire, the reverse was the case. John Philip (1775–1851), the director of the London Missionary Society's South African operation, wrote that while our missionaries 'are everywhere scattering the seeds of civilization, social order and happiness, they are, by the most unexceptionable means, extending British interests, British influence and the British Empire'.[35]

Although most missionaries did not set out with the self-conscious aim of spreading British power and influence, that bare assertion tends to push aside the question of cultural imperialism or what we might call the laws of unintended consequences. For example, the rage for missions was itself a cultural product that was consumed through voluntary societies, periodicals, annual meetings and church gatherings focused specifically on foreign mission. And on the ground, British missionaries were both conscious and unconscious spreaders of British civilizational mores including labour practices, cultural expectations and educational imperatives. Missionaries may not have fully understood how their preaching, schooling and circulation of the Gospels in translation were tied inevitably to particular forms of social and economic change, but they were. Hence it is possible to position missionaries as conduits for the flood of Western concepts and structures, both material and symbolic, with or without their self-conscious intention of being conduits. In that respect, missionaries in various locations around the world were simultaneously agents of European social and economic structures and creators of indigenous Christian traditions.[36] Even the ineffectuality of missionaries as agents of imperialism could have the unintended consequence of facilitating colonialism, because they eroded native traditions and weakened native leadership without ever being able to serve as cohesive advocates of native rights. In addition, some take the view that *both* missionaries and natives were being affected by modernity and hegemonic culture (political, economic and ideological).[37] In other words missionaries were simultaneously agents of the spread of modernity to non-European societies and products of its emerging hegemony. For example, to what extent does conversion of the Protestant Evangelical variety depend upon the modern notion of the autonomous individual which also has deeper economic and cultural salience?

In the eighteenth century both Catholic and Protestant missionaries can be found operating outside the geographical boundaries of imperial power; openly criticizing the cruelties of colonial officials and their policies; trying to place themselves as buffers between the acquisitive and predatory behaviours of colonists and native peoples; disregarding the advice and instructions of colonial officials; and even cultivating a desire for sacrifice and martyrdom that was based on no apparent imperial calculus. On the other hand, whether self-consciously or not, they were unremitting exporters of European cultural mores. Even as they fought against the naked exploitation of native peoples by European colonists, and even as they appealed to imperial governments to protect the rights of natives against colonial rapaciousness, missionaries were themselves colonizers as well as evangelists. They may have wanted to usher in the Kingdom of God on earth, but their interpretation of how that kingdom worked was rooted inexorably in their European faith traditions and their countries of origin.

A number of important points emerge from this brief foray into world Christianity in the eighteenth century. Perhaps the most important is the realization that Christianity in all its Roman Catholic, Protestant and Orthodox forms was a remarkably diverse religious tradition with a surprisingly extensive global coverage. However, its global expansion was inextricably bound up with its predominantly European roots and assumptions, and with the empires, Catholic, Protestant and Orthodox, which facilitated and shaped its expansion. Not surprisingly, therefore, Christian expansion was profoundly shaped both by the cultures that promoted it and by the indigenous cultures it encountered. Neither of these categories remained static and stable over the course of the eighteenth century, but were constantly shifting in response to some of the great structural forces of the century including the rise of empires, competition between Protestants and Catholics on the one hand, and between Christians and other religious traditions on the other, the ubiquity of the slave trade, the Evangelical Revival, and complex changes in thought, notions of governance and views of 'the other' which are inadequately, and often confusingly, summed up in the term 'Enlightenment'. With some of the preliminary mapping done the next few chapters seek to delve more deeply into the following questions. How do we account for the expansion of Christianity into new spaces? What drove that expansion? What kinds of people were involved in it? And perhaps most difficult of all, what were the relationships between Europeans and 'others' and what kinds of Christianity emerged from diverse cultural encounters in different parts of the world?

CHAPTER 2

Heart Religion and the Rise of Global Christianity: New Selves and New Places[1]

The purpose of this chapter is to shed fresh light on the processes by which Western European Christianity, both Roman Catholic and Protestant, extended its missionary compass to all parts of the globe in the early modern period. This is no easy task, for it must bring together the self understanding and religious motivation of missionaries themselves with the structural forces that were making it possible for Europeans to encounter native populations in different parts of the world. On the whole, the former is less well understood than the latter, and the work that has already been done tends to replicate the confessional division into Protestants and Catholics that so characterized Christianity's rise to globalism. But it is also possible, as this chapter will suggest, that, allowing for their different confessional traditions, both European Catholics and Protestants were developing parallel traditions of spirituality based on the 'religion of the heart' that enabled their missionary cohorts to move around the world in search of new converts in culturally unfamiliar places. It is important to state at the outset that my attempt to penetrate to the heart of missionary motivation in the lives of some key individuals and missionary traditions in terms of religious self-formation is not meant to be a substitute for, or replacement of, the conventional explanations for Christian expansion in this period. In short, nothing in what follows is meant to *subtract* anything from the well-established explanations of Christianity's rise to globalism in this period. The voyages of reconnaissance, the European revolution in cartography, the rise of the European seaborne empires (first Roman Catholic and then Protestant), the ever expanding tentacles of trade, trading companies, and the execrable slave trade, the growth of printing and Bible translation into vernacular languages, the burgeoning of travel literature, the resurgence of an optimistic and expansive millennialism,[2] and the mobility of disenchanted and often persecuted populations displaced by the brutalities of the Thirty Years' War all played significant parts in extending the geographical boundaries of European Christendom in the centuries after the Protestant Reformation.[3] All of these categories of explanation require detailed elucidation, but they do not of themselves explain why individuals were prepared to venture, risk, sacrifice and travel for the sake of a message that had reshaped their own lives and views of the world in profound ways. Nor do they shed much light on the personal spiritual formation and self-understanding of missionaries, both Catholic and Protestant and men and women, who left Europe for the New (to them) World.

To explore this theme in more detail I propose to say something about the spiritual formation of the two most potent missionary forces of the early modern period, the Catholic Jesuits and the Protestant Pietists, and then follow the lives of three important figures who made significant contributions to Christian expansion and whose unusually well-documented lives illustrate the symbiotic relationship between spiritual discipline, self-formation and missionary service. The chapter will conclude by establishing tangible connections between early modern spiritual formation, newly reconstructed selves and commitment to global mission.

Jesuits: the religion of the heart and the heart of mission

The Society of Jesus, founded by Ignatius of Loyola, arose out of a gathering of university students at the University of Paris in the 1530s and was given formal approval by Pope Paul III in 1540. It soon emerged as the largest mission organization in the world. Although comprised only of men, Jesuits were also spiritual directors of women and sometimes used women associates as catechists. Recent scholarship has paid attention to their immense investment in colleges and their cultural contributions to education, theatre, music, architecture, agriculture and industry.[4] They expertly raised money, built libraries, educated Europe's Catholic elites, promoted civic engagement, pioneered scientific inquiry, constructed maps, employed the visual arts and produced any number of grammars, vocabularies, catechisms and confession manuals. Hence, they were not only enthusiastic missionaries, but also inexhaustible cultural dynamos. Although much depended on whether Jesuits entered foreign missions on the coat tails of conquering armies or as missionaries to non-subjugated civilizations (black robes versus mandarin robes), they built a reputation for engaging foreign cultures not as domineering imperialists but as skilful adapters to local sensibilities.[5] But Jesuits also underwent a rigorous programme of spiritual formation based on their founder's *Spiritual Exercises*, which helps explain not only their personal discipline but also their enthusiasm for global mission.

My intention here is to explore further a connection Michelle Molina has made between 'the history of western subjectivity and the history of early modern global expansion', or, less technically, 'how individual efforts at spiritual transformation had global significance'.[6] In particular, Molina explores how 'new thinking about self and world were key components of Jesuit evangelical efforts', and how Jesuit spirituality proceeded from self-reform to the reform of others. Central to her investigation is the comment by Arnold Davidson that 'in trying to capture the different forms in which the care of the self has appeared, it is essential to understand not only the ways in which the self became an object of concern, but also the ways in which one went beyond oneself, relating the self to something grander than itself'.[7] With that in mind, she shows how the enormously influential Ignatian *Spiritual Exercises* were designed to reform one's self internally in the interest of a greater cause, namely the conversion of the world's population. Beginning with introspective exercises of self-scrutiny, practitioners were encouraged to look outward to imagine the whole world. Originally conceived as a four-week exercise in spiritual formation, the first week was devoted to 'spiritual exercises to overcome oneself, and to order one's life'. The second week was devoted to 'the contemplation of the Kingdom of Jesus Christ: the call of the temporal king as an aid towards contemplating the life of the eternal king'. In these exercises the practitioner was encouraged to *imagine* the life of Jesus as he moved through synagogues and villages preaching the kingdom, and then to follow him. The practitioner was to ask for 'an interior knowledge of Our Lord who became human for me, that I may love him more intensely and follow him more closely'. Following meant bringing together the interior knowledge of Christ with an expansive vision of the redemption of the whole world. The practitioner was urged,

> to see the great extent of the circuit of the world, with peoples so many and so diverse. ... I will see the various persons, some here, some there. First, those on the face of the earth, so diverse in dress and behaviour: some white and others black, some in peace and others at war, some weeping and others laughing, some healthy and others sick, some being born and others dying, and so forth. ... I will listen to what the persons on the face of the earth are saying; that is, how they speak with one another, swear and blaspheme, and so on. Likewise, I will hear what the Divine Persons are saying, that is, 'Let us work the redemption of the human race.'[8]

Originally conceived as a 30-day retreat, the Jesuits adapted and abridged the *Exercises* in various programmes to suit the individual needs of the laity. What was new about this in the early modern period was not so much the religious content of the *Exercises*, which are well known to have had any number of medieval precedents, but the audience – 'the laity was being monasticised'. A combination of shortened *Exercises* to be completed in only eight days (or less) and the growth of retreat houses, where the *Exercises* could be directed, expanded the range of Jesuit spirituality to a much larger group of people, both religious and lay. Moreover, these disciplines occurred within a context of European imperial expansion and the growing circulation of the *Jesuit Relations* (missionary reports) about what was happening in different parts of the world.[9] In short, self-discipline and spiritual formation, a key component of which was a desire to see the rule of Christ over all nations, was a way of universalizing the Christian message, and personal submission was a prelude to missionary action. Put another way (using early modern language), in Jesuit spirituality the religion of the heart was an expression of love for the Sacred Heart of Jesus and the Sacred Heart of Jesus was in turn capable of embracing the whole world.

What is being suggested here is not that writing about the religion of the heart and the spirituality associated with it was an invention of early modern Europeans, which it most certainly was not. Nor is it possible to argue even more grandly and absurdly that conceptions of the self or traditions of interior writing were somehow inventions of modernity, which they were not. No reader of classical texts, or of Augustine's *Confessions*, or of the ubiquitous medieval traditions of 'writing on the heart' could make such a case.[10] What is being suggested, however, is that in the early modern period a number of factors combined to give the renewed emphasis on heart religion by both European Catholics and Protestants an unprecedented global salience. These include the greater sense of religious competition ushered in by the Reformation and Counter Reformation, the sense of religious responsibility attendant upon the spread of European overseas empires, the greater volume of encounters between Europeans and non-Europeans (and the accompanying sense of 'difference'), the increased laicization of spiritual disciplines, and the circulating medium of travel and missionary literature which encouraged European Christians to imagine themselves in new and exotic places. As they became more aware of 'others' European Christians also became more aware of themselves. How then do these tidy theoretical ideas of the relationship between the self and the universal, and between spiritual formation and missionary zeal, play out in the real lives of missionaries and their converts?

Molina has drawn attention to a book on the Sacred Heart published by a Mexican Jesuit named Juan Antonio Mora in the 1730s, which was a translation of a book published in Rome in 1726 by the French Jesuit Joseph Gallifet. These transnational connections are themselves emblematic of the ways in which the Jesuits circled the world in the seventeenth and eighteenth centuries. Gallifet was trying to establish a feast day dedicated to the Sacred Heart of Jesus and he enlisted three notable Catholics for support. They were St Bernard, the twelfth-century Cistercian, St Gertrude, a thirteenth-century Benedictine nun, and Marie de l'Incarnation, the seventeenth-century Ursuline missionary for whom the Sacred Heart, under Jesuit direction, was no longer only a personal dwelling place but became a universal emblem for the conversion of the world. How did this happen, and what does it mean for the early modern expansion of Catholicism into the New World?

Marie de l'Incarnation (1599–1672)

Perhaps the best recorded life of an early modern Catholic female missionary is that of Marie Guyart (Marie de l'Incarnation), who founded the first Ursuline convent in North America (Quebec) in the mid-seventeenth century and whose life was an inspiration to Catholic women in the eighteenth century. Her self-declared aspiration was to 'go around the whole world looking for souls to be redeemed with the precious Blood of my beloved spouse, and to have them satisfied by your most holy Heart. ... My God! Don't permit it to pass that JESUS will be for one more moment unknown and ignored by so many souls!'[11] But how did this baker's daughter from the textile town of Tours in France end up as a missionary/educator in New France? The most important forces at work were a combination of melancholic mystical devotion, the influence of spiritual directors, the mortification of the flesh, the reading of the *Jesuit Relations*, visions of strange landscapes and a kind of Catholic millennialism in which all nations would be converted as a gift to the suffering Christ.[12] Although she had previously read François de Sales (1567–1622) and the lives of St Theresa (1515–82) and François de Xavier (1506–52), the call to missionary work and the move from personal discipline to bringing the church to the world came to Marie in a dream about a far away place which was subsequently identified by her Jesuit spiritual director as Canada. She wrote, 'My body was in our monastery, but my spirit was tied to that of Jesus and could not be enclosed. ... I walked in spirit in those great vastitudes, accompanying those working for the gospel.'[13] As she negotiated the boundaries between freedom and enclosure, what she asked for was a 'voice powerful enough to be heard at the ends of the earth, to say that my divine Spouse is worthy of reigning and being loved by all hearts'.[14]

Revealing details of Marie's own conception of herself are conveyed in her writings to her abandoned son in France, Claude Martin. As her private self gained public expression she wrote letters, contributed to the *Relations* and penned a spiritual autobiography which was subsequently edited and added to by her son for publication five years after her death in 1677 (*La Vie de la vénerable Mère Marie de l'incarnation, première supérieure des Ursulines de la Nouvelle France, tirée de ses lettres et des écrits*). What kind of self-understanding emerges from these materials? Two episodes in her life are worth paying particular attention to. The first is Marie's behaviour during the fire that destroyed the Ursuline convent in Quebec in December 1650. She tried to save the most important of the convent's records by throwing them out of the window, then she looked at 'the manuscript of the first version of her spiritual autobiography. She hesitated for a moment, touched it, and then, led by her unerring sense of sacrifice, calmly left it to burn.'[15] From this account it seems obvious that her written self, however diligently reconstructed and deeply valued, was nothing compared to the preeminence of the work of God to which she had been called. This is expressed in even clearer terms in a *Relation* edited by her son. '"C'est mon moi" ("he is my me") Marie says of an embrace between her soul and the Person of the Word (Jesus). Claude draws the line: "Il est comme un autre moi-même" ("he is like another myself").'[16]

This capacity for self-awareness and self-denial expressed in terms of a loving embrace with the 'Person of the Word' has an obvious gender dimension which emerges even more clearly in a letter written by Marie to the wealthy funder of her mission, Madeleine de La Peltrie: 'My heart is in yours, and the two together are only one with the heart of Jesus amid those large and infinite spaces where we embrace the little Savage girls.'[17] This imagined embrace between the female missionary, the female funder and the female savages shows that Marie imagined her mission as a semi-autonomous female venture dedicated to the world-embracing power of the Sacred Heart of Jesus.[18] Moreover, her repeated use of the religion of the heart shows the extent to which Marie was trying to articulate and translate for others her felt experience of divine love. In her Quebec Ursuline convent Marie described her teaching style as an attempt 'to make my heart go out through my tongue to tell my dear Neophytes how the love of God feels'.[19] This language of felt experience and the compulsion to tell it to others, though deeply Catholic in its formation, could easily have been uttered by Protestant Pietists who also embraced the 'religion of the heart'.

Pietism: from introspection to internationalism

On the Protestant side, explanations for the remarkable surge of extra-European missions in the eighteenth century after two centuries of relative quiescence have concentrated on the importance of European Pietism and transatlantic Evangelical revivals, Bible translation into vernacular languages and the rise of voluntary societies. Conversionism, translation

and voluntarism were thus the abiding Trinitarian trademarks of the Protestant missionary movement. In work that bears comparison with that on
Jesuit spirituality, however, scholars have recently made important contributions to a new appreciation of self and spiritual formation in the Pietism
and Evangelicalism of the late seventeenth and early eighteenth centuries.
Far from coincidentally (as with the Jesuits), these were also the traditions
that were at the forefront of the global expansion of Protestantism in the
eighteenth century. For example, the ubiquitous Evangelical conversion
narratives appeared along with new conceptions of the self at what one
historian calls 'the trailing edge of Christendom and the leading edge of
modernity'.[20] According to this view, the Renaissance made people more
aware of themselves as individuals while Reformation Protestantism made
them more aware of themselves as sinners. Penitential traditions of Christianity with their emphases on anxiety, awareness of sin and guilt were
thus brought into contact with modern conceptions of the self arising
from a complex of social and cultural changes associated with commercial
individualism and Lockean empiricism. The result of this encounter was
allegedly to produce modern selves with increased awareness of sin and
guilt to which the Evangelical message brought new possibilities of release,
re-formation and refashioning. Similarly, others have suggested that populist Evangelicals employed spiritual discipline as an instrument of self-
fashioning, freedom and modernity. They cultivated spiritual discipline not
as an instrument of elite or self-repression, as Marxist historians like E.P.
Thompson once supposed, but rather as a way of producing the necessary
self-control within which personal agency (however restricted and circumscribed by social realities) could work more effectively.[21]

Here I want to build on these insights by investigating the ways in which
European Pietism, and later, forms of populist Evangelicalism, helped
initiate a new Protestant enthusiasm for global mission through its dialecti-
cal emphases on holy introspection and the priesthood of all believers.[22] As
a more radical and personal expression of Lutheranism, Pietism, though
variegated and eclectic, was essentially a reaction against scholastic orthodoxy and academic theology. Its characteristic emphases were on heart religion ('Piety must first of all nest in the heart'), biblical devotion, religious
experience, the new birth and telling the experience (conversion and the
inner life), holy living, prayer and hymnody. There is also a strong emphasis
on millennialism, specifically of the postmillennial kind, or the idea that
God was preparing a splendid future for the church on earth as in heaven.
Largely operating outside ecclesiastical and political power structures,
Pietism was 'a Bible-centred movement concerned for holy living that flows
from the regenerate heart'.[23] Given the complexity and internationalism of

Pietism it is not surprising that it has been subjected to a wide range of by no means mutually exclusive interpretations.[24] It has been variously interpreted as a religious renewal movement within European Protestantism; a kind of completion of Luther's Reformation; a reaction against the incorporation of the churches into the modern state with all the attendant evils of Constantinianism and corruption; a yearning for peace and heart religion after the confessional turmoil and psychic shock of the Thirty Years' War (1618–48); a drive towards social discipline and social control, in the midst of chaos; and as a sibling movement of the Enlightenment, a religious version of the attempt to discover the means and the way to a better life.[25]

Pietism also gave a renewed stimulus to Christian mission. The Moravian Church in particular was a kind of trailblazer for the missionary awakening of Protestant churches at the end of the eighteenth century.[26] But how did this happen, not only in organizational terms, the story of which has been well told, but also in terms of the spiritual formation and Christian imagination of those who actively sought the extension of Christ's rule on earth?[27] Some of the most characteristic expressions of Pietism supply the clues for a possible answer. These include Pietist written culture with its emphases on diaries, autobiographies and letters; Pietist organizational culture with its emphasis on *ecclesiolae in ecclesia* (classes and conventicles); and Pietist vocational culture as expressed in the curriculum of the University of Halle, with its emphasis on training schools for pastors, charitable institutions, medical dispensaries and laboratories.

Another way of framing this triptych in more theological terms is to present it in terms of spiritual introspection, the priesthood of all believers and Christian vocation, all of which were inextricably connected in Pietist spirituality.[28] Consider, for example, Philipp Jakob Spener's *Pia Desideria*, first published in 1675, which is appropriately regarded as one of the foundational texts of the Pietist movement. Spener wrote that 'Our whole Christian religion consists of the inner man ... hence it is not enough that we hear the Word with our outward ear, but we must let it penetrate to our heart.'[29] This heart religion was different from mere formal observance and needed to be nurtured by word, sacrament and song. In short, the new self was in essence an inner self that could only be developed through the arts of spiritual discipline. This new inner self was part discovery, part construction and part formation, and fits Charles Taylor's view of the 'inner self' as an essentially modern move in the evolution of personality and self-consciousness. But in Pietist spirituality new selves were not to remain in atomic isolation from one another. Spener set forth six proposals for reforming individuals and the collective church. The first was a more extensive use of the Word of God by which ordinary people could exercise more control over their consciences without relying on the efficacy of a priest. The second proposal, following directly and logically from the first, is the 'establishment and diligent exercise of the spiritual priesthood'. Spener, borrowing from Luther, asserts that all Christians are priests and that the lack of missionary dynamism in the Christian church throughout history was owing to the monopolistic priesthood promulgated by 'papal Rome'. 'One of the principal reasons the ministry cannot accomplish all that it ought,' he wrote, 'is that it is too weak without the help of the universal priesthood.'[30] Freed from these foundational errors, and trained and disciplined in love and the religion of the heart, Christians would have newly sanctified vocations to take the whole Gospel into the whole world and make converts. Spener's third proposal therefore is 'to win the erring' and his fourth is 'a practice of heart-felt love towards all unbelievers and heretics'. Reading almost like a missionary manifesto Spener's injunction is to love our neighbours as Christ loved the non-Jewish Samaritan and to 'regard them as our brothers according to the right of common creation and the divine love that is extended to all', for to 'insult or wrong an unbeliever or heretic on account of his religion would be not only a carnal zeal but also a zeal that is calculated to hinder his conversion'.[31]

Here then is how the Pietist triptych worked. Individual selves would have their inner lives renewed by the word and the spirit; they would then act together as a universal priesthood both inside and outside the structures of the formal church, and would then work for the conversion of the 'common creation'. This triptych alone, however, was not enough to propel Pietists into global mission; that task was accomplished by the unfavourable historical context in which they found themselves in Europe after the Thirty Years' War (1618–48). A combination of state persecutions, confessional cleansing, low Protestant morale and migrations (both forced and voluntary) across Europe and then to the New World helped turn Pietist introspection into a movement of international renewal and revival. Pietism borne on the wings of mobile populations then influenced other movements of Protestant reform and renewal, such as the Methodists and early Evangelicals. Well served by the training available at the University of Halle, armed with a voluntaristic ecclesiology that could survive the hostility of Europe's established churches and propagating new conceptions of selfhood in the early modern world, Pietists fused introspection and internationalism, and the religion of the heart with a heart-shaped world of previously unimagined ethnic diversity. No image better encapsulates what was going on than the Moravian Johann Valentin Haidt's monumental painting of *The First Fruits* (1747) depicting the first converts of the Moravian overseas missions begun in 1732.[32] He depicts 21 men, women and children meeting the ascended Jesus in the clouds. The painting is part millennial vision, part missionary propaganda and part colourful celebration of a riotous ethnic diversity embraced by the bared heart of the wounded and resurrected Christ. Among the 21 there is a Persian, a Caucasian, an Armenian, a Greenlander, a Hottentot and several American Indians, Africans and mulattos. The unmistakable message is that the Pietist religion of the heart had gone global. Moreover, as Pietism morphed into Evangelicalism, the early Evangelicals, such as John Wesley and George Whitefield, burst on the scene initially as authors of voyage journals and missionary letters not 'unlike the earlier Jesuit relations from New France'.[33]

For both Roman Catholic and Protestant missions in the early modern period the disciplining of the self for a life of service may be a necessary but not a sufficient explanation of the way in which a new spiritual self-consciousness became a truly global consciousness. This is a large topic requiring not only a command of how perceptions of new worlds were formed and transmitted in the age of Enlightenment, but also how these new perceptions played out in the spiritual imaginations of those who pioneered the global expansion of Christianity. The first of these questions, namely how perceptions of new worlds were formed and transmitted, has been addressed in a number of different but related historical discourses.[34] Historical geographers have investigated how early moderns developed mental or cognitive maps of the world; historians of cartography have shown how early modern Europeans, beginning with social elites, mapped and disseminated new pictures of their expanding world; historians of trade and empire have shown how Europeans imagined other civilizations in relation to their own; and historians of travel literature have shown the manifold different ways by which the exotic was popularized.[35] Geographical grammars, works of fiction, Royal Society reports, newspapers, periodicals, travel narratives, printed maps and expanding libraries all nurtured a new interest in the extra-European world. For those Christians influenced by the Evangelical Revival there were additional factors at play. The territorial growth of the 'Protestant Empires' reinforced and recalibrated ideas of divine providence and fused them with Evangelical activism and opportunism. Especially in Britain, the freshly perceived evils of the transatlantic slave trade prompted a fresh consideration of religious and moral responsibilities to indigenous peoples. These new stimuli destabilized entrenched theological notions such as the notion that Christ's command to the Apostles to teach all nations applied only to the apostolic era or that divine sovereignty somehow trumped human initiative in the growth of the church. In short, spiritual cartography was now on the agenda and humans were responsible agents, not passive divine collaborators, in the world's transformation.[36] But how did these processes work out in the lives of individuals and new missionary organizations?

Protestant missions and 'spiritual cartography': William Carey and Thomas Coke

The period between 1790 and 1815 saw the formation of a remarkable wave of new Protestant missionary societies: the Baptist Missionary Society (1792), the (London) Missionary Society (1795), the Edinburgh (Scottish) and Glasgow Missionary Societies (1796), the Society for Missions to Africa and the East (1796, and known as the Church Missionary Society from 1812), and the Wesleyan Methodist Missionary Society in 1813. Arising in part out of Evangelical connections with one another and with the wider world for almost half a century, and partly facilitated by the sense of British national crisis and imperial obligation in the 1790s, the missionary societies aimed to seize a 'providential moment' to convert the world. The story of their formation and expansion is well known, but for present purposes what is most interesting is how their founders thought of themselves and their mission. Perhaps the two most influential Protestant purveyors of global mission in the late eighteenth century were the Baptist William Carey (1761–1834) and the Methodist Thomas Coke (1747–1814). Carey was the founder of the Baptist Missionary Society and the author of *Enquiry into the Obligations of Christians to Use Means for the Conversion of the Heathens* (1792), which is widely regarded as the most significant missionary appeal of the eighteenth century.[37] He was influenced by coteries of Evangelical Baptists and accounts of Moravian missions; he had his imagination fired by Captain Cook's voyages to the Pacific; he regarded the rise of trading companies, empire and new navigational technologies as providential opportunities for the expansion of Christianity; and he believed from his reading of biblical prophecies that the church was on the brink of a new era of millennial bounty.[38] In light of these influences much has been made of the individual words used in the title of Carey's famous *Enquiry*. 'Obligations of Christians' suggests a moral imperative; 'to Use Means' speaks of human initiative; and 'the Conversion of the Heathen' supplies both a sense of religious superiority and a missionary rallying call to action.

In the remainder of what is a very long title Carey gives clues about how he constructed his own mental map of the world. His map was not so much a physical and geographical representation of the world as much as an Old Testament style representation of nations and religions occupying certain spaces. Andrew Fuller records a visit to Carey in which he saw 'hanging up against the wall a very large map, consisting of several sheets of paper pasted together by himself, on which he had drawn with a pen, a place for every nation in the known world, and entered into it whatever he met with in reading, relative to its population, religion, etc.'[39] This visual aid accords completely with the intellectual and verbal structure of Carey's *Enquiry*. He viewed the world not as countries or nation states demarcated by clear geographical boundaries, but as Old Testament-like 'nations' or 'peoples' characterized by their religion and their occupancy of land. In short, his world was personally created, biblically informed and conceptually ordered around his religious predilections and his interpretation of global civilization – past, present and future. He personally mapped time, space, religion and demographics, and his map was then made to fit the maps of empire, trade and civilizational conquest that were being constructed all around him. Carey saw all this as a providential opportunity to take the Gospel message to all humankind, but he was far from uncritical of European Christendom and its colonial adventures. 'It is also a melancholy fact,' he wrote, 'that the vices of Europeans have been communicated wherever they themselves have been; so that the religious state of even the heathens has been rendered worse by intercourse with them!' Chief among the culprits were the Greek and Armenian churches who were 'more ignorant and vicious than the Mahometans themselves', the 'Papists' who were also 'ignorant of divine things, and very vicious', and the established churches of Europe which presented 'a dreadful scene of ignorance, hypocrisy, and profligacy'. There could be no clearer announcement that the expansion of Christianity as envisaged by Carey was not to be the business as usual of European Christendom, but was rather a renewed vision of presenting 'the truths of the gospel' and ushering in 'the kingdom of our Lord Jesus Christ'.[40]

If William Carey was the most important missionary pioneer for the Baptists, Thomas Coke performed a similar role for the Wesleyan Methodists.[41] His missionary journals, which are part travel narrative, part self-reflection, part spiritual pilgrimage and part self-conscious heroic endeavour, offer a particularly clear account of how an Evangelical Protestant conceived of himself and the world he wished to convert. A combination of intense personal discipline and an awakened sense of global opportunity and responsibility operate like the magnetic points of a solenoid in generating the remarkable energy of Protestant mission in the late eighteenth century.

Born in Brecon in Wales and educated at Jesus College, Oxford, Thomas Coke was forced out of his curacy in Somerset in 1777 for Methodistical leanings. He became one of John Wesley's most trusted associates and with Francis Asbury (1745–1816) was ordained as fellow-superintendent (later changed to bishop) of the Methodist church in America. His social pedigree, scholarly aspirations and penchant for cultivating those more important than himself made him unpopular at times with rank-and-file itinerants on both sides of the Atlantic (especially America), but he nevertheless displayed an unparalleled commitment to the worldwide expansion of Methodism. He is justifiably regarded as the father of Methodist missions, which became the most prolific of the Anglo-American missions of the nineteenth century. His journals are unusual in that they deal only with his life outside Britain. Accounts have survived of his first six visits to America and his four Caribbean tours in the 1780s and 90s.[42] Although his firsthand observations of the rise of Methodism in Ireland, North America and the Caribbean islands in the revolutionary epoch are unusually penetrating, what follows is not so much an account of his activities as a pioneer missionary for the Wesleyan cause, but rather an attempt to uncover his view of *himself* as an agent in the religious transformation of others. From a close reading of his journals, it is possible to identify the deeply personal meanings he attached to the overseas missions he was undertaking.

The first is the way he imagined himself as part of a heroic Christian tradition. When he first sailed for America in September 1784, Coke was reading Augustine's *Confessions*, the *Life of David Brainerd* (a biography of the missionary to Native Americans compiled by Jonathan Edwards) and the *Life of Francis Xavier*. This heady combination of self-reflection and missionary heroism provoked Coke to write of Xavier, 'O for a soul like his! But glory to God, there is nothing impossible with him. I seem to want the wings of an eagle, and the voice of a trumpet, that I may proclaim the Gospel through the East and the West, and the North and the South.'[43] Similarly, after reading the life of David Brainerd, Coke wrote, 'O that I may follow him as he followed Christ. His humility, his self-denial, his perseverance, and his flaming zeal for God were exemplary indeed.'[44] This example could only be imitated through ruthless self-discipline. Those familiar with the diaries of early Methodists will not be surprised by the extraordinary discipline of Coke's life, which enabled him to log tens of thousands of miles, preach thousands of sermons, compose lengthy scholarly works and sustain a wide-ranging correspondence. His devotional disciplines were equally demanding. A typical entry for 31 October 1784 reads, 'I devoted the morning to fasting and prayer, and found some degree of refreshments, and a sacred longing after more fervency and activity in the service of my God.'[45] At other times he set aside a day a week for fasting and abstinence. Nowhere are the fruits of Coke's disciplined spirituality more in evidence than in his remarkable stories of fortitude in storms, floods and persecutions.

Second, Coke's self-understanding as a British Christian missionary developed in response to his encounters with 'others' in different parts of the world. Although Coke never quite lost his sense of British superiority in dealing with American Methodists, and was capable of writing with great condescension about African slaves, a close reading of his *Journal* suggests that his missionary endeavours among transplanted Africans in exotic new locations persuaded him that in *his* divine economy there was a growing equality of people and locations. Like many of the early Methodists he was vigorously anti-slavery and then slowly moderated his tone in response to pressure from Caribbean and American colonial planters. But he was equally aware of the potential of popular Evangelicalism to garner immense harvests among black slaves. He writes from Charleston, 'Since my visit to the islands I have found a peculiar gift for speaking to the blacks. It seems to be almost irresistible. Who knows but the Lord is preparing me for a visit in some future time to the coast of Africa.'[46] On his fifth visit to North America and the West Indies in 1793, Coke tabulated the number of Methodists in societies. The figure came to 6,570, only 100 of whom were whites. He wrote:

> The Blacks, who nearly make up the whole of this number, have been brought out of heathenish darkness, more or less, to a knowledge of the truth, and a knowledge of themselves. They have left, as far as we can find, all their outward sins, even polygamy itself; and a considerable part of them give so clear and rational an account of their conversion, and of the influence of religion upon their hearts and lives, as is exceedingly animating and encouraging to their pastors, the Missionaries.[47]

Fortified by such stories, Coke came to believe that the New World offered even greater possibilities for the future of Christianity than the old. In 1789 he writes that Antigua 'is the favourite of heaven. It is supposed that it contains 7,000 whites and 30,000 blacks: and out of these 2,800 are in our society; and I believe the Moravians have not fewer than 2,000 in theirs. So great a leaven is not known perhaps in so small a country throughout the world.'[48] What was achieved among Caribbean blacks Coke believed was equally possible among Native Americans, West Africans and Indians. In this heady optimism about the conversion of native selves neither race nor geography, religious tradition nor cultural dissonance, seemed to stand in the way of the triumphant march of populist forms of Evangelical Protestantism. The only thing lacking was the will and the self-discipline to do it.

Although Coke's *Journals* are records of his missionary journeys he does not spend much time on the missiological disciplines of ethnography or strategy, but occasionally he does make observations about the 'other'. For example, he felt attracted to the black Caribs he encountered on the island of St Vincent. He writes about them with the same mixture of condescension and admiration that suffuses Methodist accounts of Irish Catholic peasants in the same period:

> I feel myself much attached to these poor savages. The sweet simplicity and cheerfulness they manifested on every side, soon wore off every unfavourable impression my mind had imbibed from the accounts I had received of their cruelties – cruelties originating probably with ourselves rather than with them. They are a handsomer people than the negroes, but have undoubtedly a warlike appearance, as their very women frequently carry cutlasses in their hands, and always knives by their naked sides.[49]

According to Coke, Carib religion consisted mostly of warding off evil spirits; Carib social life was organized by lazy, polygamous men who ruthlessly exploited the industry and vulnerability of women; Carib customs, whether of diet, dress, language, law or use of alcohol, were primitive and coarse; and Caribs had been more corrupted than improved by their contact with other colonial powers, especially the French. Hence, for the mission to have any chance of success it would have to be based on the education and civilization of children. Nevertheless, Coke was ultimately optimistic about the prospects for the Methodist message in the Caribbean islands and the Americas, and was also hopeful about what could be achieved in India and Africa. His most negative comments were reserved for the Muslims he encountered on board ship for India: 'The gospel-door, as it respects that people, seems entirely shut. Their religion was established by the sword, and I fear that the sword must go through their nations before they will bow to the scepter of Jesus.'[50] When it came to Muslims, millennial missionary zeal is replaced with ambivalence and resignation. Coke ruefully suggests that 'the sword' can sometimes accomplish what the missionary cannot.

Third, Coke's view of himself was further refined in response to his perceived personal relationship with God and his experience of God's creation, especially in new and exotic landscapes. On his third visit to the West Indies in January 1791 Coke arrived in Montego Bay in Jamaica to find little going on there. He writes: 'But we were without a friend or single acquaintance: and to those who are endued with the tenderest social feelings, this is no small trial: though I do know in the general, to the glory of the grace of God be it acknowledged, that the Lord is a sufficient consolation in every place.'[51] This sense of the self of being lonely yet of never being alone supplies the key to much of Coke's itinerant life as a man of no fixed abode. Despite the harsh privations of 18 transatlantic voyages, Coke seems to have welcomed the times of solitude on board ship when his God transformed his cabin into my 'sanctum sanctorum, the Holy of Holies, filling it (my soul at least) with light and glory', and when he could 'sweetly to retire into him (God) as my blessed Asylum and my only Home'.[52]

On his first voyage across the Atlantic Coke finished Virgil's *Pastorals* which 'by a kind of magic power, conveyed me to fields and groves and purling brooks, and painted before my eyes all the feigned beauties of *Arcadia;* and would have almost persuaded me that it is possible to be happy without God. However, they served now and then to unbend the powers of the mind.'[53] Pastoral scenes from classical literature nourished Coke's aesthetics of nature, and his favourite landscapes were ones that either reminded him of his Welsh homeland or awakened in him a romantic love of nature. He writes from Georgia on 9 March 1791:

> I have again entered into my romantic way of life. For there is something exceedingly pleasing in preaching daily to large congregations in immense forests. O what pains the people take to hear the Gospel! But it is worthy of all pains. 11th I am now come among the peach trees, and they are in full bloom. Truly they assist a little, under the Supreme Source of Happiness, to make the heart gay. It is one of my most delicate entertainments, to embrace every opportunity of ingulphing myself (if I may so express it) in the woods. I seem then to be detached from every thing but the quiet vegetable creation, and MY GOD.[54]

This desire to hide oneself in an enchanted location to commune with self and God is an important theme in Coke's *Journals,* especially as he gets older. On a visit to Grenada in 1790 he goes trekking in the hills and discovers a lake surrounded by wooded peaks. He writes, 'If I was to turn hermit, I think I should fix on this place, where I would make circular walks, and fix an observatory on one of the Peaks, and spend my time in communion with God, and in the study of Astronomy and Botany.'[55] Coke's capacity to fantasize about being a hermit, a mystic and a scientist on this occasion, along with his more realistic fantasies of being a revivalist, scholar and leader of a universal church, shows the extent to which he was able both to imagine and realize different kinds of self-fulfilment.

Fourth, some of Coke's most profound statements about himself and his life's mission come in bouts of Pietist self-reflection. In October 1792 Coke was en route from England to North America and had settled into a reflective mood. His boat was becalmed, placing in doubt his attempt to be present for the American General Conference in Baltimore. He was working diligently on a new Bible commentary and had his spirits lifted by the daily singing of six canaries. One of the canaries died, apparently from starvation and neglect. Coke was deeply affected by its death. He wrote that the

> little creature sung almost incessantly the morning preceding its death, hoping, I suppose, to gain our attention, and induce us to fill its seed-box. A misfortune of this kind may seem ridiculous to many on land: but to those

who are surrounded with an immense ocean, the loss of a favorite bird is great; and their feelings will, at least, be excused by ingenious minds.

The next day was his birthday and the weather changed from very fair to rainy dark and gloomy. He writes:

> What a comfort it is to be able to retire into God at all times, in all places, and in all weathers! This is my birthday. I am now forty-five. Let me take a view of my past life. What is the sum of it all? What have I done? And what am I? I have done nothing; no, nothing; and I am a sinner! God be merciful to me![56]

Four years later, in what can only be called a voyage from hell, Coke became ill and was confined to his bed.

> During this time the Lord did truly speak to my heart. ... I had sincerely loved GOD for many years, and had no ambition but to be the instrument immediately and remotely of converting millions to him. I had been long willing to die, but not to be inactive while I lived.[57]

These reflections point up the negative and positive poles of the spiritual dynamo that generated so much of the energy of the Protestant missionary awakening at the end of the eighteenth century. On one level, the individual self was no more than a sinful wretch journeying through a gloomy world, but on the other hand, the self when disciplined to the purposes of God could dare aspire to the transformation of millions of other lives. Such aspirations required more than mere discipline of the natural self, they also demanded sacrifice. During a stop in Brunswick County, Virginia, Coke wrote:

> At Mr. Myrick's, I found a lovely family, and spent much time ingulphed in the woods, and reading the younger Racine's celebrated Poem de la Religion. Many might imagine, that my natural disposition leads me into busy life; but it is the very reverse. If the principle of duty did not carry me forth into scenes which call for activity and exertion, I should certainly settle in some solitary place, where I might enjoy the company of a very few select friends, and the pleasures of a retired rural life.[58]

But as we shall see, sacrifice had its earthly as well as its heavenly compensations.

Finally, Coke's journal is quite revealing of his ego, his desire for self-fulfilment, and his sometimes ambiguous enthusiasm for the pursuit of happiness. Both in the letters of Marie de l'Incarnation and in Coke's *Journals* there is a tension between defining the missionary call as one of self-sacrifice and denial and of enjoying the experience of missions because they allowed for a type of liberty and fulfilment that the home context did not. In Marie's case she largely gave up the painful self-mutilations that had characterized her religious discipline as an Ursuline nun in France and found real joy in her new career as a missionary teacher in Quebec: 'Everything concerning the study of languages and the instruction of the Savages … has been so delectable to me that I have almost sinned in loving it too much.'[59] Coke, who often contrasted the opportunities his new life as a roving ambassador for Christ afforded him by comparison with his earlier life as a local Anglican priest in a small parish, was less prone to asceticism than Marie. Coke enjoyed being wined and dined by every dignitary he came into contact with and he is quite open about his sensuous enjoyment of the wild landscapes of the Americas. Like Marie, however, he sometimes wonders if he is having too good a time. On a visit to Antigua he writes, 'Our friends who invite us to their houses, entertain us rather like princes than subjects: herein, perhaps, lies part of our danger in this country. The country is very romantic. The cocoa-tree is very magnificent; and the milk which the nuts yield, is most cooling and delicious.'[60] In his *Journals* Coke self-consciously sees himself as a naturalist, anthropologist, ethnographer, diplomat, political trouble-shooter, missionary preacher, world transformer, elite networker and divine instrument. What vocation could possibly be more exciting and fulfilling? Certainly not that of a parish priest in a remote Anglican diocese in the Celtic fringes of the British state.

Connections and conclusions

By looking at influential spiritual texts and the lives of important individuals, this chapter has attempted to demonstrate a connection between the rise of early modern subjectivity, the religion of the heart, the cultivation of spiritual self-discipline, and the concurrent rise of global Christianity in both Roman Catholic and Protestant missions. Dana Robert has recently made a similar set of connections. She states that the Ignatian *Spiritual Exercises* was 'a powerful tool of missionary spirituality that enabled individual practitioners to maintain self-discipline and focus, even if deprived of a supportive community and familiar surroundings. The spiritual and intellectual preparation of the Jesuits made them ready to travel across cultures, and capable of working alone even in hostile circumstances.'[61] In short, spiritual self-discipline enabled one to be oneself anywhere at any time regardless of geographical location, social supports and commonplace familiarities. She makes a similar point about the historic breakthrough in Protestant mission history in 1706 when the Lutheran King Frederick IV of Denmark recruited Pietist students from the University of Halle to service his small colony at Tranquebar on the Indian coast. Pietists, she writes, 'embodied on a grassroots and personal level the cultural shift towards literacy and self-direction that marked the founding of Protestantism'. For both Roman Catholic and Protestant traditions of global mission self-abnegation, self-discipline, self-formation and self-realization were important precondititions for missionaries who followed the sinews of empire and the lucre of the trade routes to engage other cultures and religious traditions.

How these European selves then encountered other selves and native cultures is a question to be addressed in the next chapter. However, processes of self-formation in European religious traditions often had deep and lasting implications for the kind of Christianity minted in foreign locations. For example, Natalie Zemon Davis offers a helpful analytical framework in her observation about Marie de l'Incarnation's Ursuline convent in Quebec that in its combination of European educational discipline and birchbark cabins, Amerindian food and multiple languages 'it was a hybrid space rather than a transplantation of European order'.[62] How this played out in different locations varied not only according to social context but also with gender and with the kind of self-formation practised in different Christian traditions. For example, Coke's *Journals* point to a figure who had fully embraced the Methodist concept of a preaching itinerancy. As a result he was particularly untethered by his missionary locations and did not express much connection with the communities he preached to apart from helping them to organize themselves as Methodist societies. Moravians by contrast deliberately promoted a rooted hybridity. They brought their very particular Herrnhut model of community wherever they went, yet they also invested a great deal in learning languages, customs and grammars in their surprisingly flexible negotiable exchanges with local cultures. In Catholic missions, as with Methodists, Jesuits were at first more like itinerants than settlers, and were much more mobile than Ursuline women in convents. Thus religious tradition, styles of self-formation and gender affected the ways in which European selves encountered 'others' in Christianity's post-Reformation rise to globalism.

The way in which this could play out in the lives of those being instructed in the 'new world' by European spiritual directors is still a neglected subject. However, a recent study of the letters of Mexican women to their Jesuit spiritual directors in the eighteenth century reveals a similar pattern to European versions of spiritual formation. Often opaque and frustratingly veiled, the letters are not so much concerned with self-expression as on complex attempts at self-abnegation, but without drawing attention to the self in a way that could be considered as mere vanity. Here was a delicate psychological balancing act. The self had to be denied, but not celebrated in its denial, lest it resulted in pride. Hence, from the 'union of Christian asceticism with the technology of writing, emerged a science of the self that contained both renunciation of self and constitution of self within the same spiritual practice'.[63] But the selves that were being constituted were fixed more on virtue, salvation and eternal life than on personal self-realization in any conventional or modern sense. In short, self-discipline was the way and the means to spiritual maturity and a life of service to others.

One obvious question that arises from this kind of material, and one for which there is not yet a clear answer, is to what extent was the spiritual formation of the self in relation to global Christianity worked out differently for Roman Catholics and Protestants? The sources suggest that both Protestants and Catholics who were interested in global mission had a particular focus on the person of Christ, but whereas Protestants located that focus in the Bible, Catholics were more inclined to concentrate on Eucharistic theology and the spirituality of the Sacred Heart. Yet heart religion, whether of the Catholic or Protestant variety, clearly had some things in common, especially devotion and obedience to the sacrificial and wounded Christ, which is at the centre of both Moravian and Jesuit spirituality.

In terms of their respective reading materials, Protestants were reading the *Life of Xavier*, and had access to a surprisingly rich vein of Catholic writing (see John Wesley's cheap editions, for example). They were also aware of the worldwide expansion of Catholic missions, and often used Catholic sources in their early attempts to construct grammars, lexicons and translations. But to what extent were Catholics aware of Protestant sources such as John Eliot's mission to the Native Americans, the *Life of David Brainerd* or the *Halle Reports* which were smaller Lutheran versions of the *Jesuit Relations*? There is abundant evidence to suggest that Catholics were reading works produced by Protestant Enlightenment thinkers, but how far did that reading extend to Protestant missions? Was there a common body of circulating texts about global Christianity in the European universities or were collections shaped almost completely by confessional and/or national/ linguistic traditions? In short, to what extent were each other's traditions of spiritual formation and global expansion known to one another? How then should one slice up this question? Were differences between Protestants and Catholics more or less important than differences between all those interested in global mission and those with no such interest? How important are differences of gender, class, nationality and access to good libraries in universities or colleges in self-formation within a context of global awareness? Do some categories trump others, or are the patterns too complicated to establish priorities based on identity? These and other questions suggest the rich possibilities of trying to connect the spiritual disciplines of post-Reformation churches with spiritual formation and the rise of global Christianity.

The worldwide expansion of Christianity, which came in the wake of the European Reformation and Counter Reformation, was carried out by men and women who employed spiritual discipline to construct selves able to travel and to promote heart religion in new locations. Nevertheless, the kind of spiritual discipline represented by Jesuits, Franciscans, Pietists and Evangelicals varied greatly in form, content and expression. Some have calibrated these variations chronologically and culturally as movements from medieval to modern while others have connected them to faith traditions and styles of spiritual formation. New kinds of religious self-formation were being undertaken at the same time as Europeans were seeking to expand Christianity's reach in tandem with conquest, commerce and conversion. The combination of the two helps account for much of the dynamism of early modern Christian expansion. It is the task of the next chapter to determine if the same kinds of hybridity (an admittedly insufficient term) that one sees in architecture, symbols, rituals, dress and language (creolization) are also detectable in the refashioning of native selves. As in other areas of negotiated encounters, the extent to which these selves were recast in European Christian mode was dependent on a clutch of variables including gender, power, violence, economic opportunity, literacy and longevity of missionary influence. European Christians, both Catholic and Protestant, carried in their DNA centuries-long traditions of penitential devotion which were 'modernized' and then transplanted in different parts of the world in the early modern period. The extent to which missionary selves were able to produce penitent Christians committed to self-refashioning depended ultimately either on their ability to create similar tools of formation as in Europe (catechesis, education, liturgy, symbols and the vernacular Bible) or on the particular appeal of creating new selves to non-European peoples. Examples of the former are not hard to find. Perhaps the most powerful example of the latter, as we shall see, is those freed slaves who migrated back to Africa eager to construct new lives out of the brokenness and brutality of the slave experience.

How then did Christians minted in European traditions of penitential Christianity encounter 'others' without such religious formation in various non-European sites experiencing the expansion of Christendom in the eighteenth century? Perhaps the best way to proceed is to look at case studies of actual encounters between European missionaries and native cultures, to tell their stories and explain their meanings. That is the task of the next chapter.

CHAPTER 3

Encountering the Other:
Stories and their Meanings

The expansion of Christianity from its bases in Europe to other parts of the world in the early modern period is really a product of the growth of the Iberian Catholic empires and the missionary enthusiasm of the Catholic religious orders, especially the Jesuits. Both of these factors were still in operation in the eighteenth century, but were now joined by other forces gaining momentum, including the rise of the Protestant seaborne empires, the intensification of the Atlantic slave trade, the growth of Pietist missions and population migrations, the Evangelical Revival, and the formation of Protestant missionary societies. More attention will be given to all of these developments in other parts of our study. The point of this chapter, however, is to look more specifically at *encounters* between the bearers of European religious traditions and the native peoples they sought to convert to Christianity in different parts of the world.

What was at stake in these encounters? What kind of Christianity was being offered and how was it altered by the process of encounter with people of very different cultural and religious traditions? How deep was the penetration of Christianity in new places and what strategies of resistance and/or accommodation were adopted by native peoples? If Christianity did take root in new places, how much remained of pre-existing traditions, and in what forms did they survive? How did religious encounter affect other aspects of culture – everything from gender relations and sexuality to religious rituals and the raising of children? Finally, what are the most satisfactory analytical and metaphorical categories (as we shall see later, scholars often use metaphors or images for understanding encounters) for explaining the complexities of encounter and the kind of Christianity that emerged from it? My intention is to explore these encounters by telling stories that are at once quite particular but are also more generally repre-sentative of the scope and scale of Christianity's rise to globalism. Through stories, the aim is to expose the sheer complexity of religious and cultural encounter in the eighteenth century, which is not easily encapsulated by a single concept such as hybridity. In what follows, three encounters are situated within three different geographical areas – Latin America, China and India. Three other encounters are based on the personal stories of individuals whose lives reveal yet more about Christianity's rise to globalism in the Caribbean islands, colonial North America and West Africa. The three people are the freed Caribbean slave Rebecca Protten (1718–80), the ex-slave, Baptist preacher in the American colonies, Nova Scotia and West Africa, David George (1740 or 1742–1810), and the Native American Evangelical convert Samson Occom (1723–92). As with the regional case studies, they have been chosen not only for their remarkable personal journeys, but also because their lives highlight some of the most powerful forces in the shaping of global Christianity in the modern period, including slavery, empire and the rise of Protestant missions. But enough of scene setting, let the story telling begin.

Places

Latin America

In April 2007 a panel appointed by *Church Times* magazine selected the top 50 religious films of all time. Number one on the list is *The Mission* (1986), a film set in South America in the 1750s during the War of the Seven Reductions, which is also called the Guaraní War after the native peoples who fought against Spanish and Portuguese forces. The film, with considerable artistic licence, tells the story of a saintly Jesuit priest whose mission to the Guaraní falls victim to the complex forces of colonial rivalry and military brutality perpetrated by the Iberian empires. The immediate catalyst of the violence was the Treaty of Madrid signed by Spain and Portugal in 1750, an attempt to settle long-standing boundary disputes between the two empires in South America based on the principle of giving legal possession to those who had settled the land. Not everything was tidily arranged, however. According to article 14 of the treaty, Portugal ceded the town of Colônia do Sacramento to Spain in exchange for land east of the Uruguay River (present-day southern Brazil) comprising the territory of seven Jesuit reductions (the term itself is revealing of Jesuit intentions), which were planned settlements for indigenous peoples.

These settlements, some of which dated back to the 1630s, had by 1750 become sophisticated social and economic units and the Guaraní were in no mood to cede the fruits of decades of building and cultivation to Portuguese associated in their minds with raids by slave-takers known as Paulistas or *mamelucos*. Given only a year to pack up and go or accept their new masters, Guaraní leaders, with Jesuit help, petitioned Spanish colonial officials to think again. Central to their understanding was the notion that the king of Spain could not possibly have endorsed such a malevolent proposal and that if it was brought to his attention 'he would get very angry ... and would not approve the order to make us relocate'. One *Corregidor* (native leader) informed the Governor of Buenos Aires:

> This land, our children say, only God gave it to us. On this land our holy teacher Father Roque González and many of our relatives have died among us. They have raised us. Only for us they got tired. Well, why do the Portuguese desire the land so much? It is not theirs. Only our hands have worked it and prepared this land. Neither the Portuguese nor the Spaniards have done such things as build a magnificent church, a nice town, ranches for our cattle, yerba maté and cotton plantations, farms. What was achieved came about through our hard work. Well, how is it that you wrongly want to take our possession from the fruit of our labor? They wrongly want to make fun of us. That will not happen. God our savior would not want this. He would not know how to do such things nor is it the will of our good Holy King. We have not done anything wrong. We have not taken anything away from the Portuguese. Never for what we have worked will we get paid. Never have our ancestors spoken to us about resettling elsewhere.[1]

This fusion of ancestral legitimacy, Jesuit sacrifice, anti-colonial protest, celebration of labour, settlement pride, Christian faith, monarchical loyalty and utter bewilderment about the vagaries of imperial policy cut little ice with Spanish colonial officials or their masters in Madrid. The Guaraní ended up fighting against not one but two coercive colonial powers, and predictably paid a heavy price for their 'rebellion'. In the decisive battle of the conflict, their bows, arrows, lances and bamboo cannons proved no match for European artillery. Over 1,500 Guaraní soldiers perished on the battlefield at Caaíbaté on 10 February 1756, compared with only four combined Spanish and Portuguese troops. The central irony of the War of the Seven Reductions is that the Guaraní fought to defend the very reductions into which they had been so disruptively organized generations before, and that they did so using the weapons and military training they had received from the Jesuits. Just as the Guaraní rebelled against what they saw as 'bad government' even while protesting their loyalty to the king, so too did they display hostility towards priests, whom they saw as acting in collusion with Spanish officials, while still maintaining vestiges of Catholic observance. Unlike most other native rebellions against colonial rule in the early modern period such as the Pueblo Revolt of 1680 in New Mexico, the Guaraní War was a conservative rebellion in defence of existing conditions, not an attempt to overthrow Jesuit or Spanish rule. How can this be explained? What were the characteristics of the Jesuit reductions in defence of which the Guaraní were willing to fight, and what was the nature of their Catholic faith into which many of them had been baptized?

The Guaraní people of the Río de la Plata region lived on the margins of the Spanish Empire and in the borderlands between the Portuguese and Spanish empires, so that they easily became victims of both the depredations of Spanish *encomenderos* and Portuguese slave-takers. Although initially resistant to Christian missions as part of a wider opposition to colonial subjugation, the Guaraní, who by the early seventeenth century had experienced a severe demographic collapse, began to respond more favourably to the relatively sophisticated missionary methods of the Jesuits. Financed partly by the Spanish crown and animated by evangelistic zeal, European Jesuits combined an immense sense of cultural superiority over the Guaraní with a willingness to adapt to native lifestyles as a means of gaining respect and acceptance. For example, they were able to bring together Guaraní myths about Sumé, an old wise man who had taught them agriculture and religious precepts, with their own myths about the apparently inexhaustible travels of St Thomas, to forge a powerful 'principle of attachment'.[2] Moreover, Jesuits brought tangible advantages in the shape of metal tools, agricultural know how, and the possibility of acting as more humane intermediaries between the Guaraní and the cruel edges of the Spanish colonial world. Of course resistance did not melt away. Guaraní shamans relentlessly combated the 'religious magic' of their celibate Jesuit competitors. In addition, many Guaraní refused to submit to Jesuit instructions about monogamy and changing work patterns between men and women, and thousands fled the reductions. Still others outwardly conformed to Jesuit expectations but retained deep attachments to their own rituals, beliefs and practices. Indeed the encounters between Jesuits and Guaraní are laced with subversive rituals, such as baptizing and then unbaptizing by boiling, scouring, and scraping; corporal punishments including ritual killings; and endless contests about almost everything from clothes to haircuts and from sexual regulations to marriage customs.

Although resistance was endemic, a combination of power differential, Jesuit perseverance and the tangible benefits afforded by the reductions eventually contributed to their relative success by the early eighteenth century. By then a virtual 'Jesuit Republic' of over 30 reductions had been settled along the Paraná and Uruguay rivers. What were they like and what was the nature of the Catholic Christianity they sustained?

The reductions were much larger communities than the Guaraní were accustomed to living in. While Guaraní villages were home to about 200 people, the Jesuit reductions could have as many as 6,000, comparable in size to the Spanish regional capital of Ascunción. Although frequently decimated by disease and desertion and limited by extraordinarily high rates of infant mortality, the Guaraní reductions were the most populous missions in Spanish America, reaching a peak of almost 150,000 in the early 1730s. Normally built on high ground and with baroque churches at their centres, which were often decorated with distinctive forms of Hispanic-Guaraní artwork, the reductions were laid out in a simple grid plan with houses made out of easily available natural materials. One unusual feature of the reductions was the *coty guazú*, a physical space set aside for women of all ages whose personal circumstances were deemed by the Jesuits to require a place of safe retreat. Comprised mostly of orphans, younger single women, widows and those who were perceived as in need of moral reformation, the *coty guazú* represented a mixed blessing for Guaraní women. On the one hand it seems to have contributed to the safety and social status of women; on the other it clearly restricted their freedom of movement and made them more susceptible to Jesuit social control.

The existence of the *coty guazú* not only raises questions about how Guaraní women were treated within the confines of a particular designated space but also how gender relations were envisaged more generally by the Jesuits. They sought to enforce monogamy, patrilocality (married couples were to live with the male relatives) and an economic redistribution of labour away from a virtual female monopoly of farming to a pattern based more on European models of male tillage and artisanship and female tillage and domestication. Although research on the role of women in the Jesuit reductions is still in its infancy, it seems that there was almost certainly a substantial female majority within the reductions, and over the long run a larger number became more devoted Catholics and displayed a more intense devotion (sometimes accompanied by visions) to the Virgin.[3]

Children were also a focus of special attention. The Jesuits taught Guaraní children in mission schools in their own language, paying particular attention to the sons of the elite and to instruction in Catholic doctrine. Indeed, the Jesuits mounted a sustained daily effort to disseminate Catholic teaching. The Guaraní began their day at dawn, attended Mass, worked in the fields until noon, rested for a few hours before returning to work and were then gathered in late afternoon for prayer and recitation of catechism and rosary before retiring to their homes with allocated rations. All this was supplemented by holy festivals and processions, wooden images of saints and the Virgin, and singing and dancing. Efforts to convert, baptize, socialize and Christianize were unstinting, but how successful were they? The tightly controlled nature of the reductions, and the predominantly Jesuit sources on which historians must depend, make it difficult to ascertain what sort of hybrid Christianities or surviving Guaraní beliefs may have been present in the lives of their inhabitants. The Jesuit strategy here, as elsewhere, was to eliminate or reform Guaraní beliefs and practices that they believed were incompatible with Christianity while permitting those customs they regarded as neutral or inoffensive.

Jesuit recorders, and until relatively recently traditions of European scholarship, have tended to emphasize the ecclesiastical and administrative roles of missionaries and have depicted the Guaraní as passive receptors of European Catholic culture. More recent work, often based on studies of language, art, artefacts and rituals, and shaped by post-colonial and feminist theory, has drawn attention to native agency (however circumscribed by external circumstances) and cultural survival. Even with the best of intentions, however, historians, anthropologists, missiologists and ethnographers struggle with inadequate evidence and unsatisfactory conceptual frameworks. For example, the encounter between Europeans and native peoples is often framed in terms of negotiable exchanges, unequal power dynamics, manifold hybridities and mutual transformations, but none of these categories quite gets to the heart of the sheer complexity of cultural encounter, especially since neither European nor native culture was fixed or static. Similarly, the emphasis on native agency is both laudable and necessary, but agency is never pure or unidirectional. For example, to modern eyes the most distinctive feature of the reductions is the degree of social control the Jesuits exerted on the Guaraní community, but in reality the distribution of power and authority in the reductions was quite complex. The Guaraní were of course under the jurisdiction and economic control of both the Society of Jesus and the Spanish government, but power was also mediated through their *Corregidor* and the native council, or *cabildo*, which had considerable powers over regulating land use, appointing lesser officers and managing day-to-day public services. The Jesuits were ultimately the local masters, except when they were circumvented to solve larger disputes with the Spanish, but in the practical functions of everyday life the Guaraní were most often directly controlled by other Guaraní.

Similarly, even a brief excursion into the world of Guaraní art and artefacts reveals a rich aesthetic tradition for which the term hybridity seems particularly sterile. Many of the surviving sculptures and paintings of the Guaraní reveal not only an expected transportation of New World plants, animals and facial features into Catholic baroque art, but also display an emotional variety and intensity suggestive of much deeper resonances. Moreover, symbolic materials as well as motifs from earlier Guaraní art get re-appropriated in new Catholic venues. The use of the bat motif over the door lintels of mission churches, for example, may have had some resonance with the traditional Guaraní creation story in which the creator god scattered the eternal bats of darkness in order to make the world, and thus stood for spirits put to flight by new light.⁴ A similar point could be made about the Guaraní practice of taking wooden sculptures of saints or the Virgin into the fields, which can be interpreted either as an indication of the omnipresence of Catholic symbols in the lives of the Guaraní or as an extension of traditional shamanic talismanism to protect crops and sacred spaces, or more likely both.

However one comes to terms with the religious beliefs and practices of the Guaraní under Jesuit control, there is no disputing the fact that by the mid-eighteenth century they had become so invested in the reductions they had helped build that they were not prepared to up and leave them at the whim of colonial mapmakers in Madrid and Lisbon. Despite what was reported in Madrid, the Jesuits did not directly orchestrate the Guaraní rebellion. On the contrary, most Jesuits, though unhappy with the prospect of relocating the seven reductions, had little choice but to obey the command of their Commissioner Altamirano, who in turn had little choice but to obey the instructions of his Spanish overlords. It seems likely that no Jesuits either participated in battles or ordered the Guaraní to fight, though many seem to have muddled their way through the rebellion with dislocated minds and broken spirits. Some fled, some were imprisoned by the Guaraní, and some remained at their stations to administer the sacraments and assist the sick and wounded. The War of the Seven Reductions was ultimately a blow from which the reductions never recovered. Nor did the Jesuits. Less than a decade after the end of hostilities the Jesuits were expelled from the Spanish colonies and the reductions entered a phase of inexorable decline characterized by Guaraní migration, disease, neglect and incompetent management. Ironically, the bold Jesuit experiment in native evangelization and social engineering was defeated more by events in Europe from whence they came than by resistance on the ground. Most of the surviving Jesuit Guaraní missions were destroyed by the early nineteenth-century wars of independence against colonial rule, but in truth their demise had begun over half a century earlier.

Telling the story of the growth of the Jesuit reductions and their ultimate demise is an easier task than assessing the degree of Catholicization the Jesuits were able to accomplish. Generally speaking most Jesuit accounts of the reductions, at least until recently, exaggerate their missionary success while ethnographers, anthropologists and historians have tended to emphasize complexity and limitation. For example, scholars have drawn attention to the persistence of shamanism, ancestral bone cults, ancient customs and the Guaraní language, but they also acknowledge the profound impact of the Jesuit missions on Guaraní beliefs and practices. The sheer persistence of the Jesuit missionary strategy, embracing as it did men, women and children, and religion, economy and society, left an indelible impression on the native culture and religious practices of the borderlands of Argentina, Paraguay and Brazil. No single metaphor, conceptual device or theoretical model, useful though many of them are, can ever hope fully to encapsulate the 'intricate patterns of adaptation, resistance, and accommodation' in the encounter between European Jesuits and the Guaraní.[5]

Across the Andes from the Guaraní homelands and the Jesuit reductions, a more common form of encounter between Spanish Catholicism and native religion took place in Lima, the capital city of the Spanish Viceroyalty of Peru and one of the great port cities of Spanish America. Here in 1710 a revealing ecclesiastical trial took place. The trial came in the midst of a series of ecclesiastical investigations undertaken sporadically in the archdiocese of Lima from the mid-seventeenth to the mid-eighteenth centuries. The purpose of these investigations was to extirpate idolatry, destroy native religious objects and defend Christian orthodoxy against the unacceptable remnants of Andean religion. It is worth bearing in mind that this campaign to extirpate idolatry was launched over 100 years after the Spanish conquest of Peru at a time when the Roman Catholic administrative system of dioceses and parishes was already well established. Extirpation was therefore primarily not a tool of mission but an agent of ecclesiastical control – more in the tradition of inquisition than evangelism. The trial involved a local healer called Juan Básquez whose healing arts comprised a powerful combination of native Andean practices and avowed Christian piety. Básquez, who took no money for his services, attributed his healing powers to the gift of God, which, he explained, came to him in a series of visions, dreams and stigmata. Moreover, even the Spanish priests who benefited from his healing acknowledged that he used Christian prayers, creeds and acts of contrition as part of his healing armoury. But Básquez also employed a range of more traditional Andean practices including saliva divination, blood offerings, medicinal beverages and rubbings with animal and plant compounds.[6]

The case against him was brought by a priest, Don Bartolomé de Alberca, whose poor eyesight was not helped by Básquez's healing methods. Alberca's allegation portrayed Básquez as a superstitious charlatan, a medium for demons and an exponent of the secret knowledge of the *huacas* (Andean sacred places and ancestors). During the trial, Dominican friars testified that Básquez used demonic powers and mixed 'sacred prayers and vain observance'. The defence rested on more rationalist ground by stating that Básquez had already recanted his more colourful claims about visions and stigmata, and then presented medical evidence from the University of

San Marcos to the effect that the natural remedies employed by Básquez may indeed have discernible healing properties. After a lengthy trial Juan Básquez was judged guilty of 'superstition' and was entrusted to the reformatory care of the friars of the Bethlehemite order. He was ordered to cease his healing practices and avoid all discussion of them.

Básquez's trial was one of hundreds of cases brought by ecclesiastical officials during the Peruvian Extirpation. Others dealt with traditional *chanca* divinities, ritual 'superstitions' and the continued use of Andean sacred spaces. One historian has called the Peruvian Extirpation 'the most systematic attempt ever made in colonial Spanish America to repress Indian religion and uproot its alleged perversions of Catholicism'.[7] What are we to make of it? The first point to emphasize is that the speed, extent and depth of Catholic penetration in Iberian Latin America vary enormously according to region and chronology. Plenty of examples can be found throughout the Americas of intense Catholic devotion or, on the contrary, of successful strategies of native resistance. But what the Peruvian Extirpation suggests is that in most places Iberian Catholicism had an easier time decapitating older traditions of faith and practice than in eradicating their residual popularity among native populations.[8] As the case of Básquez makes clear, it was perfectly possible for native peoples to embrace some aspects of colonial religion without entirely repudiating their native traditions.

Historians have struggled to find adequate terms to describe this complex reality. Concepts such as hybridity, syncretism and hierarchies of power, while not without their uses, do not capture the intricacies of how native peoples could adopt new forms of religious belief and practice without necessarily repudiating older forms. In the complex business of warding off evil, reducing suffering and sustaining communal traditions, help could be sought and welcomed from any number of places. At the heart of the extirpation campaign, however, was the notion of religion as a zero sum game in which Catholic Christianity could only be sustained at the expense of pre-existing religious traditions. The surviving records, with their criminal trials, breaches of ecclesiastical discipline and rooting out of heresy, privilege that interpretation as does the deafening rhetoric of colonialism and post-colonialism, which quite properly draws attention to the power differential between Europeans and natives. Even the religious assumptions of Spanish and Portuguese churchmen, rooted as they were in Augustinian dichotomies between Christians and idolaters, good and evil, and light and darkness, reinforced the idea that Catholic Christianity and Andean religions were incommensurable and incompatible.

But historians delight in emphasizing the complexity of religious and cultural processes. Writing of the limits of religious coercion in mid-colonial

Peru, one historian suggests that there were many 'faces of Christianity' and many 'degrees' of what has been called the process of Christianization, and that these 'degrees' were affected by, among other things, the nature of previous evangelization and the strength of native resistance. As a result, the dissemination of Christian symbols, doctrines and rituals depended on 'the decisions – and sometimes the whims – of a varied indigenous society'.[9] If not exactly free agents in the fashioning of their own religious cultures, Andeans at least had strategies of resistance that included keeping options open, performing religious rites in secret and maintaining silence in the face of Catholic inquisitions.[10]

The Peruvian Extirpation was in a way a sacramental illustration (literally an outward and visible expression) of the attempt to impose Catholic orthodoxy throughout the length and breadth of Latin America in the early modern period. In one sense what was at stake was not that much different from the effort to impose Catholic orthodoxy on the European peasantry whose religious cultures also had geological deposits of pre-Christian beliefs and of pre-Tridentine Catholic practices. But on another level, the native peoples of the Americas were 'others' in a way that European peasants were not. Cultural chauvinism, enhanced moral obligation, fear of persistent strains of rebellion and some colonial guilt all made the need for ecclesiastical surveillance greater in the New World than the Old.

The Básquez trial, however unique in its precise details, is also illustrative of wider themes in the process of Catholicizing Latin America in the mid-colonial period, the period after the shocking violence of the *conquistadores* and before the onset of organized independence movements. The fact that the trial occurred over a prolonged period of time during which careful testimony and scientific evidence were produced shows that early Enlightenment ideas were affecting Catholicism everywhere. At the beginning of extirpation in the mid-seventeenth century Andean religion was portrayed as devilish and demonic. As the eighteenth century progressed, however, Catholic authorities began to regard Andean practices as 'superstitious' or 'mixed' resulting from a lack of knowledge or of devotion to an earlier form of supernaturally exotic Catholicism. To some extent what was at stake in the Peruvian Extirpation was not only the elimination of Andean religious practices but also the modernizing of Catholic practices throughout the world. In short, the unavoidable fact was that the process of colonialism and Christianization had brought Old and New Worlds into a much closer relationship. As the eighteenth century unfolded, major events in Europe had their inevitable colonial aftershocks. The Enlightenment, Bourbon attempts to reform ecclesiastical institutions and exert power over the Church, the growing unpopularity of the Jesuits in Europe and overseas, and the need to harness the economic resources of empire all played out as much in Lima and Buenos Aires as they did in Madrid and Lisbon.[11]

China

In December 1701 Pope Clement XI (1649–1721) appointed Charles-Thomas Maillard de Tournon (1668–1710), the son of a Savoyard nobleman, as his legate to Mughal India and imperial China. De Tournon's unenviable mission was to resolve conflicts among Catholic missionaries in India and China and to represent the official theology of the European Catholic Church to the Christian churches of the East. De Tournon arrived in China several years later at both a propitious and an unpropitious moment.[12] Propitious because at the turn of the century the numbers of Christian converts in China probably reached their early modern peak (estimates range from 200,000 to 300,000) and Christians enjoyed unprecedented toleration in the wake of the Kangxi Emperor's Edict on Christianity issued in 1692. The Edict famously stated that Europeans, since they have been living amongst us,

> have merited our esteem and gratitude, by the great services they have rendered us in the civil and foreign wars, by their diligence in composing useful and curious books, their integrity, and their sincere regard for the public welfare. Besides this the Europeans are very quiet; they do not excite any disturbances in the provinces, they do no harm to anyone, they commit no crimes, and their doctrine has nothing in common with that of the false sects in the empire, nor has it any tendency to excite sedition.

The Edict of 1692 essentially placed Christians in the same category as Buddhists and Daoists who were allowed to practise their rituals in their own places of worship so long as they did not pose a threat to Confucian state orthodoxy or otherwise cause trouble. With eerie resonances of the Edict of Milan issued by the Emperor Constantine in 313CE, Kangxi's edict, however limited in extent, seemed to be a vindication of a Jesuit missionary strategy pioneered and implemented by a distinguished lineage of mainly Italian Jesuits including Alessandro Valignano (1539–1606), Michele Ruggieri (1543–1607) and Matteo Ricci (1552–1610). These Italian humanists believed that China was a great and unconquered ancient civilization, that Confucianism facilitated belief in a monotheistic God not incompatible with Christianity, and that successful Christian mission depended on cultural adaptation. As practitioners of what might now be called accommodation, indigenization or enculturation, Jesuits at the imperial court wore mandarin robes, studied classical Confucian texts, communicated advanced European thinking in the era of the scientific revolution and sought to adapt Christianity to prevailing Chinese beliefs and customs.[13]

Inevitably such tactics bred suspicion among those with a stronger sense of the superiority of Christianity and European civilization, and who equated accommodation with syncretism, adaptation with capitulation, and harmonization with heresy.

When de Tournon eventually arrived in China in 1705 the tide was already turning against the Jesuits. They faced increasing opposition from many directions. To begin with not all the Jesuits were on the same page on the most vexed questions at stake in the so-called Chinese Rites Controversy. At its most basic level the Rites Controversy was about whether it is necessary to change deeply entrenched cultural traditions in order to adopt a foreign religion, or whether Chinese Christians had to adopt some aspects and assumptions of Western culture in order to practise their Christianity.[14] More specifically, the issues at stake included the so-called 'Term question' about how to express in Chinese the name for God and other concepts regarded as vital to Christianity, the participation of Christian converts in Confucian ceremonial rituals surrounding funeral customs and ancestor worship, and finally whether Christians should be permitted to engage in communal celebrations of non-Christian divinities. As with many missionary encounters the most controversial issues at stake involved language and meaning, the relation between traditional and new practices, religion as an agent or subversion of social cohesion and stability, and competing views over bodies and sacred rituals. Although there were any number of nuances expressed in the century-old debates on these issues, the nub of the matter was that Jesuits in the tradition of Ricci regarded many of the ceremonial rites of Confucianism as primarily civic (social and political), not religious in nature, and thus, properly understood, posed no direct threat to Christian sensibilities. However, within late seventeenth-century Roman Catholicism this Jesuit tradition was coming under greater scrutiny as a result of an increasing emphasis on order and orthodoxy in Europe and greater competition from other Catholic religious orders on the ground in Asia. Representatives of the mendicant orders such as the Franciscans, Dominicans and Augustinians, who were more accustomed to mission as a corollary of conquest, as in the Spanish and Portuguese empires of South America and Indonesia, were dismayed by the extent of Jesuit accommodation.

These views had powerful supporters in Europe among the ubiquitous enemies of the Jesuits, the Jansenist-influenced Paris Society of Foreign Missions and the theologians of the Vatican. Moreover, while the Jesuits were helping to export some of the more agreeable aspects of the European Enlightenment to the Chinese Empire, other aspects carried more than a whiff of European civilizational superiority, which of course boded ill for the Jesuit mission. In short, the Jesuits were being squeezed by more stringent formulations of Christian orthodoxy in Europe on the one hand and heightened suspicion of European intentions in China on the other. Ironically, as pioneers of early modern globalism through their travels, maps, clocks and publications, the Jesuits in China fell victim to the consequences of globalization, namely the reduced freedom to cultivate a foreign field in relative isolation from centralized control. These were the complex forces at work when de Tournon, himself an agent of papal jurisdiction, reached Canton in April 1705.

The omens for a successful mediation were not propitious. De Tournon was not a Chinese speaker and his mission was not so much to find a negotiated settlement of long-standing disagreements as to enforce papal policy. Although the slow delivery of early modern communication meant that de Tournon did not have Clement XI's decree of 1704 in his hand when he reached China, he would not have been surprised by its contents. Clement ruled against the use of the terms *Tien* (heaven) and *Xang Xu* (highest emperor) for the 'true God', forbade the hanging of plaques with these inscriptions in Christian churches and issued clear instructions preventing Christians from participating in Confucian rituals. The language was hardly conciliatory: 'Moreover, believers in Christ cannot under any circumstances whatsoever be permitted to preside over, assist or participate in the celebrations of the offerings that are brought by the Chinese to Confucius and to the ancestors in the yearly ceremonies of the equinox, because these celebrations are tainted with superstition.' In similar vein, Clement forbade Christians from taking part in 'any sort of offering, rite or ceremony, together with pagans or separately, at ancestor shrines in private houses, at the graves of the ancestors, or at the graveside before the burial of the deceased, as would usually be done to honour them'.[15] Armed with such uncompromising views and assisted by the ultra-conservative Vicar Apostolic of Fujian, Charles Maigrot (1652–1730), who proved not to be a happy choice, de Tournon predictably alienated a delegation of Beijing congregations, Chinese intellectuals and crucially the Kangxi Emperor.

The climax of the de Tournon mission came in Beijing in the summer of 1706 with a series of discussions between the contending parties instituted by the Confucian Emperor. On one side were the papal legate, de Tournon, Maigrot of the Paris Society of Foreign Missions, and representatives of most of the mendicant orders, all supported by papal authority. On the other side were Chinese intellectuals, government officials, most Chinese Christians and Jesuit missionaries, and the Kangxi Emperor. At stake in the discussions were the perceived purity and distinctiveness of Christianity, the national and cultural pride of Europeans and Chinese, the jurisdictional authority of pope and emperor and the future of Christianity in China. The discussions did not go well for de Tournon and Maigrot, whose lack of knowledge of literary Chinese and the classics irritated the emperor and made them appear outsiders to the culture they wanted to Christianize. The outcome was sealed.

The emperor expelled Maigrot from the empire, instituted a more rigorous examination of missionaries before they could be issued an imperial permit and ordered the imprisonment of de Tournon in Macao where he died in 1710, ironically soon after receiving news that Clement had made him a cardinal. Although more battles over the Chinese Rites ensued after de Tournon's death, his 'diplomatic mission' buttressed by Clement's inflexible views, marked the beginning of the end of the Jesuit accommodationist style of mission in China. Clement's papal bull *Ex illa die* (1715), followed by Pope Benedict XIV's *Ex quo singulari* (1742), were met with implacable hostility by Chinese emperors. The Jesuit mission to China was living on borrowed time long before the official dissolution of the order in 1773 weakened, but did not end, Jesuit influence.

Before leaving the story of de Tournon's ill-fated mission, a number of significant points need to be made. In the first place the issues at stake in the Chinese Rites Controversy were complex and not easily resolved. Not only were the theological and cultural, and what we might now call the anthropological and missiological, debates complicated in themselves, but they had to be handled in the context of shifting power dynamics in the relations between Europe and China, Jesuits and other Catholic religious orders, and imperial and adaptive constructions of Christian mission. Moreover, the European Enlightenment promoted both a sense of intellectual and cultural superiority over the 'other' and fascination with the 'other'. Depending on one's point of view, therefore, the defeat of the Jesuit approach to mission in Japan and China may be regarded either as 'a vision betrayed' or as a necessary assertion of Christian orthodoxy against the enculturation strategy of an autonomous and increasingly unpopular missionary order. In a sense what is most interesting about the Rites Controversy in China was not the way it was finally resolved but what the mechanisms of resolution reveal about the nature of European Catholicism in the age of the Enlightenment.

A second point to bear in mind is that the Jesuit mission to China was not by any means the whole story of Christianity in China in the eighteenth century. Indeed an over-concentration on the Rites Controversy may itself be regarded as a manifestation of an unacceptably Eurocentric approach to Chinese religious history. Chinese converts to Christianity from a myriad of different missionary encounters and indigenous efforts practised a form of Christianity that was deeply imbedded in the culture and customs of

Chinese society.[16] For most of the time the Rites Controversy was played out over their heads with little direct impact on the way they lived their lives or practised their faith. Moreover the Rites Controversy did not alter one of the most distinctive features of Jesuit missions in eighteenth-century China, namely the high proportion of abandoned infants as a percentage of all baptisms performed by the Jesuits. Consistently running at over 80 per cent of baptisms from the 1680s to the 1750s, this practice was a Jesuit response to both infanticide and abandonment. What did change, however, was the sociology of conversions, which became much less common among the literati and more concentrated among the middle and lower orders. One inevitable consequence is that Christianity became increasingly associated in the minds of elites with other kinds of destabilizing sectarian deviance. There is evidence, for example, that Christian symbols and rituals were sometimes appropriated by millenarian sectarian traditions, which inevitably led to an increase in state persecution and soured relationships between Jesuits and Chinese elites. In 1748, after three years of persecution under the Emperor Qianlong (1711–99), the Jesuit musician Florian Bahr (1706–71) wrote from Beijing that 'the continuous persecutions of three years have ruined the mission; this Chinese Empire, which was so highly praised in books because of its laws, customs and politics, has now, however, earned the name of a barbarian empire'.[17]

Jesuit ambivalence about China as both an exotic and ancient colossus, and as a giant repository of antichristian superstition and idolatry, became the predominant view of China in Europe, for the Jesuits were formidable collectors, editors and publishers. The seminal work was Jean-Baptiste du Halde's (1674–1743) *Description, Géographique, Historique, Chronologique et Politique de l'Empire de la Chine et de la Tartarie Chinoise* (1735), based on du Halde's editorial work on the 'the best-known missionary series of all time, the *Lettres Édifantes et Curieuses* published between 1703 and 1776'. European perceptions of China and its religions in the eighteenth century were essentially Jesuit perceptions, and this was true even in Protestant Europe, which accepted Jesuit observations of Chinese society while repudiating what in their view were Jesuit hypocrisy, superstition and idolatry.[18]

If du Halde supplied the preeminent source for European views of China in the eighteenth century, it was the fate of de Tournon's legatorial mission 30 years earlier that more than anything sealed the fate of the Jesuit mission in China. The history of the Rites Controversy in general, and de Tournon's papal mission in particular, showed how contested were European conceptions of Christian mission to non-European peoples, especially those who had not been conquered by Europeans and who could lay claim to a civilization even more ancient than the Greeks and Romans. Whether a vision betrayed or a vision ill conceived, the Jesuit approach to China emanating from Ignatian spirituality, Italian humanism and long traditions of engagement with Eastern civilizations was largely buried beneath the rubble produced by a renewed emphasis on Catholic orthodoxy, an Enlightenment-produced sense of European superiority and Chinese fears about what Europeans would do to their civilization. De Tournon, unfortunately for him, did not fully appreciate what he was getting himself into.

What then was the impact of the Chinese Rites Controversy on the future of Christianity in China and what would have happened if the Jesuits had won the argument? To begin with, it is important to emphasize that although there were almost a thousand Jesuits who participated in the China mission between 1552 and 1800, a great many others were associated with other Catholic missionary orders, including the Franciscans who predated the arrival of the Jesuits and had a very different missionary strategy. Generally speaking the Franciscans worked among lower social groups, vigorously promoted confraternities (lay brotherhoods and sisterhoods) and participated in quasi-underground versions of Christianity associated with secret meetings and ascetic rituals. As a result of the manifold endeavours of the Catholic missionary orders, by the beginning of the eighteenth century Christianity had already sunk deep roots into some of the more remote areas of China and was able to survive the periodic persecutions of the eighteenth century because of its generational transmission. The Chinese emphasis on filial piety enabled Chinese Christians to remain loyal to the Christianity of their ancestors and helps explain the survival of the Chinese Christian church, not only in the eighteenth century but also right down to the present.[19] Indeed, one by-product of the episodic bursts of persecution to which Chinese Christians were subjected is the existence of legal records showing that by the mid-eighteenth century Catholicism had become a genuinely popular religion, replete with abundant supernatural manifestations, millenarian fantasies, extravagant displays of emotion, rituals, festivals, fast days, images, songs and folk customs blending Confucian and Christian rites. On the whole these legal records show that Chinese Catholics mostly lived at peace with their non-Christian neighbours and periods of strife were occasioned more by social and economic rivalries and grievances than by explicitly religious differences.[20] In short, if one moved outside Beijing, the imperial court, and the purview of Jesuit missionaries there was in eighteenth-century China vigorous and distinctive traditions of popular Chinese Christianity in many of the provinces including Fujian, Zhili, Shandong and Sichuan. Chinese Christianity suffered from, but was far from eradicated by, the decline of European missionary support.

For obvious reasons, estimates of numbers of Christians in eighteenth-century China are scarcely precise, but it seems likely that there were only half as many in the mid- to later eighteenth century as there had been in 1700 despite the fact that the Chinese population more than doubled in the same period. It also seems likely that numbers began to grow again at the turn of the century and probably returned to something like 1700 levels by the early 1800s. The number of priests also declined in the eighteenth century, but on the other hand the proportion of Chinese priests increased dramatically from 6 out of 117 in 1700 to 80 out of 111 in 1800. Some were trained in Europe, others in Manila or China itself.[21] Moreover, Chinese Christianity was by no means entirely dependent on the offices of priests. Male itinerant catechists, lay congregational leaders and the remarkable contributions of the women associated with the Institute of Christian Virgins all contributed to a vigorous Catholic Christianity which was especially strong among the more mobile populations of the remote province of Sichuan. The Institute of Christian Virgins was an order of Chinese Catholic women who lived with their families, remained celibate, taught Chinese girls, instructed catechumens for baptism and baptized dying infants. Although church authorities were often ambivalent about the activities of the virgins, and repeatedly tried to impose controls on their activities, there is no denying their significance in sustaining the lived religion of Chinese Catholics in the eighteenth century.[22]

Thus Chinese Christianity was far from extinguished by the combination of government opposition and Jesuit decline and suppression, but its influence among Chinese elites waned dramatically as did its toleration by the empire. Although the Jesuits in China were never entirely free from the European context from which they came, their attempts to imagine, translate and propagate Christianity outside a Western European cultural matrix was a bold enterprise. That it ran into the ground by the late eighteenth century not only reveals a good deal about the dynamics of European modernization and expansion, but also boded ill for the fate of Christianity in an emerging era of imperial competition.[23]

The Chinese Rites Controversy not only stirred up conflict at the time but has been the subject of disagreement among historians ever since. Some have seen the controversy as a watershed both in the history of Christianity in China and in the history of Sino-Western cultural relations. Historians of the mendicant orders, including the Franciscans, take a different view, claiming that by the beginning of the eighteenth century Christianity had reached a point of either continuing down the accommodationist path or else making a determined stand for its unique and essential traits. What these writings show is that the issues at stake in the Chinese Rites Controversy were fought out among Jesuits, between Jesuits and other Catholic missionary orders, and between the papacy and the Chinese emperor. In addition, as the distinguished sinologist Jonathan Spence has shown, historians of the Chinese Rites Controversy need to take into account the interplay of the key personalities, including the irascible Emperor Kangxi, the cultural and linguistic complexities of the issues, the ways in which friendship connections and information transmission affected outcomes and an underground world of rumours, plots and machinations that made it difficult to reach agreements.[24] Many of these factors reappeared in different guises in the nineteenth century when Protestant missionaries ran into some of the same difficulties as their Catholic predecessors had done. Exporting Christianity from the West to an ancient civilization in the context of justifiable Chinese suspicions of Western intentions was never going to be an uncontested task. The fissures that were opened up, especially in the long controversy over Chinese Rites, reveal a great deal about the early modern expansion of Christianity to places Westerners had never conquered.

How then does the Chinese Rites Controversy look from the Chinese side of the encounter? The short answer is, probably not as significant as it does from the European perspective. Every religion of foreign origin with any chance of making headway in China, including Judaism, Islam and Buddhism, had to adapt to a fundamental Confucian framework. In that sense Jesuit accommodation to Confucian practices and Confucian adaptation to some aspects of foreign religious traditions was neither new nor unusual. From the perspective of the Western missionaries, the burning question was to what extent could Christianity relate to the established verities of Confucianism without betraying its essence, however that was construed, while from the Chinese side the burning question was to what extent could Confucianism absorb the insights of other religious traditions without undermining the ethical and civic traditions of the empire. Confucianism was so all pervasive 'that any religious tradition from outside was caught in its field, and was bound to gravitate towards that centre'.[25] That did not mean that the Christianity espoused by the converted Christian literati was shorn of theological content or that they had no interest in seeing Christianity grow, but it did mean that they could still hope to 'protect the orthodoxy of Confucian ideology while being loyal to the sacredness of the foreign religion', and that the spread of Christianity in China did not carry with it either as prerequisite or inevitable consequence the spread of Western cultural hegemony.[26]

The central issue in the Rites Controversy was whether the rites to Confucius and the ancestors were religious or civic in nature. Were those practising the rites honouring real gods and were they hoping for tangible benefits as a reward for their devotion, or were they merely honouring ancestors out of filial gratitude? These questions, wrapped up as they were in centuries of folk traditions and practices, were not easy to answer. The Jesuits staked their missionary strategy on the belief that Confucianism could be effectively Christianized, while their opponents alleged that Christianity had become debased in the process of cultural mediation. As is the way with bitter conflicts, part of the problem lay with the intrinsic difficulty of the issues themselves, but another part rested with the motives, methods and machinations of the major protagonists.

India

The history of Christianity in India is a largely southern story; it is also remarkably complex and shrouded in antique mystery. When the Pfarangi (European) fleets of Portugal reached southern India at the turn of the fifteenth and sixteenth centuries in search of spices, the merchants, soldiers and Franciscan missionaries who stepped ashore encountered ancient traditions of Christianity that they scarcely recognized as Christian. With roots perhaps as deep as the Apostle Thomas, and with better-documented traditions linking Indian Christianity to Orthodox Syrian and other eastern varieties, the Thomas Christian communities of India baffled the Portuguese with their diversity as much as they have done scholars ever since. The Christianity brought by the Portuguese was an especially militant form of Christendom, nourished for centuries on the unremitting Iberian struggle against Islam and armed with the *Padroado Real* that gave papal permission for Portuguese monarchs to conquer, subdue and make religious provision for their new territories. With the *Padroado* mandate behind them, representatives of the Roman Catholic missionary orders, especially Franciscans and Jesuits, arrived in their hundreds at the Portuguese port of Goa and then fanned out along the coastline and into the interior. Far from presenting a united Christian front against Muslims and Hindus, however, south Indian Christianity was riven with disputes between Rome and Lisbon, Franciscans and Jesuits, Roman Catholic and Thomas Christians, and Indians and Europeans. Thomas Christians refused to accept the Virgin Mary as the 'Mother of God', objected to the veneration of images, performed distinctive sacramental rituals, danced and sang to local idioms, practised allegedly 'magical' rites and celebrated festivals in distinctive ways. On the other side, they viewed with disdain the 'vulgar' Pfarangi habits of meat eating, lewd sexual behaviour, physical violence and inquisitorial demands. To social, cultural and religious differences were added complicated jurisdictional disputes which were inconclusively refereed by popes and patriarchs.[27]

Beyond the colonialism and the conflict, Jesuit missionaries such as

Roberto de Nobili (1577–1656), John de Britto (1647–93) and Constanzo Giuseppe Beschi (1680–1747) embraced some of the same methods as their contemporaries in China, but without reaching the equivalent apex of political and cultural power. Mughal emperors were simply less accessible to European Christians than were those at the Chinese imperial court. The Jesuits nevertheless built libraries, established colleges, spread scientific knowledge and produced a formidable corpus of Tamil scholarship. The further they travelled from the *Padroado* of Goa the more Catholic missions manifested transcultural adaptability; but while Catholic missions had their successes, the reality is that they made no substantial impact on Mughal India and never fully succeeded in reducing the Thomasine traditions of Indian Christianity to Roman Catholic orthodoxy.

What then of the eighteenth-century history of Christianity in India? I wish to tell two stories of mission, one Catholic and the other Protestant, that started within a few years of one another in the first decade of the eighteenth century. The first concerns the French Jesuit Father Bouchet (1655–1732), who came to India in 1689 and was appointed in 1702 to lead the French Carnatic Mission in South India. The second story is about Bartholomäus Ziegenbalg (1683–1719), a graduate from August Hermann Francke's Pietist University of Halle.

Father Bouchet was a French Jesuit who first went to Siam before being ejected and fetching up in Pondicherry in 1689. In *Fr. Bouchet's India: An 18th Century Jesuit's Encounter with Hinduism*, Francis Clooney uses Bouchet's lengthy letters to evoke the nature of the encounter between Jesuits and Hindus in the early eighteenth century. Having neither the gifts nor the intellectual range of someone like his distinguished predecessor Roberto de Nobili, Bouchet's opinions are all the more interesting for their typicality. He was a significant player in the Malabar Rites Controversy, in which he supplied information to de Tournon but did not support the rigorous decree against hybrid forms of Catholicism and Hinduism issued by de Tournon. Bouchet was not a progressive advocate of inculturation, but neither did he want to see the mission harmed by excessive calls for Catholic purity for Indian converts. Bouchet and Fr Laynez were sent to Rome 'to argue vigorously against the alleged inaccuracy, severity and rigidity' of de Tournon's decree and in favour of a more complex view of the religious and cultural situation in south India and how best to respond to it.[28]

Bouchet's letters are full of judicious reflections on the legal system or up-to-date commentary on the state of mapmaking, but they also contain a sustained theological engagement with Indian religion. His views were based on the idea that conditions in eighteenth-century India were similar to the state of the Mediterranean world in the first century. Thus he viewed

India as reliving the birth of the Church with all of the attendant risks of persecution (blood seed) and inadequate public confession of sins. As with the early Christian centuries he believed in the reality of demons and evil spirits and appealed to the miracles of the early church in opposition to the growing impact of Enlightenment ideas within some aspects of European Catholicism. He believed, unhistorically of course, that the religions of India derived from the Bible and the ministry of the original Apostles. According to this scheme, in ancient times India was Christian and could be so again.[29] Similarly, in the spirit of the early church Bouchet advocated missionary austerity and faithfulness in the face of manifold trials and tribulations as the most important attributes of Christian mission. Bouchet was a steadfast opponent of one of the aspects of Hinduism he liked least, namely its belief in reincarnation, and he appealed to Cartesian principles to prove that animals do not have souls. In contrast with de Nobili, there is more than a hint of contempt in Bouchet for his Brahmin interlocutors. But what did they make of him? There is in fact very little information about what seventeenth- and eighteenth-century Hindus made of European Jesuits and the Catholicism they represented. Unlike de Nobili, who had a richer encounter with Hindu texts and seemed much less nervous about the state of European Catholicism than Bouchet, there seems to have been no serious intellectual discourse or mutual engagement of any kind between Bouchet and Hindu religious elites.[30] He was nevertheless able to construct pastoral writing in Tamil for Christian converts.

In short, Bouchet's missionary strategy was based on the twin notions that Christianity in India was of ancient lineage and that eighteenth-century India resembled nothing so much as the ancient pagan world of the Mediterranean. His life and writing is more instructive in revealing what European Christians made of India than the other way round. He is an earnest, compassionate, faithful, condescending figure eager to show the superiority of his Bible, his church and his culture over those he ministered to.

Not long after Fr Bouchet took control of the French Carnatic mission in South India two Europeans from a different Christian tradition, Lutheran Pietism, arrived on Indian soil. In 1706 two young German missionaries, Bartholomäus Ziegenbalg and Heinrich Plütschau (1678–1747), landed on the south-eastern coast of India in the Danish colony called Tranquebar. When Ziegenbalg left Copenhagen in 1705 he knew almost nothing about south Indian culture and religion; by the time of his death in 1719 he was perhaps the foremost authority. He made a determined effort to learn the Tamil language, which paid immediate ethnographic dividends. He made detailed notes on politics, civic life, language, climate, work habits, diet and of course religion. He could not endorse the polytheistic and pantheistic dimensions of Tamil spirituality. He also disliked image worship, astrology, sacrifices and caste. On these issues he could come across as culturally arrogant and insensitive. On the other side, Tamils did not much admire the virtue and behaviour of many Europeans who seemed addicted to flesh eating, drunkenness and coarseness. Ziegenbalg's approach also reflected divisions within European Christian culture between Pietist and Orthodox Lutherans, and between Protestant Pietists and Roman Catholics. Ziegenbalg was critical of Jesuit missionaries for their weak language skills and their toleration of pagan ceremonies, but he was also critical of traditional Protestants for their lack of serious heart religion. Although no enthusiast for Islam he had a mostly respectful relationship with the relatively high-status Muslim community in Tranquebar.

As Pietist graduates of the University of Halle, Ziegenbalg and Plüt-schau were sent to India by the king of Denmark not primarily to service Europeans or to study native culture but actively to promote Protestant Christianity among 'Moors' and 'pagans'. In other words they were there to make converts, but to what? The Ziegenbalg-led mission tried to spread orthodox Lutheran doctrine with an Evangelical Pietist slant that included an emphasis on Godly struggle (*bhakti*) and the new birth. The methods employed by Ziegenbalg included preaching, catechizing, Bible study (hence the need for translation), the disciplining of believers and education. The aims and objectives of Spener's *Pia Desideria* were to be put into effect to produce new Pietist selves on the Indian sub-continent just as they had been among Lutherans in continental Europe. Ziegenbalg's religious mission also needs to be placed in a wider context of European engagement with India. As one scholar has it, 'Pietism unwittingly fit a notion of individual value and autonomy that was developing socially through a laissez-faire capitalism represented by the East India Companies.'[31] Central to Ziegenbalg's message, therefore, was not just the idea that the Malabarian people were to give up their Indian gods in favour of the God(s) of European Christians, but also that they were to live completely reconstituted lives set free from sin and guilt. In the characteristic language of German Pietism, Ziegenbalg informed his hearers that 'if you barely change the Name, and not the Heart, then the coming over to our Religion, and the taking upon you the Name of a Christian, will do you no good at all'.[32]

To effect such a radical change in the lives of his hearers, Ziegenbalg embarked upon an industry of translation and publishing that included the Gospels, Luther's Small Catechism, expositions of doctrine and letters explaining conversion. We know from Ziegenbalg's other distinguished writings on Indian culture that although he knew better than anyone that the culture he was evangelizing differed in very significant ways from the Europe he had left behind, the means and ends of his mission were Pietist through and through. Central to his whole enterprise was the recruitment of Tamil-speaking pastors and laypeople who could act as preachers and catechists. Indeed catechizing seems to have served the same kind of function (spreading basic Christian knowledge, creating awareness of sin and inculcating a need for penitence) among Tamil converts as it did in some parts of Europe. Not surprisingly, however, Ziegenbalg was at first more successful in sweeping up the descendants of earlier Roman Catholic and Dutch Calvinist missions than he was in converting Hindus and Muslims, but the Pietist mission nevertheless experienced slow but reasonably steady growth over the course of the eighteenth century.

What kinds of converts were being fashioned? Here the evidence is predictably thin. What we know for sure is that Tamil church leaders were both unwilling and unable to transcend the barriers of caste that separated Tamil Protestants into high-status Vellalans and low-status 'pariahs'. New Christian selves were certainly not equal selves, at least not in the way Europeans imagined. In the hybridity that emerged from the encounter between Halle Pietists and Tamil varieties of Indian culture, Tamil Protestants embraced their Lutheran catechisms, liturgies and sacraments, but also adapted them to Tamil customs, language and kinship.

Part of that successful adaptation was the maintenance of caste, because it was so deeply embedded in Tamil notions of family, purity, body, food and social relations. For eighteenth-century Evangelical Malabarians it was therefore perfectly possible to 'pray together, but not eat together, and yet love one another'.[33] This apparently un-European pattern (though of course the realities of hierarchy and social class could play out in similar ways in Europe) came under intense pressure from English, Calvinist, colonial and contractual missionaries in the nineteenth century. It nevertheless lay at the heart of the encounter between Halle Pietists and Tamils in the eighteenth century and probably shaped the way the Lord's Supper was celebrated. Vellalans and 'pariahs' very likely did not share the same cup and were separated within a communal worship space (they sat together separately), although they did read the same catechisms and hear the same sermons. What is less clear is how Pietist conceptions of the new birth and disciplined selves were mediated by Tamil conceptions of caste identity, temple rites and purification rituals.

Given the absence of hard evidence, especially among non-Vellalan Christian converts, it is probably unwise to speculate about how Pietist emphases on heart religion and strict personal accountability translated into Tamil. What we do know is that the Pietists preached and translated texts on penitence, heart religion and the new birth and that they made converts in reasonable numbers among different castes. Some low caste ('pariah') converts became respected catechists and evangelists, but ultimately they occupied a restricted space between the exclusive demands of higher caste sensibilities on the one hand and European missionaries on the other, who had no alternative but to pay attention to caste conflict in the interests of missionary expediency. There is nevertheless sufficient evidence to suggest that Evangelical Christianity helped empower some lower-caste Tamils through literacy, expanded opportunities and a strong sense of truth possession against both 'Catholic heretics' and 'pagans'.[34] Indeed, what is remarkable about the Pietist mission to Tranquebar is the extent to which European religious conflicts between supposedly 'literate' Protestants and 'superstitious' Catholics could achieve new salience on Indian soil.

Ziegenbalg was essentially a *dubashi* (an agent or go-between) missionary brokering Pietist and Enlightenment Christianity to India, and the riches of Tamil culture to Europeans. Central to his method was a painstaking study of language and culture that enabled him to write his monumental works, *Malabarian Heathenism* (1711) and the *Genealogy of the Malabarian Gods* (1713), and translate the New Testament into Tamil in 1715. Ziegenbalg was a relentless collector of Tamil books and artefacts, a regular contributor to the *Halle Reports* (a kind of eighteenth-century Pietist version of Reuters news service) and a conduit for European technological innovation to India, including the use of Tamil fonts for printing. He was equally at ease in discussions with Tamil pandits and poets and with the common people for whom he established a network of charity and orphan schools based on the Halle model. Although scarcely a radical proponent of acculturated Christianity, Ziegenbalg occasionally fell foul of the Danish authorities in Tranquebar, and also occasionally displeased Francke who stated that, 'Missionaries were sent to extirpate heathenism, and not to spread heathenish nonsense in Europe.'[35]

Perhaps the most remarkable feature of Ziegenbalg's mission was that it did not end with his death in 1719 but rather continued under a succession of *dubashi* missionaries who included Benjamin Schulze (1689–1760), a pioneering Telugu linguist and translator, Johann Phillip Fabricius (1711–91), who translated the Old and New Testaments into Tamil, and, most eminent of all, Christian Friedrich Schwarz (1726–98), a brilliant linguist who acted as military chaplain, diplomat, secretary of state and regent in the midst of the protracted colonial conflicts between the French and the English in the later eighteenth century. Collectively they also helped train generations of Tamil Christian leaders culminating in impressive numbers of mass conversions under native leadership at the end of the eighteenth century. German Pietist missionaries whose own religious tradition was associated with European revivalism were eventually able to produce similar results generations later among the Tamils of south India; but it took native leadership to produce the results. It seems that no mass movement of conversions in India was ever led by a European.

The Tranquebar mission, though relatively small in scale and scope, was disproportionately influential in the history of Protestant missions because of its methods, connections and timing. In terms of methods Ziegenbalg and his successors emphasized five things: the importance of the mother tongue as the most central aspect of culture; the translation of the Bible into spoken Tamil, not literary Tamil; the need to practise a careful observation of indigenous culture as a foundation for thoughtful mission; the priority of establishing an indigenous church; and, as befits Halle Pietists, the central role of education both of children and pastors.[36] This model became widely distributed through the well-established connections between Halle, Copenhagen and London, and through the auspices of the SPCK. News of the Tranquebar mission reached Cotton Mather in New England, influenced Zinzendorf and the Moravians, attracted the attention of the British East India Company and became a source of inspiration for Danish, German and English missionary societies in the eighteenth and nineteenth centuries. Moreover, the methods of the mission, the circulation of the *Halle Reports* and the distribution networks of Halle University made an impact both on intellectual culture and popular opinion in eighteenth-century Europe. In short, the Tranquebar mission, for good and ill, helped put India and foreign missions on the mental maps of European Protestants in the eighteenth century.

What Catholic and Protestant missions to south India in the eighteenth century showed is that there were multiple layers of encounters, between old Thomasine traditions of Christianity and the Portuguese, between Jesuits, Pietists and Hindu culture and between different national traditions of European mission. Hindu reinforcement of caste was a significant problem for all European traditions of Christianity, even if there was little agreement about what to do about it. English missionaries went one way, German Lutherans another; French Catholics respected caste divisions, Irish Catholics were more reluctant. Pope Benedict XIV (1675–1758) in 1744 insisted on all Christians hearing the same Mass, in the same building at the same time, but this seems to have been modified in practice. Most missionaries to India were not agents of imperialism, but they partly benefited from imperial expansion and trading networks and in the nineteenth century anti-imperial nationalist movements often received support from missionaries. In truth, neither Catholic nor Protestant missions quite achieved what they hoped for in India, but there is no denying the serious-ness of their efforts or their enthusiasm for understanding the religion and culture they were seeking to convert.

People

Rebecca Protten

In the mid-1720s a young six- or seven-year-old girl of mixed European and African descent (a 'mulatto' in eighteenth-century parlance) named Shelly was kidnapped from Antigua in the Caribbean islands and sold into slav-ery on the Danish sugar island of St Thomas. Shelly's owner was Lucas van Beverhout, a prominent Dutch-speaking planter who owned almost 200 slaves. As a domestic slave, Shelly was brought up in the Reformed religion of her Dutch Calvinist owner and soon displayed an unusual apti-tude for learning and teaching other black women. As an adolescent she was baptized by a Roman Catholic priest from Puerto Rico, was renamed Rebecca and set free by her owner. These events took place in the shadow of one of the bloodiest slave insurrections of the eighteenth century on the neighbouring Danish island of St John in 1733. With a ratio of five people of African descent for every European, the Danish islands, as with most slave societies, were ruled by 'an elaborate choreography of terror', which both provoked resistance and then squashed it with unspeakable brutality. Rebecca's early Christian ministry to black women took place within the anxieties produced by the violence endemic to slavery and the colonial slave trade.[37]

Rebecca's ministry to the black slave population of St Thomas was soon to be transformed by events taking place over 3,000 miles away in Europe. In 1731 a chance encounter between Count Zinzendorf (1700–60), the leader of the German Pietist group known as the Moravians, and Anthony (also known as Anton Ulrich), a black ex-slave from St Thomas, at the corona-tion of the Danish king Christian VI (1699–1746) resulted in the dispatch of two Moravian missionaries to St Thomas. The origins of the Moravi-ans, otherwise known as the Renewed Unity of the Brethren, are complex but important, for they were the most significant of the early pioneers of the Protestant missionary movement, which did much to reshape the reli-gious geography of Christianity in the eighteenth and nineteenth centu-ries.[38] With some of its roots reaching deep into Jan Hus (1369–1415) and the Bohemian critique of Roman Catholicism a century before Martin Luther (1483–1546), the eighteenth-century Moravians were essentially refugees under Christian David's (1690–1751) leadership who fetched up on the Berthelsdorf estate of Zinzendorf in 1722. Part ancient church, part new Pietist sect, part interconfessional and international religious movement, and part Zinzendorf's aristocratic creation, Moravians established a new Pietist settlement at Herrnhut from which they expanded out to form new religious communities in Europe and North America. Moravians shared with other Pietists an emphasis on heart religion, cell groups, biblical devotion, religious experience and the new birth, but added their distinctive emphases on mission, community and what has been called 'blood and wounds' theology. Moravian hymns and some of the religious paintings of the Moravian Johann Valentin Haidt reveal a spirituality deeply focused on Christ's blood and wounds, especially the side wound of Christ within which Moravians sought refuge, comfort and security. Disturbingly gory for many, and too crypto-Catholic for Orthodox Lutherans and contemporary revivalists like George Whitefield, this aspect of Moravian spirituality sometimes got out of hand and had to be reined in by the brotherhood itself.

Along with its emphasis on the blood and wounds of Christ, the characteristic expression of Moravian belief was 'not the confession of faith, in the Reformation tradition, but the accumulation of archives, the evidence of the way God operated in history'. Less concerned with creeds and confessions, Moravians wrote little autobiographies, journals, letters and missionary reports as testaments to the active work of God and the millennial spread of the Gospel.[39] Mission became their passion. Their first attempt at foreign missions was the dispatch of two missionaries, Leonhard Dober and David Nitschmann, to St Thomas in 1732. Although their mission ended in relative ignominy, one of their successors, Friedrich Martin, arrived in St Thomas in 1736 and soon after encountered Rebecca. Thus began an association between Rebecca and the Moravians that was to shape the rest of her life. In association with the Moravians, Rebecca soon found herself at the centre of a spiritual revival, resulting in the formation of the first black Protestant congregation in the Americas. By 'mobilizing conversion from within the slave community', and by 'making Christianity a religion of and for people of African origin', Rebecca and her associates were the forerunners of one of the most dynamic movements of the early modern period, namely the emergence of the black Protestant church in North America.[40] Up until the mid-1700s the great preponderance of African Christians in the Atlantic world were Catholic, the product of both Catholic missions to West Central Africa and the colonial expansion of the Spanish, French and Portuguese. But as with other aspects of global Christianity, the balance of power between Protestants and Catholics began to shift decisively from the 1730s. The Moravians were catalysts. Here then are the roots of one of the major transitions in world Christianity. Unlikely as it seems, slaves of African descent encountered populist forms of Evangelical Pietism in the

Caribbean islands and the American colonies and were able to construct communities of faith of surprising durability.[41]

Of note here is the fact that Rebecca was a female itinerant evangelist and class leader on the small island of St Thomas some years *before* George Whitefield and John Wesley took the revolutionary step of preaching outdoors to large gatherings in England in the late 1730s. Just as Wesley was indebted to Moravian spirituality, so too was Rebecca. Although resolutely pro-slavery (unlike Wesley) and anti-polygamy, Moravian spirituality, with its emphases on Christ's blood and wounds, the sacredness of water baptism (conferring new names), its enthusiasm for dreams and revelations and its focus on kinship and community, made symbiotic connections with the African religious traditions they encountered in the Caribbean islands and the American colonies. The congregation they helped establish on St Thomas, as with most Pietist Protestant congregations in the eighteenth century, was predominantly female with a ratio of three women for every two men. This partly reflected the work of women like Rebecca, but also created avenues of female leadership and responsibility. Despite their endorsement of slavery, Moravians treated people of African descent with respect, reflected in social encounters involving direct eye contact, handshaking and submissive rituals. Moreover, Rebecca's facility with languages (German, Dutch and Creole), along with her mixed-race background, enabled her to translate, embody and create the transcultural connections upon which successful mission depended.

One consequence of Rebecca's association with the Moravians was her gradual awareness that she was now part of an international community of Christians and a sisterhood of faith that stretched far beyond the island confines of St Thomas. In common with other converts, she was encouraged to write a brief faith statement, which she sent to the Single Sisters of the Moravian congregation in Herrnhut. As with most eighteenth-century conversion narratives and spiritual autobiographies it is always hard to know how heavily edited and constructed they were by those responsible for their creation and transmission. Nevertheless, the letter is revealing of Rebecca's sense of unworthiness ('I want to be with the Lord and reveal my puny form to you'), her sense of discovery ('I never knew there was such a thing as a spiritual life'), her enthusiasm for Moravian heart religion ('Oh, how good is the Lord. My heart melts when I think of it. His name is wonderful. Oh! Help me to praise him, who has pulled me out of darkness'), her earnestness of purpose ('I will take up his cross with all my heart and follow the example of his poor life'), and her sense of being part of a community of faith ('If we cannot be together in person, let us be together in the spirit').[42]

Rebecca not only worked with the Moravians, she also married a white

Moravian missionary, an event that scandalized the white planters of St Thomas and led to a trumped-up charge of burglary against Rebecca, her husband and the leader of the Moravian mission. But for the intervention of the visiting Zinzendorf, whose social rank conferred persuasive power, Rebecca would probably have been sold back into slavery. Rebecca migrated with her husband Mattäus Freundlich and their child back to the European Moravian settlements of Marienborg and Herrnhag. Sadly, Rebecca's husband died en route and so did her child a few years later. As was their custom, the European Moravians plotted a new marriage for Rebecca, this time to Christian Jacob Protten (1715–69) who was born on the Gold Coast of West Africa to an African mother and a Danish father. A gifted linguist, he too was an insterstitial figure with roots in both African and European cultures. While in Europe, Rebecca not only found a new husband but was also given a more formal role in ministry. She was ordained a deaconess, which allowed her to preach to other women, celebrate communion and preside over other Moravian rituals such as foot washing. In fact, Rebecca Protten 'may well have been the first black woman to be ordained in western Christianity', thereby taking part in an 'emerging spiritual revolution that was quietly beginning to undermine centuries of Christian doctrine propping up the subordination of women and people of color'.[43]

As was often the way in enclosed Pietist communities, the Prottens soon ran foul of communal disciplines. They left the Moravian settlements in Germany and eventually made their way to Christiansborg in the Accra region of the Gold Coast, the Danish centre of the West African slave trade. Here the Prottens taught school, fought with colonial officials and maintained a rather chequered relationship with the Moravian community that initially sponsored them. Rebecca's gifted but unpredictable husband, who seems to have had a penchant for alcohol and indiscipline, predeceased her by a decade. Rebecca died in Christiansborg in 1780 at the age of 62 having migrated along the lines of the slave trade in reverse. She grew up in Antigua, had her most significant accomplishments in St Thomas, resided for a time in the heartland of German Pietism and then ended her life in the West African slave-trading port through which her own ancestors were brutally sent to the New World. In this way Rebecca sowed the seeds of a black Protestant international movement and struck a small blow for the emancipation of Christian women.

Rebecca's life, though singular and untypical, connected with some of the most significant developments of the eighteenth century: the triangular trade of African slaves, plantation produce and European consumption; the fierce violence of colonial exploitation and racial subjugation; the rise of Pietism and of Protestant missions, especially the exotic, but immensely important Moravians; the creolization of language and the symbiotic relationship between populist forms of white and black Christianity in the Atlantic world; the surprising mobility of populations, literature and Christian rituals; and the spread of Christianity from its European heartlands to new populations and new landscapes. That this expansion was accomplished through a mixture of brutality and kindness helps explain the remarkable life of Rebecca Protten.

Little remains of the writing of Rebecca Protten, but, thanks to the painting of the Protten family by Johann Valentin Haidt (1700–80) in 1751, we have some idea what she looked like, at least in idealized form. Born in Danzig in 1700 Haidt met the Moravians in London and spent some time in the Moravian settlements in Germany before eventually finding his way to the North American Moravian outpost of Bethlehem, Pennsylvania. Deeply influenced by the religious paintings of the European classical tradition, Haidt became the Moravians' most significant painter. As we saw in Chapter 2, his large canvass of *The First Fruits* is an allegorical celebration of the global first fruits of Moravian missions. In the painting, 21 figures representing the racial diversity of Moravian converts meet the risen Christ. One of the 21 figures is Rebecca's first child Anna Maria.

Christian and Rebecca Protten with their child Anna Maria (who like her half-sister also died in childhood) sat for Haidt in Herrnhut in 1751. Although all three are of mixed-race background, Haidt seems to delight in portraying their very different skin tones (Rebecca is the most dark skinned, Anna Maria the lightest). Rebecca is painted wearing a laced-up Moravian gown, Haube and blue ribbon signifying her marital status. The face that stares back from the canvas is black, kindly, purposeful and composed. Almost saintly in demeanour, she wears a faint smile as she sits with her husband and child, the last family of colour in the Moravian settlements in Europe. The portrait of this Europeanized nuclear family seems light years away from the scenes of Rebecca's exploits on St Thomas in the 1730s or her last years as a teacher on the Gold Coast in West Africa.[44]

David George

This story is about another case of a freed African-American slave with significant implications for the globalization of Christianity in the early modern and modern periods. The person is David George and the story begins in the mid-eighteenth century in the American South, then moves to Nova Scotia in present-day Canada and finishes in Sierra Leone in West Africa, which was the location of pioneering attempts to settle freed slaves back on African soil. As with Rebecca, this story represents a geographical and chronological reversal of the traditional slave-trade routes from West

Africa to the American colonies. Its finishing point in Sierra Leone was the location of attempts by British Evangelical anti-slavery activists to set up a model settlement for freed slaves in Africa from whence they had been so violently captured.

The first such planned settlement of freed slaves in Africa was carried out under Evangelical auspices and ended in disaster. The so-called 'Province of Freedom', which was initiated by the formidable anti-slavery activist Granville Sharp in 1787 for freed British slaves, was a grim failure, wracked by disease, desertion and disillusionment.[45] Within a year of arrival more than half of the almost 400 settlers had died, run away or been discharged. But the second attempt five years later was both more unusual and more promising. Most of the 1,100 men and women of African descent who migrated from Nova Scotia to Freetown in 1792 were once North American slaves. The black Nova Scotian community from which this reverse transatlantic migration originated had its roots in the promises made to black slaves in the American colonies by the British in return for their assistance in the American Revolutionary War. Some of these unlikely empire loyalists brought with them a religious faith birthed in colonial revivals that was given a further Evangelical twist by the red-hot Evangelicalism preached by Baptists and Methodists in Nova Scotia.[46]

Out of this unlikely community of migrants came David George, born a slave in Virginia in 1743 and revived in South Carolina before the American Revolution, who then became the first black Baptist pastor in Canada and the first Baptist pastor in Africa. He has left a spiritual autobiography that was transcribed from oral delivery and published in the *Baptist Annual Register* (1790–93). According to this narrative, George, while still a slave, picked up the various Christian influences that wafted around the southern colonies in the 1760s and 1770s. White Anglican plantation religion, the influence of slave believers and New Light Baptist preaching all played their part in bringing him eventually to a classic Evangelical conversion experience of awareness of sin, self-loathing and joyful release. This was not quite a classic conversion narrative, however, for George was illiterate at the time of his conversion. Only later did he extract from the biblical narratives the formal template for his own experience. 'I can now read the Bible,' he states later, 'so that what I have in my heart, I can see again in the Scriptures,' indicating that 'the oral and the personal was anterior to the written and the discursive element in his experience'.[47] Here then is an example of how a European tradition of penitential Christianity and release from sin could be stripped of its literary superstructure and act directly in the experience of a black slave, who experienced both a real physical bondage and a perceived spiritual bondage.

George's conversion was followed by his British-assisted migration north to Nova Scotia during the American Revolutionary War. The black inhabitants of Nova Scotia were already a people in motion before a surprisingly high percentage of them decided to make the voyage across the Atlantic in the opposite direction from their enslaved ancestors. Just as West African slaves were a captive people in motion long before they arrived at the slave ports of the Bight of Biafra, the Nova Scotians had a migration history before they departed from Halifax for Sierra Leone. The dislocations of the American Revolution had resulted in the migration of substantial numbers of free blacks to the cities of Savannah, Charleston and New York. Scholars have shown how religious practices that were diversely spread across the southern plantations coalesced in more significant ways in the eastern seaboard cities during the Revolution. Partly benefiting from client–patron relationships with the British military, partly facilitated by the greater population density of the cities and partly fuelled by a new generation of black preachers, small but fast-growing black churches emerged from the chaos of war and mobility. David George, George Liele (1750–1820), Andrew Bryan (1737–1812), Jessie Peter and Brother Amos all helped preach and pastor new churches among black populations in Silver Bluff, Savannah, the Caribbean islands and eventually Nova Scotia. One scholar concludes that 'religious transformations such as George's planted among former slaves who had just become nominally free British subjects the means to engage and define their liberty across a wider terrain, an expanse once the exclusive spiritual and political domain of their masters'.[48]

Just as a popular form of black Christianity emerged from the migration of free blacks to eastern seaboard cities during the war, their subsequent migration northwards to Nova Scotia aided the process of new religious formation. Populations forced together to experience new freedoms on the move found solace, opportunity and community support networks within emerging black churches. Nova Scotia added yet another dimension, because it was already being 'revived' by transplanted revival preachers from the British Isles and North America. David George and a growing number of black migrants from the southern colonies added to the mix. In a sense Nova Scotia emerged as an ethnic and religious junction box not unlike the Azusa Street community that played such a significant role in the launching of Pentecostalism in the early twentieth century. George and other black preachers virtually had a captive audience of black refugees. George's 'peculiar antinomian blend of American southern and Nova Scotian New Light popular evangelicalism' was first preached to the black empire loyalists in Canada and was then carried back to Sierra Leone where it encountered an even more diverse cultural melting pot.

The Sierra Leone colony expanded exponentially after the act abolishing British participation in the slave trade (1807) led to African recaptives from all over the continent being settled there. British colonial administrators envisaged the colony being Christianized and civilized (the words were often interchangeable) through the creation of model villages supervised by ministers and schoolteachers and united by the universal application of rules and sacraments. This tidy reapplication of the European Christendom model of the ecclesiastical parish as the chief engine of Christianization lacked many of the elements that made it work, after a fashion, in Europe. In Sierra Leone there were no resident squires supplying a measure of economic stability and social deference, no fully agreed Christian tradition and authority to impart (there were representatives from a proliferation of European missionary societies and religious traditions, and no resident bishops) and little homogeneity among the idealized settlements. These parish-style villages, quaintly named after British people, places and battles, 'transformed Freetown into a black diaspora, a bustling entrepôt of refugees at large, with Freetown becoming a creolized, Caribbean-style cultural experience on African soil, a teeming crossroad of African and Western ideas stirred with an admixture of religious elements, Muslim, Christian and indigenous'.[49] So extravagant was the diversity that the CMS German missionary linguist Sigismund Kölle in his *Polyglotta Africana* (1847) was able to document some 120 different languages spoken in the colony.

What is particularly significant is the way in which the Freetown Nova Scotian contingent operated simultaneously both as missionaries and as the objects of mission. At the same time as they were being disciplined into model Christian settlements, they were also Christianizing, albeit African-American Christianizing, the African recaptives. Here are multiple levels of engagement that gave rise to some revealing encounters. The British organizers of the Sierra Leone colony reported in 1795 that the Nova Scotians in their religious observances were punctual, sabbatarian, well dressed and disciplined, but that some had imbibed 'very inadequate or enthusiastic notions of Christianity; a few perhaps who set up hypocritical pretensions to it'.[50] Part of what was happening in Freetown was a version of the contest between European establishmentarian Christianity and new forms of populist Evangelicalism that was being played out in many different geographical locations in the British Isles and North America, but the demographic collisions and cultural resonances of Sierra Leone also produced distinctively African expressions. The historical trail of what was going on stemmed in one direction from the eighteenth-century Great Awakening, and in another from the African-American missionary impulse, but there were also strands of European Pietism, with its radical distrust of religious establishments, and slave religion, with its heart-stirring aspiration for spiritual and physical liberty.

What came out of these different strands were not only competing visions of how Christianity should function in new colonial spaces but also different constructions of the kinds of Christian selves that should be fashioned. Consider, for example, the following three encounters. The first is between the Evangelical Anglican governor of Sierra Leone from 1793 to 1799, Zachary Macaulay (1768–1838), and David George. Macaulay, the English gentleman, regarded George and the Nova Scotians he represented as antinomians, a most 'seductive' creed in which there were 'No means to be used, no exertions to be made, no lusts to be crucified, no self denial to be practised.' Instead, they constructed their faith round instantaneous conversions, 'inexplicable mental impressions and bodily feelings', and the 'delusive internal feelings of a corrupt imagination'. After a 12-hour discussion and debate between the two men, Macaulay's observation was that if any Nova Scotian believers were asked how they knew themselves to be a child of God they would answer not from proof drawn from the Bible 'but because (perhaps) twenty years ago I saw a certain sight or heard certain words or passed thro a certain train of impressions varying from solicitude to deep concern and terror and despair thence again thro fluctuations of fear and hope to peace and joy and assured confidence'.[51] Macaulay believed that God's Evangelical kingdom in Africa could not be built from such ephemeral and transient materials.

A similar conclusion was reached by one of his successors as governor, Sir Charles MacCarthy (1764–1824), an Anglican from a Roman Catholic background and 'an establishment man, and a soldier, with a very clear idea of where his duty lies, and an acceptance of the alliance of religion and duty'. MacCarthy was certainly no Evangelical and his vision of Christianization and civilization in Africa was to divide the Sierra Leone colony and then the entire continent into ecclesiastical parishes within which universal baptism would make a uniform Christendom.[52] Not even the European missionaries with their Evangelical roots could buy into that vision, never mind the Nova Scotians, and never mind the even more eclectic recaptives. W.A.B. Johnson (1787–1823), a CMS missionary, told MacCarthy that he would not baptize more Africans 'unless God first baptized their hearts. He [MacCarthy] said that the reason why so many were baptized on the Day of Pentecost was that the Apostles despised none. I replied that they were pricked in the heart, and that I was willing to baptize all that were thus pricked in the heart. He thought baptism an act of civilization, and that it was our duty to make them all Christians.'[53] Here are two visions of how Africa should be Christianized: one is territorial, liturgical and universal, a product of the Anglican civilization that constructed it; the other is providential, experiential and emotional, a product of a very different set of experiences.

Our third encounter is probably the most significant of all. Moses Wilkinson, a blind, lame slave from Virginia escaped to Nova Scotia during the American Revolution and was one of those who sailed to Freetown in 1792. As someone who had suffered more than most from the perfidy and broken promises of white officials and who practised and preached a populist Evangelical message (he gave out his hymns and texts from memory), Wilkinson objected to the official Christianity of the Sierra Leone colony. One suspicious colonial official who showed up to mock his preaching came away impressed by his ability to affect his hearers: 'Many of the wise and learned in this world,' he wrote, 'if they were to see and hear such a man as our brother, professedly engaging in endeavouring to lead their fellow creatures from sin to holiness, would at once conclude it to be impossible for them to effect the object which they have in view. Experience, however, flatly contradicts such a conclusion. Numbers have been led by their means to change their lives.'[54] Colonial officials were justifiably nervous about the enthusiasm, antinomianism, indiscipline and potential political radicalism of black preachers like Wilkinson, but there was no denying the fact that their version of Christianity was the one most likely to succeed among the burgeoning communities of recaptives deposited by the British navy in Freetown. A shared suffering of body and spirit, and a shared sense of being marginalized by the structures of economic and political power, enabled preachers like Wilkinson to build a base of communal authority that could not be matched by colonial officials or white missionaries.

To these very different visions of how freed Africans and transplanted African Americans should reconstruct their selves, their communities and their continent, can be added still more layers of interpretation carrying enormous consequences for the globalization and indigenization of Christianity. Working out of the Sierra Leone experience, the religious independency and charismatic authority exemplified by the Nova Scotians and recaptive converts have been described as threshold phenomena that can thrive 'at the boundary between establishment values and the ideals of a people in transition'. In other words, Christianity does not have to be regarded as a mere extension of Western norms but carries within it 'prethematic local resonance' for those on the frontiers of 'disruption, dislocation, resettlement, and restoration'.[55] In short, Christianity does not have to come encased in centuries of European civilization.

For the kind of Christianity forged by ex-African slaves in South

Carolina, Nova Scotia and Sierra Leone to thrive beyond local boundaries required the practical defeat of the European Christendom model, a vernacular Bible (translation as empowerment) and the transmission of Christianity shorn of Western cultural specificities and receptive to indigenous religious sensibilities.[56] In Sierra Leone, for example, receptive Yoruba diviners who were 'thoroughly at home in the world of divination, visions, and the crowded company of unseen spirits, welcomed the challenge of missionaries saying they were happy to add the Christian divinity to the Yoruba pantheon because a place already existed for that'.[57] What Sanneh has called 'the local religious grammar' of rites, customs and language shaped the emergence of a distinctively African form of Christianity and laid the foundations for its mass transcontinental appeal in the nineteenth and twentieth centuries.[58]

It is difficult to overestimate the importance of this process for the remarkable expansion of Christianity in Africa in the modern period. In the long run, however, there was to be no happy ending in Sierra Leone, for the Christianity that was minted by the combined and often contradictory efforts of missionaries, settlers, recaptives and colonial officials was largely obliterated by the political anarchy and civil war of recent times. But something very significant had happened at the turn of the eighteenth and nineteenth centuries in colonial West Africa. Apparently inconsequential selves, refashioned in and out of slavery by the unlikely resources of populist Evangelical Christianity, had demonstrated a capacity for large-scale transformation not just in North America but also in the continent from which they had been so brutally seized and so serendipitously resettled.

David George's unlikely narrative and faith journey needs to be located within the context of the transatlantic slave trade, colonial warfare, population migrations, popular Pietism and Evangelicalism, the rise of empire, the colonization of Africa, the growth of the Protestant missionary societies and the geography of the slave trade. Although his life is singular and unique, its trajectory resonates with some of the most powerful forces of his time. His is one of the more powerful examples of the Exodus stories so beloved by black Christians, and of the rise of African Christianity in both North America and Africa.

Samson Occom

On 17 September 1768 a Mohegan Indian called Samson Occom (1723–92) finished writing a 26-page notebook intended for publication, though it was never published in his lifetime.[59] This 'Short Narrative' of his life is written in the form of a conventional spiritual autobiography but with an unconventional twist. Occom writes that he was 'Born a Heathen and Brought up in Heathenism', by which he means that his 'Parents livd [sic] a wandering life, for did all the Indians at Mohegan, they Chiefly depended upon Hunting, Fishing, & Fowling for their Living and had no Connection with the English, excepting to Traffic with them in their small Trifles: and they Strictly maintained and followed their Heathenish ways, Customs & Religion, though there was Some Preaching among them.' The picture Occom draws of his parents as 'wandering', as opposed to engaging in settled agriculture, as following their own religious traditions and rituals, as opposed to the prescribed Biblicist Christianity of the colonizers, and having little to do with the English apart from trade, is corroborated by much of the recent writing on encounters between Europeans and native peoples in North America. The preaching Occom refers to is that associated with the 'Great Awakening', an international movement of religious revivalism that began in Central Europe and spread along the Atlantic seaboard of North America in the 1730s and 1740s. Although led and directed by white Europeans, neither Native Americans nor transplanted Africans were immune from its influence. At the age of 17 Occom 'had, as I trust, a Discovery of the way of Salvation through Jesus Christ, and was enabl'd to put my trust in him alone for Life & Salvation. From this time the Distress and Burden of my mind was removed, and I found Serenity and Pleasure of Soul, in Serving God.' This apparently conventional conversion narrative, similar to hundreds of such narratives across the Atlantic world in the eighteenth century, was followed by serious Bible reading and an education at the hands of a local Congregational minister, Eleazar Wheelock (1711–79), who used Occom's example to raise funds for a school to train Native Americans for missionary service to their own people. Occom went on to serve the separate Montaukett and Shinnecock communities on Long Island as a teacher and minister from 1749 to 1761, was ordained a Presbyterian minister in 1759 and was hired in 1764 by the Boston-based Society for Propagating the Gospel in New England to minister to native peoples.

It was then that Occom's mind took an autobiographical turn, and the stimulus seems to have been a series of disputes between Occom and church and mission authorities over Occom's character, identity and loyalty. One precipitating factor was Occom's participation in a long-running land dispute, sometimes known as the Mason Controversy, between the Mohegans and the colony of Connecticut. The case, which had gone on for decades, was nearing resolution in the 1760s. Predictably the verdict went against the Mohegans, and it had a transformative effect on Occom, for whom the case operated as an instruction in the way colonialism worked. He ruefully reflected, 'I am afraid the poor Indians will never stand a good chance with the English in their land controversies because they are very poor, they have no money. Money is almighty now-a-days, and the Indians have no learning, no wit, no cunning: the English have all.'[60] With his Christian religious sensibilities shaped by the colonizers, but with his loyalties to his people shaped by perceived injustice, Occom spun in and out of a number of controversies with church and mission authorities. He spent the next few years in England on a George Whitefield-inspired tour to raise the profile of Indian evangelization and to raise money for Wheelock's Indian Charity School. In England he was celebrated as an exotic species, but he cast a cold eye on the power and pretentiousness of the Anglican episcopacy, which he found hard to reconcile with the primitive simplicity of the Gospel as he understood it. He also questioned the sincerity of the English bishops' commitment to the causes he believed in, concluding, 'I am apt to think they don't want the Indians to go to Heaven with them.' But worse was to follow. Occom believed that the money he painstakingly raised for Indian schools was being siphoned off by Wheelock to establish Dartmouth College. Meanwhile, partly due to family stresses he encountered on his return from England, Occom was prone to episodic bouts of 'intemperance' (drunkenness), which of course made him an easy target for those unhappy with his 'disagreeable' and 'arrogant' attitudes.

It was in this context of accusation, suspicion and stretched relationships with white religious authorities that Occom penned his personal narrative in 1768. Alleging that he was discriminated against because of his race, Occom concludes his narrative with the story of an Indian boy who was repeatedly beaten by his English master for supposedly bad ploughing, but in reality, according to the boy, it was merely 'because I am an Indian'. Similarly, Occom attributed his own troubles with white Christians to the fact that he was 'a poor Indian. I can't help that God has made me So; I did not make myself so.' What began therefore as a conversion narrative ended as a subdued complaint against white discrimination and exercise of power.

Occom's personal narrative is as complex in structure as the colonial circumstances that created it.[61] In its opening paragraphs Occom clearly aligns himself with the European Christians who converted him and he talks about native peoples as 'the other' even though the 'other' is partly himself. This points to a generic issue in trans-religious encounters that lead to conversion. For conversion to one religious tradition is also in part a deconversion from another. The new convert not only has to embrace a new life but also has to repudiate an abandoned life.[62] However, in Occom's case that transaction was highly charged with issues of race and loyalty to his people and traditions. When conversion takes place between religious traditions, it is often associated with power differentials between the parties, ensuring that conversion is not simply an internal bifurcation but represents wider contests of power and influence. Such was the case with Occom. Moreover, Occom's narrative, unlike more conventional Puritan and Evangelical conversion narratives, spends more time on the external material circumstances of his life and less time on the internal spiritual struggles and releases that feature prominently in European narratives. In addition, as his narrative unfolds he repeatedly uses the passive voice, not as someone being acted on by the divine as in Puritan narratives but as someone who was not fully an active agent in his treatment by white Christians. As a Christian minister and teacher he had only a partial autonomy, the power structures were outside his control and influence. By boldly proclaiming that this sad reality was not a product of white ignorance but was rather a deliberate instrument of policy, Occom's narrative is a simple acknowledgement of the way things were.

One writer has interpreted Occom's final statement in his narrative ('I did not make myself so') not as a pitiful declaration of powerlessness but 'as much an indictment of the missionaries who have shaped his experience as it is an appeal to the sovereign God who ordained his race'.[63] Occom's hard lessons in the austere classroom of colonial realities did not end in his breach with Christianity, however, or even in a decline in his determination to educate, civilize and Christianize his fellow Indians, despite the hazards of war and violence. But it did mean that he was largely shut out from the structures of power and influence within the white mission community. His most significant accomplishment thereafter was to help found the pan-Indian community at Brothertown in the Oneida territory of New York, which he served as minister and adviser until his death in 1792. Brothertown was, from inception to realization, an all-Indian affair, but its etymology was based on both Puritan notions of settlement as in John Eliot's 'Praying' Indian villages in the seventeenth century and on native notions of conflict resolution which often resulted in the dissenting party having to move to another location. In these revealing respects, even the native settlement of Brothertown was more hybridized than at first appears.[64]

What then are the meanings surrounding this singular example of the encounter between Western Christianity and native peoples in North America in the eighteenth century? A few preliminary observations are in order. In the first place, much of the writing of the past decade has attempted to look at these encounters from the perspective of the native peoples' 'East' in relation to the Europeans' 'West'. In the spirit of Daniel Richter's book title, *Facing East from Indian Country: A Native History of Early America*, scholars from multifarious disciplinary backgrounds have tried to reconstruct 'encounter' from the perspective of the native peoples.[65] Applying that principle in the eighteenth century, Richter has shown how

Indians and Europeans had already been interacting with one another for over 200 years. Before the decisive victory of the British in the Seven Years' War (1754–61 in North America, 1756–63 in Europe) eastern North America was the site of rapidly changing and fluid relations between the European colonial powers (France, Spain and England) and the manifold tribal populations of native peoples. It is a European conceit, even when motivated by appropriate guilt or humane intentions, to believe that the sole engine of change among Native Americans was European colonialism. Nevertheless, native peoples were drawn slowly and imperceptibly into the global structural changes produced by trade, consumerism and mobility. Indians traded with Europeans and both sold goods to Europeans and consumed goods produced in Europe long before it became clear that European intervention in North America would lead inexorably to a land grab and cultural annihilation. Looking backwards from the end of this process, and knowing its result, has the perverse effect of further reducing Indian agency and diminishing the complexity and longevity of historical processes.

Religious encounter adds to the complexity, for Occom's singular narrative is part of a much larger story of European Christian missions in North America, which James Axtell has characterized as a more or less sustained attempt by both Catholics and Protestants over several centuries to 'reduce' Indians from savagery to civility and from paganism to Christianity.[66] Most of these ventures, from Spanish Franciscans, French Jesuits and English Puritans in the seventeenth century to American Methodists and Evangelicals in the nineteenth century, were predicated on the notion that American Indians would have to be 'civilized' before they could be 'Christianized' and that these two objectives were co-dependent. By European standards of assessment Native Americans were deficient in order (their 'scattered and wild course of life'), industry, or, in John Eliot's words, 'we labor and work in building, planting, clothing our selves, &c. and they doe not', and in personal behaviour and manners, especially 'pride' as exemplified in their immodest dress and long hair. This list is important, for any kind of religious conversion was both interpreted and measured by the extent to which Native Americans not only understood and practised liturgical expressions of Christianity but also how much evidence there was of settled order, agricultural industry, reformed behaviour and altered appearance. All of this was of course complicated by the fact that Europeans brought not only Christianity but disease, a hunger for land, an enthusiasm for trade and a self-conscious technological superiority. All dealings between European missionaries and Native Americans were of necessity refracted through differential and continually shifting distributions of power, resources and control.

How then does all this relate to encounters between European missionaries and Native Americans? The most important point to stress is the extraordinary variety of encounters between European missionaries (Puritans, Jesuits, other Catholic orders, Anglicans, First Great Awakening revivalists, Moravians, and so on), and the multitudinous Indian tribes and civilizations. There were, for example, within Catholicism well-known differences in approach between Jesuits and others. 'Unlike the Dominicans and Franciscans within their own church and the Puritans and Anglicans without,' states Axtell, 'the Jesuits articulated and practiced a brand of cultural relativism, without, however, succumbing to ethical neutrality.'[67] There are echoes here of the Jesuit adaptive approach to missions in the East. There were also considerable variations of style and strategy within Protestantism. The praying towns established by John Eliot (1604–90) and the Mayhews (Thomas Sr and Jr) in colonial New England enforced strict prescriptions of European ways, including ubiquitous legal codes and endless schemes to promote industriousness. Coming out of a different tradition of European spirituality Moravians acted almost as hybrid shaman-missionaries. As one scholar has observed, 'During the 1740s and 1750s, missionaries listened to, recorded, and interpreted dreams, blessed hunters and their lodges, dispensed magical medicines, performed rituals over the dead and dying, and offered personal spiritual power through the blood of Christ.'[68] The Moravian focus on heart religion, the wounds of Christ and the healing power of blood (including an emphasis of Christ's blood and individual blood-letting) all found their way into the spirituality advocated by missionaries and was at least partly appropriated by their converts as expressed in their autograph narratives. For example, one 14-year-old Delaware girl begged at her 1756 baptism, 'Dear Savior, have mercy on me! I am very poor. … I would like to love him gladly, my heart strives for that, and I want to surrender my entire heart and my entire body to him gladly. He might accept it, and wash my heart and body in his blood, and give me a new name.'[69] The surrendered heart, joyful obedience to the sacrificial saviour, the cleansing by the blood and the construction of a new identity are all staples of Moravian spirituality.

It would be a mistake to underestimate the complexity of the issues at stake in these encounters or to see them as influences moving in only one direction. For example, Axtell has shown how Native Americans were often much better at acculturating Europeans into native tribes than the other way round, and Albanese has demonstrated that just as Christian missionaries were at their most effective in supplying medical remedies to Native Americans, Native American cures were in turn employed by both European whites and African Americans.[70] Even more subtly, Native Americans were perfectly capable of using the sanctimonious European Christian concepts of moral excellence as strategies of resistance against white rapaciousness. If white Europeans were willing to promote their moral vision of the righteous society, Native Americans were sometimes willing to hold them to a strict accountability for their actions, not just their claims.

Examining more closely the spate of conversions to Christianity reported during the first Great Awakening in the 1730s and 1740s, of which Occom's was the most famous, is one way of penetrating to the heart of what was at stake in the religious encounters between Europeans and Native Americans. Although the spike in religious conversions among the Native Americans of southern New England in the 1740s may not be as high as its most ardent Evangelical publicists claimed, there is no disputing the fact that there was a surge of religious conversions among the Mohegan, Pequot, Niantic, Narragansett and Montaukett in Connecticut, Rhode Island and Long Island. But why, and what sort of Christianity was embraced by the native peoples? It has been suggested that Native Americans were attracted to the New Light revivalism of the 1740s by its apparent novelty, ecstasy (as reflected in bodily movement and musical rhythms), proffered release from communal anxiety and the appeal of a new kind of society.[71] Without diminishing the importance of what took place in the 1740s, it seems that the Native American revivals were partly superimposed on earlier traditions of missionary education and occurred at a time when natives felt culturally marginalized by continual land losses.[72] To students of transatlantic revivalism this pattern of catechetical spreading of some pre-existing Christian knowledge combined with communal anxiety and a sense of temporal defeat is not altogether unfamiliar.

But to what extent did the Great Awakening's emphasis on the New Birth produce new Christian selves among Native Americans? As always, the supply of materials for answering such a question is predictably thin. Native literacy rates were low, ministers and missionaries could not and did not record native experiences, and the accounts that survive inevitably privilege the most Europeanized and long-lasting of native converts. Occom's Narrative fits this pattern perfectly. Other examples of penitential-style conversion narratives are recorded in the journal of Azariah Horton (1715–77), who was sent on a preaching tour of Long Island under the auspices of the Society in Scotland for the Propagation of Christian Knowledge.[73] However, there are also clear hints in Occom's autobiography, as in other accounts of Native American conversions, that religious conversion was partly understood as a transfer of loyalty to a different deity, a forswearing of idleness, a rejection of hunting, fishing and merry-making, a repudiation of drunkenness, and a cultivation of influence with European religious and political power. Even within this complex framework, variety was everywhere. Most Native Americans did not convert to Christianity of any description, of those that did only a minority got baptized, a still smaller minority committed to regular church membership, and a yet smaller minority built a life of Christian commitment over a decade or longer. Those who did, and who lived long enough to tell their stories in English for English consumption, emphasized penitence and the birth of new selves, but the selves that were birthed were partly cultural constructions privileging the system that produced them. Over time, many Native American tribes became expert at conceding what could not be withheld and protecting that which could not be negotiated away. Amerindian rituals, social customs, views of nature and approaches to the spirit world proved to be remarkably resistant to missionary penetration well into the nineteenth and twentieth centuries.

A significant example of that approach can be found in the writings of David Brainerd (1718–47) whose diary was published by Jonathan Edwards in 1749 and became a runaway bestseller across the North Atlantic region. During Brainerd's sojourn among the Delaware Indians in New Jersey from 1744 to 1746, he recounts conversions in terms that privileged the penitential traditions of European Christendom, but a deeper reading even of his own accounts indicates that his interpretive grid was imposed on narratives with different sorts of meanings. Hindmarsh's conclusion is that what Brainerd was seeing primarily in terms of 'the problems of conscience and their resolution was seen by the Indian converts rather more in terms of Elijah on Mount Carmel'.[74] In other words, where he read repentance and conversion, their words are as easily understood as transfers of allegiance from less potent to more potent spiritual powers as represented by the superior cultural and political power of the missionaries who were both initiators and recorders of the encounter. However one reads Brainerd's diaries, there is no disputing the fact that the wide circulation of his *Life* helped establish the idea among American and European Protestants that Evangelical preaching to native peoples would produce exactly the same results everywhere as it did among white Europeans. That historical myth, which still has some currency among British and American missionary societies, did as much to inspire the Protestant missionary movement, as it helps account for many of its subsequent deficiencies.

Meanings

The expansion of Christianity in the eighteenth century was inexorably linked to other powerful forces in the world order including the growing economic and military ascendancy of Europe, the slave trade, imperialism and colonialism and the challenge to ecclesiastical autonomy and power mounted by rulers, elites and intellectuals. No treatment of religious encounters with 'others' can afford to ignore the complex ways these conditions interacted with one another. However, even when these factors are taken into account, one is still left with the uneasy problem of coping with the Eurocentrism within which encounter is inevitably framed and with understanding how it was experienced by non-Europeans. The surviving sources of encounter are enormously weighted on the side of Europeans, and even when read sensitively by later generations they are what they are, namely accounts constructed mostly by missionaries for missionary purposes.

One way round this problem is to look harder for, and pay attention to, different forms of resistance narratives which at least help one to see what was most distasteful about European Christianity from the perspective of 'others'. Of course, resistance came in many forms, ranging from strategic subversion to outright violence, and from outward conformity to complete indifference. Styles of resistance also depended on the contingencies of power and authority within which encounter took place. Written forms of resistance are in the nature of things rare, though far from absent, especially in cultures that were not conquered by the West and which had indigenous traditions of literacy. Hence one can get a sense of what bothered Indian Hindus and Chinese Confucians about Christianity from the writings of social elites, evidence from legal cases and depositions and from the paper trails of major controversies. Moreover, every now and again one comes across a missionary corpus which treats seriously the 'other's' perceptions, even if only as a preparatory device for more targeted mission. For example, Ziegenbalg's papers contain a wide variety of Hindu complaints about Christianity. These include its comparative lack of antiquity, its lax morality, its emphasis on eternal punishment, its lack of consideration for other living things and its dependence on a saviour who was born of mean parentage, was executed as a criminal and who did not travel the world to enable all men to listen to his teachings. If the message was untenable, the messengers were unappealing. Europeans were criticized for their propensity for drunkenness, their killing and eating of creatures 'endued with Five Senses', their habit of spitting and conversing with menstruating women in public, and above all for simply being outsiders and exponents of strange doctrines.[75]

Chinese intellectuals shared some of these perceptions and added others. They also found it hard to understand how a crucified criminal could be God or how Christian formulations of a personal deity could explain the essential unity of all things. Moreover, the Christian emphasis on original sin through the Adam and Eve story posed obvious problems for a civilization rooted in the veneration of ancestors. What was to be the fate of dead ancestors, especially ancestral adulterers, who had never heard of this new religion and its teachings? Even the apparently well-received scientific knowledge of the Jesuits seemed to neglect the moral cultivation of the individual, and their maps had the effect of removing China from the centre of the world. In short, Chinese religious practices (including ancestral sacrifices), Chinese ethical traditions and the Chinese Empire itself all seemed threatened by a religion which seemed to undermine social harmony and stability and might even be the forerunner of foreign invasion. [76]

Below elite level, provincial legal records also paint a mixed picture of how Christianity was viewed by local populations. In eighteenth-century Sichuan, for example, Catholicism was outlawed as a perverse sect with sinister doctrines, but unlike the more obviously insurrectionary White Lotus sect of Buddhism, Catholics were left more or less alone unless a conflict arose out of local economic or social grievances. If that happened, being a Catholic was a disadvantage in the legal depositions that followed, but not disastrously so. In general, legal authorities knew very little about the content and practice of Catholic belief, but were more concerned that it was an underground sect spread by networks of lay teachers and relatives. Once they concluded that the Catholics were law-abiding and posed very little real threat, they were generally treated with leniency. In other words, once Catholicism was well established as a popular religion it was mostly left alone unless civil disturbance brought it to the attention of the authorities. In localities where Catholic families were distrusted over their ritual and festival practices, or because of economic or landownership disputes, they were vulnerable to legal harassment, but they were not subjected to systematic persecution.

For obvious reasons, very few texts have survived of indigenous resistance to Christianity below the level of social elites. One intriguing exception is 'The Carpenter-Preta', an eighteenth-century Sri Lankan folktale in which Jesus is presented as a delusory emanation of Mara, the Buddhist deity of delusion and desire. Mara's emanation is conceived in the womb of an outcast carpenter girl whose son is born on a rubbish heap outside the city and grows up as a ruffian who drinks liquor, eats flesh and calls himself a god. He wanders from country to country with 12 companions and he make robes of black cloth with wings of black fowls allowing him to terrorize villagers and steal their cattle. He is arrested, interrogated and executed by being nailed to a gibbet, and then buried with deeply packed rubble so that he survives only as a ghost. The folktale evidently seems to be a fusion of a Sri Lankan version of the Jesus story overlaid with a Sinhalese account of the arrival of Portuguese Jesuit missionaries. In the story the evil emerges from the margins (Portugal), and the black-robed, evil flying spirits (*rahats*) are Catholic missionaries. This folktale, written down in a palm-leaf manuscript, seems to have surfaced during the Buddhist revivals of the nineteenth century and entered the Western corpus through the collection of an early nineteenth-century British Methodist missionary. Such survivals are obviously rare, but it does offer a suggestive glimpse of how Christian stories were 'translated' into local idioms and survived as a resistance narrative.[77]

Resistance to European Christianity sometimes resulted in outright rebellion and violent revenge. One such example from the start of our period is the Pueblo Revolt against the Spanish in New Mexico in 1680.[78] The chief bearers of Christianity in this region were the Franciscans, whose spirituality was characterized by the suppression of sexuality and the sublime union with Christ nurtured by a combination of denial and self-punishment with ecstatic experience of the divine. What Ramón Gutiérrez and others have drawn attention to is the projection of Franciscan Christianity on to natives through punishment. Natives were reformed and punished in much the same ways and for much the same ends as their Franciscan punishers inflicted pain on themselves. Franciscans also portrayed themselves to Native Americans 'as supermen who controlled the forces of nature' and as spiritual machismos who could make vows of perpetual chastity. The Franciscan reformation of the soul was a threefold process of purgation of the old self, illumination modelled on the exemplary lives of Christ and St Francis and a mystical union between Christ and the individual soul. If the Native Americans were to reach God, they too would have to be led through purgation, illumination and union. There were of course aspects of Native American culture that could not be reformed by such a tidy scheme. Franciscan inability to accept non-urban settlements, sexual impurity (including homosexual practices) and unacceptable child-rearing practices led to unsustainable tensions that inevitably contributed to revolt and violence. As part of their attempt to form native Christians Franciscans introduced Native Americans to new concepts of time (linear and teleological), new work disciplines (based on production capacity) and new views of nature, sexuality and child-rearing. They were able to employ a panoply of powerful tactics from gifts to liturgical reform, and from direct confrontation over sexual habits to an attempt to replace native habits of flagellation and bloodletting with Franciscan ideals of self-flagellation as an act of devotion to the bleeding Christ. To what extent then did these vigorous attempts to school native selves after the model of Franciscan spiritual disciplines actually succeed in making conversions? Gutiérrez, while acknowledging that there were some true conversions ('defined as a fundamental change in beliefs whereby a person accepted the reality of the Spanish God and vowed to obey Him and his ministers'), especially among the boys painstakingly educated by the friars, the general tally was low. 'The simple reason is that the Franciscan model of personal re-formation and evangelism, with its pronounced emphasis on externality – transforming the "outer person" (behaviour) to change the "inner person" (the soul) – predisposed the friars to believe that Pueblo dissimulations were true conversions.'[79] In short, the Franciscans were better at eradicating native rites or substituting Christian alternatives than they were at producing penitent and refashioned converts to the Holy Catholic Church. That was a task that would require decades, or even centuries, of cultural transformation, and not one that could be accomplished in the immediate white heat of cultural encounter.

As it turned out, time was not on the side of the Franciscans. By 1680 a deadly combination of drought, famine, attacks by other Indian peoples, accumulated Spanish humiliations, a resurgence of traditional Indian loyalty to their old traditions and some inspired leadership by a Puebloan medicine man named Popé produced the conditions for a violent repudiation of Spanish rule. The revolt was accompanied by 'the most unspeakable profanations of Christian sacra', symbols and personnel. Churches were razed, crosses and images were smeared with excrement or destroyed, Christian names and marriage customs were obliterated and some of the friars were killed with ritualistic fury. Indeed the rituals of violence not only paralleled what the Spanish had done to native religious traditions over the previous century but also liturgically revealed what aspects of Christianity the Indians most disliked. Remarkably, the Franciscans accepted their fate as the will of God and embraced martyrdom as God's way of seeding the church with the blood of the friars.[80]

These examples of resistance to Christianity both from parts of the world where Christianity was imposed, at least in part, by force, and those areas where it was introduced by persuasion show that resistance could operate at a number of different levels and could be provoked by many different stimuli. These include the apparent perversity of some of the more controversial Christian doctrines and practices (especially the incarnation and the sacrament); the uncouth behaviour of 'Christian' Europeans – especially flesh eating, drinking, physical cruelty and sexual practices; the challenge Christianity brought to indigenous social, cultural and religious traditions such as ancestor worship in China and the all-pervasive reality of caste in India; the disturbance it could bring to well-established social harmonies; and the fact that it was associated with a wider European onslaught which carried trading and military dimensions. The most difficult times were either when

Christianity was first introduced, or was associated with cultural domination, or was thought to be responsible for disturbances or insurrection. The longer Christianity was established, the less it was associated with coercion, and the more respectful it was of local customs the greater the likelihood that it could take its place as an exotic but not very threatening religion among others.

Not all encounters between European Christians and native peoples in the eighteenth century should be framed in terms of opposition or resistance. Self-evidently, Christianity established durable cultures that were capable of indigenization and propagation by native peoples. It is impossible to comprehend the longevity of Christian penetration in non-European parts of the world, even after instruments of coercion were removed, without acknowledging that reality. The question then presents itself of how encounter, in all its diversity, can be interpreted and expressed in appropriate language. In answering this question, cultural historians have either explicitly, or unconsciously, resorted to metaphors. Hence encounters are described in terms of borrowing (economics), hybridity (zoology), the melting pot (metallurgy), the stew (cooking), and creolization (linguistics). But all these metaphors have a way of flattening out the sheer life and complexity to be found in early modern religious encounters. The artefacts (architecture, images, and objects), texts (and their translations), rituals (worship, music, healing and festivals), bodies (dress, decoration, taboos and degrees of nakedness), sexual mores and economic practices resulting from encounters admit of no easy categorization.[81]

In more advanced forms, we talk of acculturation and transculturation, of accommodation and negotiation, of imitation and appropriation, of syncretism and translation, and of homogenization and globalization. None of these linguistic turns will suffice in itself. As our stories have shown, narratives of encounter require terminology that leaves room for agency (however circumscribed by coercion), flexibility, complexity, differential power dynamics and a clear sense of change over time and place. European Christians' encounters with the wider world in the eighteenth century have thrown up a dizzying array of different patterns that had important consequences not only for the church in the eighteenth century but also for the shape of world Christianity ever since.

BOOK TWO

THE TRANSFORMATION OF CHRISTENDOM

CHAPTER 4

Enlightenment and Society: Glimpses of Modernity

The Thirty Years' War (1618–48), which started as a religious conflict between Catholics and Protestants in the Holy Roman Empire before rippling outwards through dynastic conflicts to engulf much of Europe, was one of the most destructive and shocking events in European history. Arising out of the devastation caused by the war, and the scientific revolution which pre- and post-dated it, there emerged new ways of thinking about the impact of religious conflict on human well-being and about the relationship of the earth to the motions of the planets. It seemed that traditional Christianity in Europe, whether Catholic or Protestant, faced unprecedented challenges to its intellectual foundations and its moral and social utility. The aim of this chapter is to look at the nature of those challenges in the later seventeenth and eighteenth centuries under five main categories: the Enlightenment, science and religion, religious toleration and religious liberty, the rise of anti-slavery sentiment and secularization. In each of these areas traditional ways of thinking and behaving were revolutionized and Western Christianity changed faster and more dramatically than at any time since the Roman Empire. Emphasizing change and modernity, as this chapter does, carries the risk of underestimating deep structural continuities, so it is appropriate to list some of these right at the beginning.

By the end of the eighteenth century the fundamental divisions of European Christendom, Roman Catholic, Protestant and Orthodox, were still in place, and sectarian religious conflict was far from over. The supernatural framework of Christianity was profoundly shaken, but it was not eradicated. Religious acquiescence in the ubiquitous human trafficking of slavery was challenged, but slavery was far from over. Some of the roots of secularization were already in view, but as the next chapter will show there were also unmistakable signs of renewed religious vitality, especially within the Protestant world. Confidence in the divine inspiration and authority of the Bible among educated elites was eroded, but the century ended on the brink of its widest dissemination in human history. Brave new statements of religious toleration and religious freedom were enshrined in the constitutions of revolutionary regimes, but the tawdry limits of religious toleration were still experienced by millions of Western Christians. We could go on and on in this vein, but the recognition of continuity, which is after all what one expects, is not the subject of what follows. I have chosen these categories among many possibilities because they best encapsulate the stresses and strains of new ways of thinking on Western Christianity and the civilization it helped to build.

Enlightenment

Described by one historian as the first sustained attack on Christianity from within Europe since the time of Constantine in the fourth century, the Enlightenment, however it is to be defined, has been the subject of fierce disagreement among its interpreters.[1] The reasons are obvious. The Enlightenment is the name given by late eighteenth-century thinkers to a complex set of intellectual and cultural changes that affected most parts of Europe from the late seventeenth to the late eighteenth centuries. Not only were new ideas bitterly contested at the time, especially with regard to their implications for traditional Christianity, but the Enlightenment also came to be viewed through the prism of the violent revolutions that rocked the Western world at the end of the eighteenth century. The French Revolution in particular had the effect of dividing the European mind between optimistic radicals who looked to the Enlightenment as a justification for their bold new political and social aspirations, and pessimistic conservatives who thought that the Enlightenment had unleashed furious forces of godlessness, terror and immorality. In addition, many traditional Christians, both Protestant and Catholic, have come to see the Enlightenment as the root cause of European secularization, with all its allegedly pernicious consequences. By emphasizing reason over revelation, secular aspiration over ecclesiastical authority, and human potential over divine sovereignty, so the argument goes, the Enlightenment eroded the very foundations of Christendom. With so much at stake, with so many intellectual traditions to consider over the course of a whole century and with such a wide geographical area to cover, it is not surprising that the Enlightenment has trumped even the Renaissance and the Reformation as perhaps the most hotly contested topic in the history of Christianity. It is best to start with some ground clearing.

In the first place, although it is possible to distinguish different characteristics of Enlightenment in different national traditions in the eighteenth century, the Enlightenment was a European-wide phenomenon. Newspapers, magazines, libraries, salons, coffee houses, learned journals and academies, and international distribution networks all ensured that the traffic in ideas was supra-national in scope. One of the most ardent advocates of this position, Jonathan Israel, states that the European Enlightenment was a 'single highly integrated intellectual and cultural movement, displaying differences in timing, no doubt, but for the most part preoccupied not only with the same intellectual problems but often even the very same books and insights everywhere from Portugal to Russia and from Ireland to Sicily'.[2] However, even allowing for a transnational circulation of books and ideas by the most significant thinkers, and for a common stock of intellectual problems to be addressed, there were many different characteristics of Enlightenment that showed up in different locations over the course of the century. It is possible, for example, to distinguish a more moderate from a more radical Enlightenment, a specifically antichristian from a more reformist Christian Enlightenment, and even different expressions of Enlightenment according to religious tradition, national context and social location. In short, in studies of the Enlightenment there does not have to be a stand-off between the coherence of some of its most important personalities and ideas and the variety of their expression in different parts of Europe at different times. How then should we define the Enlightenment, and what were its implications for traditional Christianity?

The seventeenth-century conditions that provoked new ways of thinking included a reaction against the devastating effects of confessionally motivated violence during the Thirty Years' War, the fear of Catholic absolutism and arbitrary government, the possible resurgence of religious warfare, the persecution of religious minorities and the implications of new scientific discoveries by Galileo Galilei (1564–1642), Johannes Kepler (1571–1630) and others associated with the scientific revolution. Whether looking at the cosmos or at the devastation caused by religious conflict, it seemed that confessional religion neither aided understanding nor produced social harmony. If there is a single thread running through the complexity of Enlightenment thought, it is that human reason and reasonableness offered a better way forward for human flourishing than religious dogma, inherited opinions and ancient habits of intolerance. Behind the desire to construct a 'reasonable' Christianity lay dark memories of confessional violence and ecclesiastical sophistry.

The Enlightenment critique of traditional Christianity over the long eighteenth century was deep and wide-ranging. At the centre of it was a sustained attack on revealed religion and ecclesiastical authority. The more radical enlightened figures rejected among other things the traditional

Judaeo-Christian understanding of creation, the intervention of a providential God in human affairs, the existence of a divinely ordained social
hierarchy, the divine origin and authority of the Bible, the Christian supernatural framework of the Virgin Birth, the resurrection and miracles, the
idea of reward and punishment in an afterlife (especially the existence of
hell), the reality of Satan, demons and spirits, the authority of a priestly
caste and the notion that there was a divinely revealed morality which
humans were expected to live by. More moderate enlightened figures were
less sweeping, concerned more to establish the 'reasonableness' of Christianity by removing its most 'superstitious' and irrational elements than to
attack it head on. Moderates were primarily interested in what Christian
Thomasius (1655–1728) called *philosophia practica*, namely the application of
new ideas to improve government, administration, social policy, the legal
system and the better functioning of church and state.[3]

Over the course of the eighteenth century moderates and radicals fought
with one another and with conservatives who wished to defend Christian
orthodoxy against the new onslaught of ideas. In that sense the Enlightenment was not so much a unitary phenomenon as it was a dynamic set of
interactions among thinkers interested in a similar set of problems. Positions also hardened over time. In the second half of the eighteenth century
the radical Enlightenment became more associated with atheistic materialism, sexual libertinism and political republicanism. Moreover, changes
in the world of thought had repercussions in the wider society. In France
and the Netherlands there is evidence of the secularization of wills, fewer
recruits to the priesthood and a decline of interest in religious confraternities in favour of Masonic lodges. As one scholar has it, by the late
eighteenth century the radical Enlightenment had made possible a 'world
where statesmen like Thomas Jefferson could rewrite the Bible to expunge
its mysterious elements, scientists like Darwin [Erasmus] in England and
Laplace in France could dispense with God, revolutionaries in Paris could
empty the churches of crosses and statues and make them into temples of
reason'.[4]

There was of course a wide variety of responses to the Enlightenment critique of Christianity, from Voltairean scepticism to outright
atheistic materialism, and from rationalistic deism to serious attempts to
bolster orthodoxy by demonstrating its rationality.[5] In more recent times
the assumption that the Enlightenment was essentially and uniformly an
antichristian movement has come under attack from those who think that
there were was something approaching a 'Christian Enlightenment' in the
eighteenth century, as European Christians in all faith traditions sought to
reconcile their faith with new scientific knowledge. Advocates of the idea

of a Christian Enlightenment believe that our knowledge of the Enlightenment has been skewed by an over emphasis on the coterie of mostly French
or French-speaking intellectuals such as Voltaire (1694–1778), Diderot (1713–
84) and the contributors to the great *Encyclopédie*. However, if a wide-angle
lens on broader European religious developments replaces the telephoto
lens on the French atheists and deists, a good case can be made for both a
Protestant and Catholic Enlightenment. A quick tour of some of the most
important sites may help make the point.

Generally speaking the enlightened critique of Christianity emerged
first among Protestants, especially in England. Nevertheless, English
Christianity also supplied important responses. Some historians have
referred to the notion of an English 'conservative Enlightenment', which
had as its central feature a determination to safeguard the painful gains of
the seventeenth century, most notably the achievement of a mixed constitution, the survival of the Anglican establishment, the supremacy of law, the
security of property and the achievement of a limited measure of religious
toleration. The religious version of all this was John Locke's *The Reasonableness of Christianity* (1695) with its appeal to reason as a counterweight
to unbridled enthusiasm and superstition. Thus one interpretation of the
English Enlightenment is to see it as a movement to protect a civilized
society from the ravages of religious enthusiasm, superstition and intolerance, which were thought to have emanated principally from the respective
religious capitals of Rome and Geneva, and were regarded as responsible
for the religious and political chaos of the English Civil Wars. Presented
in that light, the English Enlightenment could be regarded as a distinctively English fusion of conservation and modernization operating within
an ordered providence, polite discourse, the rhetoric of improvement and
the repudiation of religious enthusiasm. Although the English church
had been rocked by the deist (belief in a non-interventionist god of nature
against revealed and supernatural religion) controversy that lasted for some
50 years after the Glorious Revolution (1688–89), there was a widespread
consensus by mid-century that the deists effectively had been answered by
the combined orthodox onslaught of George Berkeley (1687–1753), Joseph
Butler (1692–1752), Daniel Waterland (1683–1740) and William Warburton
(1698–1779), who appealed both to reason and revelation in their defence of
orthodoxy. For the rest of the century the chief threat to the intellectual and
ecclesiastical ascendancy of Anglican enlightened conservatism came not
from atheism or materialism but from the rational dissenters who mostly
wanted religious liberty and equality, not an end to Christianity. Even
their embrace of heterodox theology was not a way of evading Christian
disciplines and practical piety, as some nineteenth-century Evangelicals

perversely thought, but as a way of protecting themselves from the corrosive influences of establishment persecution on one side and enthusiasm and fanciful notions on the other.[6]

In Scotland, where the established church was Presbyterian (Calvinist), a different pattern emerged. The Scottish Enlightenment brought forth talent of truly international significance, spanning three generations from Francis Hutcheson (1694–1746), through Adam Smith (1723–90), David Hume (1711–76), Thomas Reid (1710–96) and William Robertson (1721–93), to James Beattie (1735–1803) and John Millar (1735–1801). The scope and depth of the Scottish Enlightenment defies easy compression, but it was distinctively Scottish in essence as well as international in scope. Unusual among the thinkers of the European Enlightenment, most of the Scottish literati worked in institutions, were not alienated intellectuals, did not run state bureaucracies and did not wish for the overthrow of the existing order in any political sense. They were mainly professional and practical men who made their most significant contributions to the fields of political economy, jurisprudence, natural science, anthropology and moral philosophy, especially the commonsense tradition that made such a deep impact on the religious life of the American colonies and later the United States. Within the Scottish Presbyterian established church, the Moderates who came to dominate the Church of Scotland by 1760 tried to inculcate a rational and urbane form of Presbyterianism some distance removed from John Knox's hard Calvinism and David Hume's arch scepticism. They emphasized public virtue, ethical obligations, social improvement, religious tolerance and freedom of expression. Their ideas were rooted in civic humanism, classical republicanism and moderate Whig constitutionalism. Above all, they wanted their church and their society to be models of cultivation and virtue, a Presbyterian 'godly commonwealth' of a more enlightened kind than Knox's Reformation vision.[7]

Largely a creation of the migration of Lowland Scots, the Presbyterian dissenting community in Ireland experienced similar tensions between old orthodox Calvinism and 'New Light' influences. 'New Light' intellectuals gathered around Francis Hutcheson's dissenting academy in Dublin in the 1720s and both influenced and were influenced by the Scottish Enlightenment through their close links with the Scottish universities where many Irish Presbyterians ministers were trained. Central to 'New Light' thought was a more optimistic view of human nature than was to be found in orthodox Calvinism. Their emphasis on human rationality, benevolence, natural law and religious toleration made them unwilling to subscribe to the Westminster Confession (1646), which they regarded as a mere product of its time and place. Moreover, required subscription to a human formulation seemed to be an offence against voluntary commitment, which they saw as the best guarantor of religious and civic virtue. The resultant subscription controversies rocked Irish Presbyterianism throughout the eighteenth and early nineteenth centuries, but they also had the effect of keeping alive a vigorous debate about the essence of Irish Presbyterianism that sustained a surprisingly rich intellectual tradition.

A central component of that tradition, and, given its Irish situation, its most contested feature, was its enthusiasm for religious toleration. Unfortunately, what was worked out in the relatively calm atmospheres of Irish dissenting academies and Scottish universities could not easily stand up to the social and political turbulence of the 1790s, when Irish Presbyterians faced hard choices about how much religious toleration and political emancipation should be extended to Roman Catholics. Revolutionary violence in France, bitter social disturbances in the Irish countryside and the United Irish risings of 1798 divided and chastened Irish Presbyterians. The 'New Light' tradition of Presbyterian liberalism was far from extinguished by the brutal events of the 1790s, but its optimistic view of human nature had suffered a rude shock from which other traditions, more conservative and Evangelical, stood to benefit in the nineteenth century. Some of the seeds of future conflicts between Protestants and Catholics in Ulster in the nineteenth and twentieth centuries, with which the world is now all too familiar, were sown in the turbulence of the 1790s when enlightened aspirations for religious equality could not trump the stark realities of sectarian conflict.[8]

Protestantism in continental Europe also had expressions of Christian Enlightenment. In Geneva theologians such Jean-Alphonse Turrettini (1671–1737) and Jacob Vernet (1698–1789) defended reasonable Christianity by smoothing some of the rough edges of predestinarian Calvinism, confronting the enthusiasm of the Pietists and by portraying Jesus less as a supernatural redeemer than a supreme moral teacher. In Germany, philosophers and theologians such as Christian Wolff (1679–1754) and Johann Salomo Semler (1725–91) held the line against the enthusiasts on one side and the confessional scholastics on the other, and arrived at the view that Christianity was itself capable of change and improvement. This notion of 'progressive revelation' came to exercise profound intellectual influence over subsequent generations of Protestant theologians in Germany and beyond.

Continental Catholicism was also not without Enlightenment influences, even in France which is often regarded at the epicentre of the antichristian Enlightenment. Recent work has drawn attention to the better education of the parochial clergy, their attempts to eradicate the prevalent 'superstitions' of popular religiosity and their preaching of Christianity as a 'useful' and 'reasonable' faith. Attention has also been paid to the ecclesiastical reforms of so-called 'state Catholicism' in Portugal, Spain, Austria and among the German prince archbishoprics. In Catholic Europe Jansenists attacked relics and image worship, Catholic writers extolled the importance of reason as well as revelation, reformers established schools and revised liturgies, and some clergy even disobeyed two papal condemnations by becoming freemasons. Some scholars have even noted a change in enlightened Catholic discourse from the middle of the eighteenth century, suggesting that Christianity was not only compatible with reason but was the very agent of human progress down the ages.[9] In this scheme, traditional Catholics turned the tables on their enlightened critics by asserting that all the important advances of human civilization were achieved because of, not despite, Christianity.

It is therefore a mischaracterization of the Enlightenment to regard it as something that existed only outside and in opposition to the churches. For example, almost all of the major faith traditions in the eighteenth century had internally generated reforming movements: Pietism within Lutheranism; Jansenism within Roman Catholicism; Methodism within Anglicanism; and international revivalism within Calvinism. What this shows is that one way of protesting against the dry orthodoxy, pastoral inadequacy and confessional authority of Europe's established churches was not to abandon religion altogether, or even to find a more reasonable version, but rather to adopt forms of religion that had more emotional resonance and personal assurance than could be delivered by reason alone. It is erroneous to view these more emotionally satisfying forms of religiosity as expressly counter-Enlightenment; they were simply alternative visions of how to employ religion as a means and a way to a better life, which is after all one way of speaking about the central concern of the Enlightenment.

Another way of looking at these more emotionally resonant forms of religion is to view them as a religious version of the greater emphasis on sentiment and sensibility within Enlightenment thought that characterized the second half of the eighteenth century. As the Age of Reason morphed into the Age of Sentiment, novels such as those by Laurence Sterne (1713–68), Samuel Richardson (1689–1761) and Jean-Jacques Rousseau (1712–78) became more popular, as did publications such as Jacob Vernet's *Théorie des sentimens agréables* (1750). What one scholar has called Enlightened Christian sentimentalism can be discovered in many of the sermons, poems and publications at the end of the eighteenth century.[10]

Nevertheless, traditional Christianity did not emerge unscathed from its encounter with Enlightenment. By the end of the eighteenth century, the dogmatic, supernatural and hierarchical dimensions of religion had taken a fearful pounding. These included belief in miracles, a personal devil, the existence of witches and the reality of a place called hell; the authority of popes and sacred texts and clerical leaders; the interpretation of natural events as expressions of divine favour or wrath; and the idea that Christianity, or indeed any faith, held the keys to temporal morality and eternal destiny. These foundations of 'revealed' Christianity would never again be unchallenged, or indeed command the intellectual assent of most European secular elites. Perhaps most significant of all was the fact that the core sacred text of Christians, the Holy Bible, had been opened up to the withering scrutiny of new critical methods. Some of this was unintended. The almost constant search for a purer and more reliable text, and the efforts of Newton and others to harmonize the worlds of prophecy and machinery, had the paradoxical effect of making the Bible more, not less, vulnerable to critical attack. Despite remarkable intellectual ingenuity, it soon became clear that biblical chronology, scientific explanation and prophetical interpretation could not be lined up with the same mechanical accuracy as the motions of the planets. Indeed, it is one of the most ironic themes of the history of the English Bible that those who sought to defend it often contributed most to undermining it. Worse was to follow during the later Enlightenment when thinkers such as David Hume helped shift the goalposts away from textual research and accuracy to a repudiation of the whole supernatural framework that the Bible both assumed and taught. In this way Hume and his many followers degraded the Bible's supernaturalism to 'a temporal product of a primitive tribe living in uncivilized times', an approach that once adopted could never again be ignored. In the nineteenth century there was a further erosion of biblical authority from the pens of German higher critics, which in turn set the scene for the 'warfare' between Christian fundamentalists and liberals which has had such an impact on Western Christianity in the modern era.[11]

Science and religion

Little has remained stable in the interpretation of the Enlightenment over the last half century and the treatment of science is no exception. Science in this period, at least after the death of Isaac Newton (1642–1727), is sometimes portrayed as the dull intermission between the 'first scientific revolution' associated with René Descartes (1596–1650), Gottfried Leibniz (1646–1716) and Newton, and the 'second scientific revolution' associated with Charles Darwin's (1809–82) evolutionary biology and Albert Einstein's (1879–1955) physics. Historians of science are apt to challenge this opinion by pointing to important eighteenth-century developments in continental European mathematics, the chemical sciences (atmospheric gases), experimental physics (electricity, magnetism and fluid mechanics) and natural history, including Carl Linnaeus's (1707–78) taxonomic system and the early evolutionary theories of Erasmus Darwin (1731–1802) and Jean-Baptiste Lamarck (1744–1829).

Perhaps of even more significance, however, is the suggestion that the eighteenth century was the period in which new scientific ideas were consolidated, assimilated and propagated more widely. In other words this was the century in which science became in a sense 'public knowledge' and thus had to be reckoned with by educated elites including philosophers, administrators and theologians. As one distinguished historian of science has it, 'gradually, unevenly, but perhaps inexorably, the production of knowledge about Nature and the casting of discourse in natural terms were playing increasingly prominent roles in culture, ideology, and society at large'.[12] Both for those who have welcomed it and for those who have regretted it, the eighteenth century is often portrayed as the era in which 'scientific and instrumental reason became a defining characteristic of modern culture'.[13] How then was religion and theological discourse affected by this development?

The narrative with which we are perhaps most familiar is the one that portrays the age of Enlightenment as a period of changing relations between science and religion which set the stage for the 'displacement of theology, once the queen of the sciences, by more bracing sciences that promised an improvement of the world and a brighter destiny for humankind'.[14] In this scheme, the brave new intellectual world created by Descartes and Newton blossomed in the eighteenth-century sceptical writings of Voltaire and Hume, who respectively subjected orthodox Catholicism and Calvinism to withering scrutiny. As scientific reasoning 'rose', so the narrative goes, Christianity, with its dubious categories of creation stories, prophecies, miracles, virgin birth and resurrection, became less credible. Scientifically informed reason was thus the antidote to credulous superstition and revelation. Moreover, certain kinds of religious defence against the onslaught of new thought, especially the emphasis on natural theology and the argument from design, had the unintended effect of importing new forms of rationalism into theological discourse. In this way, Christian orthodoxy was as much eroded by its well-meaning defenders as by its sternest opponents. To complete the narrative, the conflicts between deists and more orthodox Christians in the eighteenth century prefigured the more intense 'war' between science and religion in the nineteenth century, and the inexorable secularization of Europe in the twentieth century. By then, a status revolution had taken place with scientists replacing clergy as the 'explainers of the world' and science replacing theology as the most reliable form of knowledge. This familiar narrative obviously has compelling explanatory power, but it needs serious revision.

In the first place, as the Newtonian universe with its natural laws of motion and gravity gained intellectual preponderance, its implications for orthodox Christianity were not entirely clear, and arguments about natural religion were surprisingly diverse. After all, Newton's *Principia* contains its own hymn to the divine as the supreme, eternal, infinite, omnipotent and omniscient God who 'rules all things and knows all things that happen or can happen'.[15] In similar mode, many orthodox churchmen such as Joseph Butler (1692–1752) in his *Analogy of Religion* (1736) viewed natural religion as a foundational defence of Christian orthodoxy and as an important confirmation of the truths of revealed religion. On the other hand, for deists like Voltaire natural religion opened up a line of attack on the dogmas and superstitions of Catholic Christianity in favour of a simple and universal creed based on reason, benevolence and virtue. Further still from Christian orthodoxy were the Parisian atheists of the 1750s, gathered around Baron d'Holbach (1723–89), for whom Newtonian science opened up the possibility of doing away with God altogether. Moreover, those who employed natural theology as a defence of orthodoxy also had to contend with nature's caprices, such as the devastating Lisbon earthquake of 1755, which could hardly be placed in the category of nature's benign laws. Biblical miracles also posed problems. Miracles were clearly more agreeable than earthquakes, but even they, as Hume ruthlessly pointed out, hardly squared with the argument from design. If God was indeed such an excellent designer, why did the design need to be tampered with?

What is striking then about the ubiquitous literature of natural religion in the eighteenth century is not a simple pattern of religious retreat and scientific advance but rather an 'interpretative flexibility' that could give rise to any number of positions depending on nationality, religious tradition, degrees of orthodoxy and views of nature.[16] One reason for that is that the dichotomous categories of science and religion with their different sets of questions and methods is not a concept that would have been recognized by most eighteenth-century figures for whom the term 'natural philosophy' included *both* empirical and theological elements. Hence, 'scientific' disagreements among protagonists often had as much to do with differing views of God's relation to the world, or what kind of religion best promoted social harmony, as on experimental reasoning. Specific local and national contexts mattered. So too did religious affiliation. Conflicts between Protestants and Catholics, or between Trinitarians and Arians, or Churchmen and dissenters, however masked, were an integral part of scientific discourse.

Although natural religion was a broad church, there is no denying that over time it could have a secularizing dynamic. The more that natural processes were understood the more the human mind was thought of in physical terms, and the more that popular lecturers could reproduce marvels such as electrical shocks (science as entertainment) the more distance there seemed to be between the creator and the creation. In *A Secular Age* Charles Taylor seeks to account for the fact that in Western society it was virtually impossible not to believe in God in say 1500, while in 2000 many Westerners find it not only easy but perhaps inescapable. Of course explaining this, as we shall see, is a big complicated story, but in his search for the roots of 'exclusive humanism' Taylor pays particular attention to what he calls the intermediate step of 'providential deism'. In the late seventeenth and eighteenth centuries he detects three important intellectual shifts towards anthropocentrism, the primacy of impersonal order, and pure natural religion stripped of its accretions and superstitions. None of these was framed initially as an expression of atheism, but taken together they had the effect of constructing a new kind of 'social imaginary' in which human flourishing became more central than God's demands, natural laws more important than divine intervention, and beneficent order more desirable than the tenets of revealed religion.[17] The cumulative effect of these intellectual shifts over the course of a century was to highlight the natural and diminish the supernatural. As one historian of science has it, 'One hundred years also separated the *Theory of the Earth* (1795) of James Hutton (1726–97) from the *Sacred Theory of the Earth* propounded by Thomas Burnet (1635?–1715). The word "sacred" was lost.'[18] Full-blown materialism, or reductionism, as orthodox Christians prefer to call it, is rarely on view in eighteenth-century scientific discourse (except for the French materialists), but increasingly nature came to be seen as having a dynamic life of its own rather than having its strings pulled by an interventionist creator.

Moreover, these intellectual shifts were not confined to the corridors of learned societies or aristocratic salons. As cultures of improvement made headway among enlightened rulers and urban elites, a scientific rhetoric of control, efficiency and order began to infiltrate voluntary societies and infant bureaucracies. Churches and clergy were not completely cut out of these developments, but over time their role as social guardians diminished. When nineteenth-century towns and cities looked to improve their industrial efficiency, sanitation, disease control, educational provision, civic amenities and poor relief, religious and moral values had to live alongside the serried ranks of reports, statistics and calculations. This 'calculating spirit' began to permeate many more aspects of life, from insurance to gambling, and from account books to nascent social policy. One does not have to exaggerate the speed and scope of these developments to appreciate their long-term significance.

The argument that the scientific revolution through its discovery of mathematical mechanisms boded ill for orthodox Christianity, notwithstanding its embrace of natural theology, should not be pressed too far, however. If natural religion was capable of many iterations, from Butler's orthodoxy to Diderot's materialism, so too was science. Newton's mechanistic natural philosophy did not conquer all. Older traditions of animism, alchemy, Paracelsianism (esoteric medical therapies) and vitalism (the idea that life processes are not reducible to scientific laws) not only remained embedded in popular beliefs and practices but were also developed and refined by a post-Newton generation of thinkers throughout Europe.[19] Many late Enlightenment thinkers abandoned the idea that nature's complexity could be reduced to a few all-encompassing laws, but instead emphasized variety, dynamism and vitalism, which drew attention to living matter and self-activating forces. This shift in intellectual priorities was also in part a disciplinary shift from mathematics and cosmology to chemistry, the life sciences, medicine and natural history. Rather than focusing on mechanical bodies and the laws they obeyed, naturalists influenced by the almost forgotten Georg Ernst Stahl (1659?–1734) attended to living systems and nature's diversity. Reacting against the 'absolute solutions and reductive rationalism' of mechanistic natural philosophy, 'Enlightenment vitalists sought to reintroduce entities such as soul and individuality into the inner core of scientific thinking'.[20] In some respects this tradition of thought seemed friendlier to religious sensibilities, especially those associated with Pietism and Evangelicalism which emphasized interiority, mysticism and experience, but in other respects it opened up a more self-actualizing world of nature even more distant from the God who had allegedly created it.[21]

By the turn of the eighteenth and nineteenth centuries it seemed that the role and authority of science had been consolidated. Ubiquitous scientific societies and encyclopaedias, a thriving publishing industry, the recruitment of science by elites as a disciplinary and regulative authority, commerce in scientific apparatus and extravagant claims about the utility of scientific knowledge all seemed indications of a powerful new reality.[22] Yet, it is a mistake to see science as 'the spirit of the future mounted majestically on an iron horse; rather it was a resource with multiple uses, and foes no less than friends'. In this spirit, it is hard to be too certain about science's impact on religion, not only because these two categories were far from separate entities but also because the lines lead in multiple directions. Newtonian science both bolstered natural theology and supplied the tools to undermine it.

In some respects Christianity seemed to have weathered the storm rather well. Scottish commonsense philosophers, notably Thomas Reid, defended belief in an intelligent deity as intuitive and grounded in the first principles of the human condition. William Paley's *Natural Theology; or Evidences of the Existence and Attributes of the Deity* (1802), with its watchmaker analogy, comfortably outsold the works of Enlightenment sceptics like David Hume. Jonathan Edwards wrote with sublime beauty about nature and nature's God. These were all resources used by religious traditions in the nineteenth century. But on a deeper level cracks had appeared that could not easily be contained. A Christian argument for intelligent design, as Hume clearly saw, and as recent court cases in the United States have confirmed, is vulnerable to all kinds of challenges from those who see it as both an unwarranted foundational claim and a far from self-evident conclusion from reading the book of nature. More serious still for the intellectual sustainability of Christianity were not so much the challenges posed by naturalistic scientific theories, whether eighteenth-century mechanical theories or nineteenth-century evolutionary theories, as the profound and indeterminate cultural impact of 'instrumental rationality' on humankind. The period of the Enlightenment produced new scientific ideas and disciplines, undermined traditional natural philosophy and disseminated new ways of thinking about the world. Theologians struggled to cope with the scale and diversity of the onslaught, clergy sensed the beginnings of a status revolution and churches felt the first icy blasts of disenchantment. Enlightenment science did not inflict mortal wounds on orthodox Christianity, but along with other developments, including the historical and moral criticism of the Bible, it made traditional Christian belief less axiomatic. Over the long term, the option of unbelief, not its inevitability, was the real threat to religion.

Religious toleration

The conventional narrative of the rise of religious toleration is that the religious bigotry and violence associated with the Thirty Years' War in the seventeenth century slowly dissipated in the eighteenth century as a result of the Enlightenment and the consequent triumph of reason over enthusiasm. In this story toleration was the beneficiary of increasingly secular enlightened elites whose rational support for toleration eventually won the battle of ideas and helped shape the policies of state governments from the American colonies in the west to the Habsburg Empire in the east. Hence, toleration had its roots in the rise of Protestantism and the war weariness of Europeans scarred by confessional conflict and wars of religion. It then grew under the influence of Enlightenment thinkers before finding its way into state laws throughout the West in the late eighteenth and nineteenth centuries. This interpretation also tended to pair the rise of toleration and the rise of secularism, with the two combining to produce an impressive meta-narrative about the emergence of liberal modernity out of the dark ages of religious superstition and absolutism. As with all compelling meta-narratives there is some truth in all of these assertions, but increasingly they have been subjected to critical scrutiny not least because of the obvious circularity and apparent inevitability of the argument, namely, those who value liberal ideas construct the past in a way that privileges the inexorable triumph of liberal ideas. What then can be said about the growth of religious toleration in the long eighteenth century?

In the first place it is important to recognize that the end of the Thirty Years' War did not see the end of religious conflict in early modern Europe. The Peace of Westphalia (1648) sought to reduce confessional conflict by recognizing the territorial rights of religious establishments – Catholic, Reformed and Lutheran – within the jurisdictions they controlled in 1624. But Westphalia made no provision for Jews and Protestant sects, gave no clear direction about what was to happen to religious minorities ruled by confessional majorities (apart from the right to immigrate) and did nothing to erode the idea that social and political stability in any state or principality was dependent on the support of a single state-sanctioned church. Throughout the early modern period, religious diversity was perceived as a weakness to be eradicated, not as a strength to be cultivated.

Moreover, Westphalia offered no remedy for the inconveniences of changes in the confessional allegiances of rulers, or for the growing problem of intra-confessional conflict within territorial units. Unsurprisingly therefore, the Peace of Westphalia did not usher in a period of religious tranquillity. In fact the litany of subsequent cruelty and conflict is ubiquitous and sobering. In pursuit of the religious uniformity that was regarded as the foundation of royal absolutism, Louis XIV's revocation of the Edict of Nantes (1685) unleashed a wave of persecution against French Calvinists resulting in the most extensive migration of early modern Europe. That in turn helped provoke the Revolt of the Camisards (1702) which manifested some of the worst civilian excesses in the name of religion since the French Wars of Religion in the sixteenth century. The grim list of religious-inspired violence and persecution trails throughout the eighteenth century, including the expulsion of 20,000 Protestants by the Archbishop of Salzburg in 1731, the anti-Catholic Gordon Riots in London in 1780 and the gruesome massacres in Ireland during the Rebellion of the United Irishmen in 1798, whose Catholic and Presbyterian leaders ironically supported religious equality. Eighteenth-century Europe was therefore anything but a model of religious peace and tranquillity. Religious toleration, defined as the equal legal right to profess and practise any faith without penalty or persecution, was not a reality anywhere in early modern Europe. Even in the Dutch Republic, where different religious traditions had extensive rights, only those of the Reformed tradition were entitled to hold public office.[23]

Yet there is another side to the story. The fact that Europe's confessional conflicts in the seventeenth century had bequeathed a territorial mosaic of immense complexity created an opportunity as well as a problem. One authority states that 'Europe's religious borders ran not just between major states, but around petty principalities, enclaves, and exclaves, cantons, noble estates, cities, ecclesiastic immunities, and even, in a few regions, parishes. These borders divided European society in a new and fundamental way. At the same time, they created a vast inner frontier land where religious contact and exchange were inevitable.'[24] In other words many European populations had no alternative but to work out some sort of pragmatic resolution to the problem of confessional diversity in order to live in close proximity with one another without the recurring resource to violence.

Such arrangements were occasioned more by the day-to-day realities of life, not determined by any sort of ideology of toleration. Although these accommodations were 'limited, tension-ridden, and discriminatory', eighteenth-century Europeans discovered that they could often manage and contain confessional conflict out of pragmatic needs and collective self-interest. The various 'experiments' that were tried with various degrees of success included immigration, confessional cleansing, practising religion beyond the gaze of established authorities (either disobediently or with *de facto* consent), declarations of indulgence granting relief from certain legal penalties, occasional conformity to avoid social and political penalties, and 'Auslaf', by which authorities would permit minorities to travel to a neighbouring town of the same confession as the minority so that they could practise legally without giving offence to the confessional majority. Auslaf was effective because it 'respected borders even as it violated them', and acknowledged the realities of confessional power without being crushed by them.[25]

As a matter of daily lived religious experience Europeans had to find strategies for coping with an apparent cognitive dissonance; on the one hand they belonged to states and confessional traditions that believed there was neither truth nor virtue to be found in the idea of tolerance, while on the other they had to work out practical strategies for living alongside people of different religious confessions. Historians who have written about this use descriptive phrases such as 'the ecumenicity of everyday life' or 'practical rationality'. What they mean by these phrases is that Europeans came to practise a degree of religious tolerance not as a self-conscious virtue but rather through avoidance, connivance, dissimulation, negotiation and sheer pragmatism. Even the much commented on Dutch tolerance of the early modern period was 'pragmatic and opportunistic rather than principled or ironclad, and it would be the source of continual conflict between the Reformed clergy, who wanted to extend the influence of the church, and the "libertine" regents of the cities, many of whom, with political power and the interests of trade in mind, favoured a non-dogmatic, laissez-faire approach'.[26] In short, there was no 'high road to toleration, signposted from the Reformation' or even from the Enlightenment for that matter, rather the practical effects of the religious pluralism of early modern Europe forced the renegotiation of confessional boundaries, case by case, in dynamic and unpredictable ways. The uneven and piecemeal growth of religious toleration, as a practical reality, was more often negotiated on the ground, in actual sites, than it was dictated from above or argued in print.[27]

More grandiose schemes of religious toleration based on ecumenical engagement or politically motivated comprehension tended not to fare so well, partly because religious divisions were rarely contained within a single state or territorial unit and therefore could not easily be solved within it. Confessional identities and loyalties transcended territorial boundaries. Nevertheless, even before the better-known toleration acts, edicts and treatises gathered pace in the later eighteenth century, Europeans, if not exactly tolerant of religious diversity, had found limited and pragmatic ways to contain the contagion of confessional violence. If this analysis may be regarded as a social history story of the slow growth of religious toleration in Europe, there is also something to be said for changes in the climate of ideas and in the formation of policy by states.

The ideological roots of religious toleration have been traced through a predominantly Protestant line beginning with Sebastian Castellio's (1515–63) protest against the execution for heresy of Servetus in Calvin's Geneva, and including Roger Williams (c.1603–83) in the American colonies, the Dutch Arminians, English Civil War radicals, and the influential writings of Pierre Bayle (1647–1706), Baruch Spinoza (1632–77) and John Locke (1632–1704).[28] In this narrative, arguments for religious toleration stemmed primarily from religious belief itself: religious persecution was contrary to the example of Christ, tarnished the cause of Christianity and was in any case not the responsibility of princes and rulers. If heresy was to be combated, that was the responsibility of the church, and the church should respond with appropriate ecclesiastical penalties, not state-enforced brutality. Over the course of the eighteenth century, the scope and depth of writing in support of religious toleration increased to include deists and freethinkers such as John Toland (1670–1722) and Tom Paine (1737–1809), English radical dissenters like Joseph Priestley (1733–1804) and German and French philosophers like Immanuel Kant (1724–1804) and Voltaire (1694–1778). Increasingly, the case for toleration was made not so much on grounds of religious purity as on reason and natural rights. Moreover, the concept of toleration itself came under attack from radicals like Tom Paine, whose goal was full religious equality. For Paine the strictly limited concept of religious toleration presupposed an established position, which he regarded as an offence against natural rights and religious equality.

Changes in the climate of thought were accompanied by, though not necessarily occasioned by, slow and often haphazard changes in state policy. The English Act of Toleration (1689) exempted Protestant Trinitarian dissenters from the penalties of certain acts provided they took oaths of supremacy and allegiance, registered their buildings, licensed their preachers and paid tithes and church rates to help fund the Anglican Established Church. Even these limited concessions were not meant to benefit Jews, Unitarians or Roman Catholics. Nevertheless, the very fact that non-Anglicans had the legally acknowledged right to dissent from the Established Church, albeit within strict limits, made it more difficult for the whole apparatus of church courts to enforce the religious and moral requirements of church and state. Increasingly, Established Churchmen had to operate more within the parameters of persuasion than persecution. That said, despite the efforts of religious dissenters in Britain and the United Provinces, allegedly two of Europe's most tolerant states, not much in the way of formal legislation was accomplished until the later eighteenth century when the British Parliament passed acts relieving some Catholic disabilities in 1778 and 1793. Notwithstanding these limited concessions, the political climate determined that the repeal of the Test and Corporation Acts against Protestant dissenters had to wait until 1828 and Roman Catholics were not allowed to sit in the British Parliament until after 1829. Although these gains were significant, both Protestant dissenters and Roman Catholics had to wage a long war against the remaining Anglican confessional privileges throughout the nineteenth century and beyond. Anti-Catholicism in particular was painfully slow in abating, not least because Britain's national and imperial identity, and its propagandist self-image, was constructed around Protestantism.[29]

Elsewhere in Europe the progress of religious toleration was also piecemeal and limited. French Protestants secured some social and legal legitimacy from Louis XVI's Edict of Toleration (1787), and Lutheran and Reformed Protestants as well as Greek Orthodox Christians in the

Habsburg Empire were afforded some freedom of worship by Joseph II's Patent of Toleration (1781). Similarly, Muslims, Jews and Old Believers were extended limited toleration by Catherine the Great of Russia. Finally, a succession of Prussian rulers employed pragmatic toleration as an instrument of state efficiency and prosperity, but it was not until 1788 that a more general edict on toleration guaranteed liberty of conscience and extended toleration for some religious minorities.[30]

However, the real breakthroughs for the cause of religious toleration occurred not as a result of the social policies of enlightened absolutists or the gradualist concessions of governments in Britain and the United Provinces, but as a result of revolutionary energies in the American colonies and France. In France the 'Declaration of the Rights of Man and the Citizen' adopted by the National Assembly in August 1789 proclaimed that no one should be disadvantaged on account of their opinions including 'their religious views, provided their manifestation does not disturb the public order established by law', though of course the subsequent history of the Revolution was scarcely kind to the French Catholic Church.

The most striking advances in religious freedom, however, came in America. Eight of the 13 American colonies had some form of religious establishment at the outbreak of the American Revolutionary War and three New England states retained Congregational establishments until well into the nineteenth century. The most important debates on the nature of religious establishments and religious freedom took place in Virginia, where a combination of Baptist and Presbyterian opposition to Anglican privileges and the political leadership of Thomas Jefferson and James Madison resulted in the Virginia Statute for Religious Freedom (written in 1777 and enacted in 1786). It declared:

> That no man shall be compelled to frequent or support any religious service, place, or ministry whatsoever, nor shall be enforced, restrained, molested, or burdened in his body of goods, nor shall suffer on account of his religious opinions or belief; but that all men shall be free to profess, and by argument to maintain, their opinion in matters of religion, and that the same shall in no wise diminish, enlarge, or affect their civil capacities.

This was the first statute in history to state that there was no religious opinion spoken or written by anyone that could adversely affect his or her property or civil capacity.[31]

The Virginia Statute was passed on the eve of the Constitutional Convention in Philadelphia and became the direct antecedent of the establishment clause of the First Amendment to the United States constitution forbidding Congress from making any law 'respecting an establishment of religion, or prohibiting the free exercise thereof'. Because of the nature of the federal constitution, the First Amendment did not instantly abolish established churches in the individual states, but the template was set for the separation of church and state and for the removal of state compulsion or financial exactions for the practice of religion. The precise impact of this amendment on the development of American religion is still a hotly debated topic, but, as we shall see later, some think that a combination of religious pluralism, voluntarism and democratization in America produced a more vibrant and popular religiosity than could be maintained by the established churches of Europe. Thus the alleged differential trajectory of secularization in Europe and the United States is partly attributed to the impact of religious freedom in promoting diversity, competitiveness and voluntary muscle. In this inter-pretation, free religion and free markets marched hand in hand.

Why then were the American colonies the pioneers not only of mere religious toleration but even more significantly of the grander notion of religious liberty? Part of the reason, no doubt, is the enlightened leader-ship of James Madison, Thomas Jefferson and others, but there are other factors that need to be taken into account. The relatively low levels of inter-religious violence in the colonies, the decline of anti-Catholic sentiment in the later part of the century, the overwhelming numerical preponderance and diversity of Protestantism, the context of the American Revolution in which the British, not other religions, were perceived to be the real threat to liberty, and the fact that the colonists wanted relief from the annoying inconveniences of being classified as a religious dissenter all played their part in opening up a window for greater religious liberty. Crucially, an elite tradition of enlightened thought, as exemplified by Madison and Jeffer-son, made common cause with the practical grievances of popular religious traditions such as the Baptists, to end the coercive powers of already emaci-ated colonial establishments of religion.

If the New World led the way, the Old World still had a way to go. Nowhere in eighteenth-century Europe was toleration 'unequivocally and comprehensively embraced either in theory or practice; and where it gained ground, it was partial, fragile, contested, and even subject to reversal. No clear and distinct metaphysics underpinned toleration claims, nor was there a single, classic foundational text, commanding universal assent.'[32] The factors resisting the claims of religious toleration included the perceived security, homogeneity and stability of the state, the construction of provi-dential national identities, the sincerely held religious obligations to enforce confessional orthodoxy and the conceptions of church and state as equal pillars holding up the arch of social and political stability. Factors promot-ing toleration included economic self-interest, political expediency, Enlight-enment ideas of subjecting religion to rational discourse, the campaigns mounted by religious dissenters against religious establishments and the very slowly growing notion that state security and prosperity did not necessarily depend on religious uniformity. Even when a measure of religious toleration was adopted, as with Roman Catholic emancipation in Britain in 1829, it was passed by legislators against the clearly expressed wishes of the majority of the population. *Demos* was not always the friend of religious equality. Hence, there was nothing inevitable or unilinear about religious toleration. Moreover, when Europeans as a result of colonial conquests were brought into contact with other peoples and their religions, the kinds of 'otherness' that confronted them most forcefully remained the religious differences among themselves. In particular, the old Reformation divisions between Protestants and Catholics were played out in multiple new locations far removed from their geographical point of origin. Protestants and Catholics disliked each other as vehemently in the Americas, Australia and India as they did in parts of Europe from which they originated. Geography was no respecter of religious tolerance and intolerance.

Slavery, abolition and progress

Slavery, particularly African slavery, was of central importance to the Atlantic economies and the new worlds they settled in the early modern period. By 1820 nearly 8.7 million slaves had left Africa for the New World and African slaves constituted a staggering 77 per cent of the total population that had sailed towards the Americas. In terms of the total numbers of African slaves carried to the New World, the Portuguese shipped the most, but in the period 1650–1810 Britain, ironically a pacesetter of European Enlightenment, topped the list.[33] Within Africa the geographic sources of slaves shifted over time, but in the eighteenth century the main slave-exporting regions were those associated with the British slave trade in the Bight of Benin, the Gold Coast, the Bight of Biafra and Sierra Leone. Overall the Atlantic slave trade drew captives 'from a vast area stretching thirty-five hundred miles along the West and West Central African coast, from present-day Senegal in the north to the Kalahari Desert in Angola in the south, and from five hundred to even a thousand miles inland'.[34] From there they were taken to the Caribbean islands, the British colonies of North America and the Spanish and Portuguese colonies of Central and South America. All the major European seaborne empires were slave traders. The chief economic engine that drove the trade was sugar production. Sugar-producing Brazil absorbed over 41 per cent of African slaves and the sugar-producing British, French, Dutch and Spanish Caribbean accounted for another 48 per cent. Only 5 or 6 percent were brought initially to the British colonies of North America. Their numbers were subsequently inflated by unparalleled natural population growth.

Historians have had comparatively little trouble accounting for the ubiquity of the slave trade, the racial assumptions that undergirded it, the cruelties that characterized it, the routes that sustained it and the economic benefits that accrued from it, but they have disagreed sharply over the reasons for the growth of abolitionist sentiment in Britain, the first country to abolish the slave trade, during the latter part of the eighteenth century. Over the course of writing on British abolitionism, historians have variously emphasized the role of heroic individuals (often motivated by serious religious convictions), changes in economic conditions and perceptions, the political calculations of the governing classes, the unanticipated coalescence of unlikely circumstances and subtle shifts in cultural sensibilities.[35] Those changes in cultural sensibilities have in turn been explored through the additional lenses of gender, race, religion, identity and economic theory.

Let us then start with the facts. Beginning in the early 1770s a number of significant events helped propel slavery to the centre of national attention. In 1772 *Somersett's Case* brought by the pioneering abolitionist Granville Sharp was interpreted as outlawing slavery in England. In 1774 John Wesley, the founder of Methodism, published his widely circulating anti-slavery pamphlet, *Thoughts Upon Slavery*. In 1781 Sharp, aided by the free Africans Ottobah Cugoano (*c.*1757–?) and Olaudah Equiano (*c.*1745–97), publicized details of the *Zong* case in which the owner of a slave ship tried to collect insurance for black slaves who had been thrown overboard during an epidemic. In 1783, at the end of the American Revolutionary War, British Quakers formed two committees to work against the slave trade. In 1787 the Society for Effecting the Abolition of the Slave Trade was formed. In 1787–78 a mass petitioning campaign against slavery got under way, and in 1789 William Wilberforce, the Evangelical MP from Hull and close friend of prime minister Pitt, introduced resolutions into the House of Commons against the slave trade. During the next two decades the war against Revolutionary France and fears about popular democratic movements in Britain and Ireland complicated and ultimately hindered the anti-slavery cause both inside and outside Parliament. Nevertheless, apparently against its immediate economic interests, the British Parliament outlawed the British slave trade in 1807, peacefully emancipated its own 800,000 colonial slaves from 1833 to 1838, paid the immense sum of £20 million to the slaves' owners as compensation, and used its imperial power to pressurize other nations such as France, Spain and Portugal to end their own oceanic slave trades. Within 50 years of the emancipation of British colonial slaves, Holland, the United States, Spain and Brazil had all followed suit. The perplexing question, however, is how and why did Britain do this, and from our point of view, what role was played by British Christians in abolishing a trade they seemed to have had little difficulty endorsing, or at least collaborating with, for well over a century?

As was the case with our treatment of religious toleration, it is good to start by casting some suspicion on a facile progress narrative based upon the notion that a greater appreciation of human rights and civilizational advance was ushered in by the Enlightenment. On the contrary, David Brion Davis, the distinguished historian of slavery, and others have conclusively shown how pro-slavery arguments for over 2,000 years have emphasized the connections between slavery and various forms of economic and social progress and that some of the Enlightenment's most eminent philosophers, including Hume, Voltaire and Kant, were capable of writing the most racist comments. It is an undeniable and sad fact that slave trading and slavery have played a significant part in many, perhaps most, of the great civilizations of human history. Hence, from the 1660s to 1807 Britain, perhaps the most 'advanced' nation in the world, carried the greatest number of enslaved Africans to the New World. Ironically, the 1780s, the very era of the supposed breakthrough into modernity and enlightenment, appears to have been the all-time peak of slave trading, not just in the North Atlantic region but in East Africa and South East Asia as well. Not only was slavery compatible with notions of high civilization in the past, but also slave emancipation seemed to offer no immediate economic and social advance. Slave emancipation, as in Haiti, often produced immediate poverty. Emancipation in the northern states of the United States produced anti-black racism. Britain's emancipation of 800,000 slaves in the Caribbean led to economic disaster. Most likely if there had been no American Civil War, slavery as a relatively successful economic system would have persisted into the twentieth century. The fact that slave emancipation has often failed to produce the economic and social improvements for the emancipated slaves for which abolitionists had hoped is of course no argument against the moral rectitude of abolition itself, but it is a reminder that abolishing slavery was not a self-evident concomitant of inexorable economic advance, at least in the short term.

One problem in dealing with the British abolition of the slave trade is that the abolitionists themselves, as with later social analysts, constructed their own versions of progress narratives. Thomas Clarkson, for example, historicized anti-slavery sentiment as an expression of the Christian Gospel of love – the inexorable growth of righteousness, or even as the expression of a distinctively British devotion to liberty, natural justice and the rule of law. The economic version of a progress narrative, namely the growth of liberal capitalism and free trade, also assumes an unrealistically hegemonic explanatory power. Why is it, for example, that Western Europeans, who were pioneers in the development of political and economic freedom, including wage labour, were also the creators and sustainers of the Atlantic slave system? That question is not easily answered.

Whatever the historical processes involved in the rise of abolitionism, therefore, they are clearly more complicated than mere progress narratives alone can explain. Moreover, on one level Britain seemed an unlikely place for abolitionist sentiment to take root and prosper at the end of the eighteenth century. Britain had no democratic revolution, and the French Revolution, together with the subsequent war with Napoleonic France, stimulated a conservative reaction against reforming movements of all kinds. In other words, it was by no means obvious that the world's leading participant in the Atlantic slave trade by the end of the eighteenth century, at a time when it was beleaguered by a costly war, should have been the place where abolitionism gained its first and most important victory. Most of the recent work on the economics of the British slave trade and colonial slavery has taken the view that there was no pressing economic reason for the inevitability of the abolition of slavery. If free-market conditions had prevailed there was no obvious reason why labour costs in New World plantations would not have fallen, leading to a corresponding drop in prices and further stimulating the international trade that slavery serviced. In short, slavery was not abolished by Britain because of widespread agreement that it was no longer economically viable.[36]

Given this complexity, how do we address the question posed by Moses Finlay some 40 years ago when he wrote, 'Nothing is more difficult perhaps than to explain how and why, or why not, a new moral perception becomes effective in action. Yet nothing is more urgent if an academical historical exercise is to become a significant investigation of human behaviour with direct relevance to the world we now live in.'? In seeking to explain how abolitionism became 'effective in action' in Britain at the turn of the eighteenth and nineteenth centuries, perhaps we need a clearer map of the terrain of abolitionism. For example, although we cannot afford to trust progress narratives completely on their own terms, neither can we afford to ignore them altogether. To put it crudely, human actors may not fully understand why they do the right things, or even why good things are done, but we are foolish to ignore the patterns of 'mental ordering' that humans engage in when good things *are* done.

In the case of abolitionism, 'mental ordering' has come in many forms which have been helpfully teased out by David Brion Davis. He has written of a 'scientific tradition', embracing otherwise unlikely bedfellows such as Adam Smith (1723–90) and Karl Marx (1818–83), which claimed that slave labour was an inefficient form of labour organization invented by primitive economies, that would become anachronistic in more modern economies. There is also a predominantly 'Evangelical Christian tradition' that presupposed an irreconcilable conflict between slavery and the Christian message that all people were created equal in the image of God. For that idea to become effective in action it needed some form of organizational catalyst to take an inward and spiritual message out into the public sphere. The catalyst came from those ubiquitous eighteenth-century voluntary associations for civic improvement that came of age in the era of the American, French and industrial revolutions. They used the rational means of print, propaganda and persuasion to achieve the partly rational but also partly apocalyptic ends of the abolition of slavery. In this way providence, prophecy and persuasion came together in a powerful way. How 'mental ordering' happens is of course important in coming to terms with the motivation of anti-slavery activists, but Finlay's question still remains tantalizingly unanswered.

Three possibilities suggest themselves from the burgeoning literature on this subject. The first is to look afresh at the complex relationship between the Enlightenment and Evangelical religion. For example, the most distinctive aspects of Evangelical spirituality, namely conversion narratives, hymns and affective poetry were vehicles through which new constructs of the self, new notions of freedom from bondage and new formulations of guilt and responsibility were widely disseminated among the English-speaking populations. It is perhaps no accident that among the most prolific of British anti-slavery petitioners in the period 1787–1833 were the Methodists, whose theological orientation and organizational structure seemed a good fit for an abolitionist toolkit: they formed a religious voluntary association with a ticket membership in the era of voluntary associations; their founder was the first British religious leader of national significance to write publicly against slavery and the slave trade; they believed themselves to be active Arminian collaborators in the working out of divine providence, not passive Calvinist automatons (their construction); they encountered the unspeakable cruelties of slavery first-hand in their missions to the Caribbean islands and the American colonies; they built a formidable organizational structure which could be utilized for petitioning and propaganda purposes; they had unusually high literacy rates among their members; and they helped facilitate the entrance of women, who were instrumental in the sugar boycotts, into the public square.

Although often overlooked both by economic historians and by those who attribute the abolition of slavery to the heroic actions of great men like Clarkson and Wilberforce, women were important in the early anti-slavery cause in manifold ways. They were often the stirrers of a more humane sensibility in some of the elite homes of early anti-slavery activists.[37] They were authors of a distinctive genre of poems and imaginative literature. They supported boycotts of slave-labour produce and subscribed financially to abolition societies.[38] Quaker and Methodist women in particular were to the fore in anti-slavery circles on both sides of the Atlantic.

A second suggestion is to link more closely the rise of anti-slavery ideas and the development of the American colonies and the American Revolutionary War as a way in which the English were forced to engage in a kind of imperial self-reflection. If England was indeed a divinely favoured Protestant nation whose values were being disseminated all over the globe, what were those values? What kind of empire was Britain building and what kind of human rights were to be acknowledged by those breaking free from that empire? In short, what was to be the moral character of colonial institutions and practices? Linked to that was the debate about what kind of religion and religious sensibilities should be exported to the colonies, and how the contemporary rise of foreign missions impacted those sensibilities. This whole debate started much earlier and was deeper than is conventionally assumed.

Finally, there is a need for a fresh way of thinking about the relationship between the familiar categories of the anti-slavery discourse, namely the respective influences of Quakerism, Evangelicalism, the Enlightenment, capitalism and humanitarianism. One way into that problem is to produce a more sophisticated set of collective biographies of exactly how, when and why people became abolitionists. Another approach is to look at the eschatological frameworks of slavery and abolition in a more creative fashion. How people matched slavery to biblical themes and biblical prophecies is an intriguing segue into their mental maps and frameworks. It is no accident, for example, that the Quakers arose in the midst of a fever of apocalypticism during the English Civil Wars, or that abolitionism in England arose at a time of a vigorous renewal of eschatological and apocalyptic writing. Is there a link between the two, such that anti-slavery political action served as a kind of national purging of blood at a time when Britain was confronting the Napoleonic Antichrist from without and unprecedented social change from within?

However we think about these grand frameworks, we cannot easily avoid an explanation for the rise of abolitionism that also places an emphasis on mere historical contingencies. It may very well be the case, therefore, that the rise of abolitionism was a 'peculiar moment' in the evolution of Western civilization – produced by an unusual combination of circumstances and personalities at the end of the eighteenth century – not its inexorable destination, as is so often assumed in various kinds of progress narratives.

Secularization

In almost all ways that religiosity can be measured by modern polling agencies, the United States, despite being a modern technological society, shows up as more religious than most parts of Europe. There are of course manifold regional variations in both North America and Europe, but in general terms religiosity, as measured by church membership, frequency of church attendance, belief in God, heaven and hell and the practise of prayer, appears to be higher in the United States than in Europe. Even allowing for the well-documented tendency of Americans to exaggerate their religiosity in polling surveys (a revealing phenomenon in itself) and for significant differences of styles in religious discourses and practices, it still seems that there is a discrepancy between the patterns of religious belief and practice in Europe and the United States that requires explanation. How then can one account for these different patterns, and how far back in history does one need to go to find their roots?

Secularization theorists once supposed that America was 'exceptional' in the strength of its religious traditions, but more recently they have suggested that by comparison with the rest of the world it is Europe, not America, that seems to be exceptional.[39] Given the fact that the United States, until relatively recently, was populated mostly by European migrants, how is it that religion there has apparently remained stronger for longer? This is of course a very complicated question to answer, involving as it must manifold categories of analysis. Moreover, there is a danger both of exaggerating the differences between the two places and of assuming too easily that these differences have been there for a very long time. Some writers on comparative secularization, for example, justifiably refer to the relatively recent decade of the 1960s as perhaps the most important period in the differential secularization trajectories of America and Europe.[40]

On the other hand, when writing about the different secularizing trajectories of Europe and the United States, Charles Taylor has pointed to the importance of historical shadows of long-term factors in national traditions, which over time produce quite different outcomes.[41] The accumulation of 'small differences' over time, even allowing for ebbs and flows and cultural negotiations, can add up to the evolution of a significantly different pattern. It is possible that the roots of some of these 'small differences' may stretch right back to the seventeenth and eighteenth centuries. The differential secularization trajectories of Europe and America were certainly not fixed in stone or predetermined in any way by, say, 1830, but even by then there were significant structural differences in the religious cultures of the two land masses which cast 'historical shadows' over their respective religious developments. In short, while it is a mistake to suggest that secularization is unilinear, irreversible or somehow inevitable given certain conditions of 'modernity', it is also a mistake simply to assume that the important elements for explaining differential patterns of religious strength are *all* products of historical conditions after 1960. Neither position is adequate.

In the huge literature that now exists on this topic it is possible to identify many major categories of difference between American and European religion dating back at least to the eighteenth century. They are the separation of church and state; the democratization of Christianity and the role of free markets; the relationship between religion and political culture; the different roles played by social elites; the impact of immigration; the relationship between religion and popular culture; the organization of Christian congregations; the impact of Evangelical Christianity; the importance of fertility rates and generational transmission; the connection between religion and modernity; and the discourse of secularization itself.

The first three categories are in fact closely linked with one another. The determination of the American founding fathers in the much quoted First Amendment that 'Congress shall make no law respecting an establishment of religion, or prohibiting the free exercise thereof' (1791) effectively guaranteed a different pattern of church–state relations in America from that in Europe where the chief device for Christianizing populations was by means of territorially organized established churches, whether Anglican, Catholic, Lutheran or Calvinist. Although some states in America's federal union retained their religious establishments until the 1830s, the broad tendency in the new republic was to move away from the European pattern of national religious establishments with their political and legal privileges and their compulsory financial exactions. Seizing on the implications of the First Amendment, and on the high degree of religious pluralism that existed, especially in American east coast cities in the later eighteenth century, American cultural historians have emphasized the contiguous ideas of a free marketplace of religion and the democratization of American Christianity. Although it was once fashionable to associate American religious diversity with secularization (through the erosion of a unifying sacred canopy), there has been almost a tidal wave of recent writing on American religious history linking religious pluralism, free markets, voluntary enterprise and democratization. All this, it is alleged, produced a more competitive, dynamic and populist religious culture in which religious traditions marched hand in hand with the rise of a market economy, consumer choice and voluntary associations. In this way the American people got to choose, own and direct their own religious traditions rather than having them established by state law, paid for by compulsory taxation and led by an elite clerical caste. The obvious conclusion is that freely chosen religion is more popular and durable than that which is imposed from above or established by the weight of inherited tradition.[42]

There is an appealing symmetry to these arguments. The phrase 'a free market in religion' has become a powerful and ubiquitous explanatory metaphor for what is distinctive about American religion, so powerful in fact that it is time to introduce some qualifying caveats. In the first place it is important to state that the American founders were much more interested in securing religious liberty than in promoting a religious marketplace. In their conceptions of church and state, they were reacting against European patterns of religious coercion in the past rather than anticipating a new age of religious competition. Second, it is a category error to conflate the choice of consumer items with the 'choice' of a religious tradition. The idea that religious affiliation was a mere consumer preference or a product of 'rational choice' is not one that squares readily with eighteenth-century sources, with their emphases on religious duty, devotion and obedience to the divine will. As far as one can determine, eighteenth-century Americans did not 'choose' a religious affiliation the way they might choose a consumer item (even allowing for category differences), but rather they either followed the religious traditions of their families and localities or they adopted another religious tradition because of a sincere 'truth' conviction that it offered a better temporal and eternal repose for their souls. At present there is too little published research on the degree of church swapping among eighteenth- and early nineteenth-century Americans for us to adopt the 'free market' metaphor with anything like the confidence of its most ardent advocates. Third, even if one were to accept the proposition that American religion was unusually pluralistic by the end of the eighteenth century, and there is considerable evidence from cities such as Charleston, New York and Philadelphia that it was, one needs to be careful not to underestimate the degree of religious pluralism of cities such as London, Manchester and Birmingham in the same period.

Nevertheless, with all caveats in place, and allowing for the accumulation of 'small differences' with which we are concerned, there seems little doubt that by the beginning of the nineteenth century American religion had developed some measurably different characteristics from those in most parts of continental Europe. That is also the case in the relationship between religion and political culture. After the American Revolution, unlike Europe, there was no *ancien régime* to react against, no church lands to secularize and no religious orders to subvert. These structural differences produced less organized anti-clericalism in the United States and more socialistic and social democratic movements in Europe. At critical moments of nation building in the nineteenth century, emancipatory movements in Europe became more secular and more anti-clerical, while in the United States the national project of more democratic politics, more free markets and more voluntary associations seemed perfectly aligned with the kind of religious traditions that emerged in the new republic. Only in countries like Ireland and Poland, where religious identity was strengthened in symbiotic relationship with the national project, namely a fusion of Roman Catholic identity and national resistance to foreign domination, did the national project and religion cohere as closely as they did in the United States, and they too gave rise to surprisingly durable religious traditions.

Another way in to the different secularization trajectories of Europe and the United States is to look at the interaction of elite and popular culture. In Europe since the Enlightenment secular elites have been more influential in shaping culture than American secular elites who have encountered much stronger popular resistance. Part of that has to do with two rather different varieties of Enlightenment discourse which gained traction in the two places. In the United States it was the discourse of liberty, as represented in the American Revolution and constitution-making, which became the most influential, while in Europe, particularly France, it was the ideology of reason and the subjection of dogmatic religion to rational critique that became dominant. Put another way, in the United States it was the Scottish Enlightenment's emphasis on commonsense, especially with regard to the plain reading of the Bible, more than the subversive anti-clericalism of the French Enlightenment, that had the most cultural significance. That is one reason, among many, why in subsequent centuries Europeans were less reluctant to accept the religious implications of evolutionary biology and other scientific modes of thinking than Americans who preferred to rely on a plain, 'commonsense' reading of sacred texts for knowledge of the truth, including scientific truth. Another consequence of the different roles of social elites is that in America a popular religiosity emerged that was less concerned about appearing to be vulgar or unrefined. In fact the opposite prevailed. A cursory look at the pamphlet literature that emerged out of the Second Great Awakening at the start of the nineteenth century reveals something approaching contempt for learned elites, wealthy professionals and clerical careerists. Authenticity was measured more in terms of ardent preaching, undiluted emotion and a plain message for a plain people.

One reason for this contrast in religious style between Europe and America lies in the differential impacts of Evangelical Protestantism in Europe and the United States. Although there are pockets of Evangelical strength in eighteenth- and early nineteenth-century Europe, most notably in parts of England, Wales, the Scottish highlands and the northern part of Ireland, Evangelicalism, with its rhythms of revivalism, grew much more strongly and for longer in the United States. Even Methodism, which origi-nated in England, achieved its most striking growth rates in the United States, and that was also the case for the Baptists and other popular Evan-gelical traditions. It is hard to account for the different cultural style of American religion since the mid-eighteenth century without paying close attention to the enduring strength and cultural mobilization of different varieties of Evangelical Protestantism.[43]

There are still other factors that need to be taken into account to help explain the apparently greater religiosity of the United States that await more serious research. For example, what are the long-term effects of emigration and mobility in sustaining religious cultures? Emigration in different contexts can yield varying results with respect to increasing or diminishing religiosity, but in America the process of integration has worked better than in Europe. Moreover, geographical mobility within the United States also seems to have sustained rather than eroded religious traditions. One area urgently in need of fresh treatment is the impact of fertility rates and generational transmission on religion. For the past two centuries, American fertility rates have been higher than European rates, and, whatever the means of measurement, American women have been shown to be more religious than their European counterparts. In addition, within America religious conservatives of all denominational traditions have long had higher fertility rates than the more liberal mainline denomi-nations. Although fertility rates are affected by a huge number of variables, which are hard to control for (region, poverty, etc.), there is a demonstrated correlation between religion and fertility and between secularization and diminished fertility. The question is how far back in time do these patterns go? Similarly, to what extent were marriages contracted by couples within a shared religious tradition, and is it possible that patterns of generational transmission are stronger in the United States than in Europe for all kinds of cultural reasons? Higher fertility rates among more seriously commit-ted members of religious traditions, and better rates of generational trans-mission among families, would over time make a substantial difference to patterns of secularization in Europe and the United States.[44]

One of the main arguments for secularization in the West is that modernity itself is a secularizing force. Once presumed to be unilinear, irreversible and necessarily secular, modernity with its concomitants of urbanization, privatization and specialization has been traditionally inter-preted as the enemy of religion. According to this model, the United States as a modern technological society should show broadly comparative rates of secularization with other modern societies. But modernity is an elastic and imprecise concept. It may be that there are many different kinds of modernity, and some are less friendly to religion than others. Hence, looking at how the United States seemed to embrace new aspects of modernity in the eighteenth and nineteenth centuries (such as democratic political structures, voluntary religious congregations and technological innovation) without eroding the social salience of religion may be a productive line of enquiry. Certainly lots of nineteenth-century European observers such as Alexis de Tocqueville thought so.

Finally, even the discourse of secularization itself seems to play out differently in Europe and the United States. At least since the eighteenth century European publics and their religious leaders interiorized the meta-narrative of secularization as a story of steady, inexorable religious decline, and have adjusted their sights accordingly. This then becomes a self-fulfilling prophecy. In the American colonies and the United States secularization discourse has often acted as a warning against religious decline or as a catalyst for religious renewal or revival. From Puritanism to the great awakenings, and from Methodism to the rise of holiness and Pentecostal traditions, jeremiads of decline paradoxically have often turned out to be the unlikely agents of religious revival.

In conclusion, the differential trajectories of secularization in Europe and the United States have roots that go back to the eighteenth century and beyond. In the United States the constitutional separation of church and state, the emergence of an exceptional degree of religious pluralism, the role of immigration and religious mobility, the depth of religious penetration into popular culture, the durability of Evangelical Protestantism and the impact of differential fertility rates have all played a part in sustaining a higher degree of measurable religiosity than in most parts of Europe. In addition, the success of the Puritan congregational experiment, as a way of organizing religious life, has proved to be remarkably resilient. The United States is now as much a federation of religious congregations (some 400,000 according to recent estimates) as it is a federation of states. If American religiosity is not as 'exceptional' as some of its interpreters claim, there is no question that in comparison with Europe it is really quite distinctive.

What these 'glimpses of modernity' have shown is that whatever the category one chooses, from science to enlightenment and from the rise of religious toleration to the growth of abolitionism, there is no obvious meta-narrative playing out towards the inevitability of 'progress' even if such a concept could be clearly defined. If history is more than the sum total of contingencies, it is also not a progress narrative. The same holds for religion. Few would doubt that the world is a better place as a result of the growth of scientific knowledge, enlightened thought, religious liberty and slavery abolition, but as this chapter has shown the relationship between Western Christianity and these developments is complex and ambiguous. Christianity was sometimes at war with modernity and sometimes was its midwife. Moreover, as we shall now see, the eighteenth century was as much a century of religious enthusiasm, renewal and revivalism, albeit influenced by the Enlightenment, as it was a century of cold rationalism and proto-secularization.

CHAPTER 5

Renewal and Revival:
Evangelicals and Methodists

The international religious revival in the Protestant world in the eighteenth century, from the Urals in the east to the Appalachians in the west, was probably the most significant event in the history of Protestantism since the Reformation, and was arguably the most important religious development of the eighteenth century. The revival influenced most of the existing Protestant traditions in Europe and North America, gave rise to a major new religious tradition (Methodism and its subsequent holiness and Pentecostal offshoots), refashioned the denominational landscape in the British Isles and the United States, and supplied new urgency to Anglo-American transcultural missions, which helped shape the world order in the nineteenth and twentieth centuries. Perhaps as many as one in three Americans and one in ten people throughout the world now identify with religious traditions than can be traced back directly to the Pietist and Evangelical revivals of the seventeenth and eighteenth centuries. The profound shift in the centre of gravity of world Christianity in the twentieth and twenty-first centuries from the north and west to the south and east has some of its most important roots in the Pietist and Evangelical revivals of the early modern period.

The roots of revival

Although there is almost general agreement about the significance of the Protestant Evangelical Awakening (often called the Evangelical Revival in the British Isles and the Great Awakening in the American colonies), there is less of a consensus about how to account for it. What caused this revival of Evangelical Christianity? What were its roots, when did it emerge and what were its chief characteristics? Who sponsored it, how was it disseminated and how did it affect the people, regions and religious traditions that came under its influence? These deceptively straightforward questions have complex answers, for not only was the Evangelical Awakening international in its scope, but it was also pan-denominational in character and was far from uniform in theology and spirituality. Not surprisingly, therefore, historians disagree vehemently about how to define or describe it, or even about how, when and where it started. What this shows is that of all the kinds of change historians have to deal with, changes in religious style and sensibility are among the hardest to explain.

Perhaps the best place to start is with the important trilogy of books by W.R. Ward, the most distinguished historian of the international revivalism of the eighteenth century, which has revised our understanding of the Evangelical Awakening, temporally, geographically and intellectually.[1] According to him the roots of the religious revivals of the eighteenth century – from Eastern and Central Europe to the middle colonies of America – are to be found in the resistance of confessional minorities in post-Westphalia Europe to the real or perceived threat of assimilation by powerful states and established churches. In the late seventeenth century Protestant morale was at a low ebb. Feeling under threat from the gains of the Catholic Counter Reformation, fearful of popes, Jesuits and Jacobites, nervous of further confessional conflict and persecution, and critical of the dry orthodoxy of their established Protestant churches, pockets of European Protestants developed an enthusiastic piety that, under pressure, had the capacity to erupt into fully fledged revivalism. How this played out in different locations in Central and Northern Europe, the British Isles and the American colonies is a complicated story, but characteristic elements appear again and again. These include an emphasis on heart religion, small groups and the priesthood of all believers; the circulation of Protestant religious classics; the forced relocation of Protestant minorities; the emergence of a revived ministry; the proliferation of children's revivals; and the growth of millennial and apocalyptic speculation about how, when and under what circumstances the Second Coming of Christ would take place. Anxiety was kept alive in Protestant environs by periods of confessional warfare and by well-publicized threats and persecutions such as the fate of the French Huguenots, the execution of Protestant Burghers in Thorn (Poland), the Jacobite rebellions in Britain and, most notorious of all, the forced migration of the Salzburg Protestants in 1731–32. Reformation Protestantism, it seemed, was on the wane, and Roman Catholicism, with all that that meant for those raised on Foxe's *Book of Martyrs* and similar literature, was in the ascendancy. If Pietism thrived on the inadequacies of the magisterial churches of the Protestant Reformation, its close cousin, religious revivalism, thrived on anxiety.

Revivalism in the Habsburg lands of Central Europe was the response of pious minorities who had to achieve quick results or else go under. Often with no time to wait for church renewal, or more likely, with no institutional church to renew, Moravians, Silesians, Bohemians and Salzburgers pioneered new forms of popular Protestantism and through writings and migrations exported them to Western Europe and then to the New World. Class meetings began with Spener in 1670; camp meetings originated with the Swedish army in Silesia in the early eighteenth century; and itinerant preaching developed as a survival strategy for Pietist communities outside the confines of the established Reformed and Lutheran churches. 'Revival had begun among Protestants deprived of their church system,' states Ward, 'and was never promoted for long by church establishments.'[2] All was accompanied by a remarkable increase in hymn writing and by revivals instituted and conducted by children and young people. The money behind the expansion came from the commercial exploitation of medicaments, Bibles and religious literature, and from the availability of Dutch credit at low rates of interest. In this way revivalism flourished outside the purview of well-established systems, whether of church, state or trade.

Taken as a whole, Ward's work has had the effect of directing attention towards the European origins of the Protestant Evangelical Revival to complement the better-known emphases on the Anglo-American part of the story. It also invites us to look for origins further back chronologically, at least to the late seventeenth century, rather than to the 1730s, the conventional date for the beginning of the Evangelical Revival, which is also the decade of the well-known religious conversions of Howell Harris (1714–73), George Whitefield (1714–70) and Charles (1707–78) and John Wesley (1703–91). Part of that looking back is investigating the intellectual culture within which Evangelicalism arose, and to ask if there was an Evangelical identity which supplied cohesion to all the major strands of early Evangelicalism, from Halle to Northampton, Massachusetts, with all the many stops in between. Early Evangelicals, though sometimes bitterly divided over both belief and practice, nevertheless constructed a global fraternity around a number of important themes.

> These themes – the close association with mysticism, the small-group religion, the deferred eschatology, the experimental approach to conversion, anti-Aristotelianism and hostility to theological system, and the attempt to reinforce religious vitality by setting it in the context of a vitalist understanding of nature ... formed a sort of evangelical hexagon lasting until the original evangelical cohesion began to fail.[3]

It is worth pausing a while over this hexagon of Evangelical characteristics, for they are rather different from the features that came to dominate the established Anglo-American Evangelicalism of the later nineteenth century, with which many are more familiar, including biblical infallibility and inerrancy, dispensational pre-millennialism, propositional belief-systems of all kinds and bureaucratic denominationalism. These features were not there, at least not in fully formed ways, at the start. Instead, in the early days of the Evangelical movement the idea of a deferred Second Coming, before which there would be an opportunity to prepare a harvest for the returning Christ, and the linked emphases on mysticism, vitalism, experiential conversion and small-group religion, supplied Evangelical-ism with an optimistic message that had an appeal both to individuals and communities. A religious faith that could offer individual assurance and communal self-discipline beyond the immediate controls of confessional states and churches had obvious appeal to populations made insecure by religious and political conflict.

Hence, one place to look for the roots of the Protestant Evangelical Awakening of the eighteenth century is among European Pietists, chiefly but not exclusively Lutheran, who were reacting against a dry scholastic orthodoxy represented by systematic theologies, church confessions and ecclesiastical bureaucracies. In important ways the new Pietist turn was also a product of the enduring tensions between the magisterial Reforma-tion, which gave rise to Protestant established churches, and the radical Reformation, which took root in more marginalized Protestant communi-ties. Hence, the rise of Pietism may be regarded in part as 'the rebirth of the radical tradition, and it gave rise to a transformation of Protestant culture that reached from Germany, Silesia, and Sweden to the woodlands of the Delaware Valley'.[4] In that sense, the rise of Pietism and Evangelicalism marked the beginning of the end of the confessional age of the magisterial Reformation, and may be regarded as a second stage in the history of Prot-estantism. Radicalized by anxiety produced by war, confessional cleansing and forced migration, sustained by an emphasis on heart religion, religious experience and the priesthood of all believers, and pragmatically equipped for expansion through its emphasis on conversion, mission, cell groups, camp meetings and itinerant preaching, European Pietism is undoubtedly one of the most significant of the root systems of the Evangelical awaken-ings. But it is not the only one.

Another root system can be located among the international networks of Reformed/Calvinist communities across the transatlantic world dating back to the geographical dispersion of the first generation of Reformed Protestants in the sixteenth century.[5] These include English Puritans, many of whom migrated to New England, English Nonconformists, Scottish and Irish Presbyterians, who also migrated across the Atlantic in substantial numbers, and French and Dutch Calvinists. Here was a rich intellectual and devotional tradition that produced some of the most important writings influencing the Evangelicals of the eighteenth century. These included the works of Joseph Alleine (1634–68), Thomas Boston (1676–1732), Richard Baxter (1615–1691) and, most famously, John Bunyan (1628–88), whose *Grace Abounding to the Chief of Sinners* (1666) and *The Pilgrim's Progress* (1678–84) became widely circulating classics of Protestant spirituality. This transatlantic community, which included religious leaders in the American colonies such as Cotton Mather (1663–1728), William Tennent (1673–1746) and Jonathan Edwards (1703–58), had an existing network of circulating literature long before George Whitefield's preaching tours converted it into a vibrantly connected network in the early years of the Evangelical awakenings in the 1730s and 1740s. Given this trajectory of Reformed influence over Evangelicalism stretching deep into the seventeenth and even sixteenth century, it is not surprising that most historians writing out of that tradition *play down* the discontinuity and novelty of the Protestant Evangelical Awakening of the 1730s, while most historians coming out of the Methodist and Arminian wings of the revival, which after all gave rise to a brand-new religious movement, *play up* the novelty of the revival.[6]

Another of the root systems of the revival can be located deep within the Church of England. After all, three of the revival's most important leaders, Whitefield and the Wesley brothers, were ordained Anglicans, and many more rural clergymen who kept their distance from Methodism experienced Evangelical conversions in 'unassisted solitude'. As observers were well aware of at the time, when the 'revival arrived, it came, paradoxically, not among the Calvinist dissenters, who had corresponded about it, published treatises about it, and prayed for it, but in an Arminian Church of England in which the old Puritan Calvinism was virtually extinct, and the prejudice against spirit-filled "enthusiasm" almost an obsession'.[7] How did this happen? Once again, anxiety and uncertainty seem to be dominant themes as the Church of England faced up to a disturbing array of intellectual, political, social and structural problems. Intellectually, the Church was rocked by the emergence of deism, which emphasized rationalism and natural religion at the expense of supernaturalism and revelation. Deism was not only deeply ensconced in the Anglican quadrangles of the University of Oxford (Matthew Tindall was a Fellow of All Souls College), but also had become widely disseminated in common rooms, salons, coffee houses and inns. Politically, the Church had been shaken by numerous crises since the Glorious Revolution of 1688–89 and found itself by the 1720s and 1730s profoundly enmeshed in Walpolean patronage networks which threatened to make the Church a mere instrument of state policy at best, and an acquiescent vehicle for the Whig Party at worst. Many Anglican Tories in the English counties were seriously disaffected, and some of them (known as Jacobites) even flirted with a Stuart restoration. Socially, the period is full of jeremiad prognostications about the state of the country and its descent into debauchery, profligacy, drunkenness and vice of all kinds. Here was the world of Hogarth prints with all its low-life frivolity and immorality. Moreover, some parts of the country were experiencing the first fruits of what economic historians call proto-industrialization, as the rise of extractive industries and small workshops seemed to create wild new populations of displaced workers (such as the Kingswood colliers) way beyond the traditional influence of squires and parsons. Structurally, the Church of England's instruments of influence and control were weakening. Convocation did not meet after 1717, church courts were in decline, religious conformity was harder to enforce after the Toleration Act of 1689, anti-clericalism seemed to be on the rise and the Church still seemed deeply mired in the ideological struggles surrounding the legitimacy of the Hanoverian dynasty and its Jacobite opposition.

With this background in mind, it is easy to see how churchmen schooled in the old disciplines of High Church spirituality were facing an existential crisis of serious proportions and how some were attracted to forms of spirituality rooted in experience and assurance. Here in a nutshell is the trajectory of the Wesley family, and of many others, who found in a Moravian-inflected Evangelicalism a religion of joy and assurance in the midst of pessimism and asceticism. As John Walsh has it, the 'reintroduction of the Reformation doctrine of Justification by faith alone, not merely as a credal proposition but as an experiential reality, set the revival in motion', and once in motion what turned it into a global missionary movement was 'the crucial determination of Wesley and Whitefield to launch into itinerancy, making the world their parish and not the parish their world'.[8] Religious experience and religious mobility together helped fan the fires of revival.

While the strongest root systems of the Evangelical Awakening can be located among international networks of serious-minded Calvinists, continental European Pietists unhappy with Lutheran scholasticism, and English High Churchmen concerned about the state of their church and nation, there are many others that added strength and diversity to the revival. Also important are traditions emanating from the old Scots-Irish Presbyterian communion revivals, or Holy Fairs, and the growth of Welsh Evangelicalism, which is often dated as having begun with the Evangelical conversions of Daniel Rowland (1713–90), curate of Llangeitho, Cardiganshire, and Howell Harris, an Anglican layman, in the spring of 1735. But at least as important in the rise of Welsh Evangelicalism is the remarkable network of Welsh schools established by Griffith Jones (1684–1761), who by the time of his death had established some 3,325 schools teaching people in Welsh how to read their Bible, Catechism and Prayer Book.[9] Indeed the commitment of the established churches in continental Europe and the British Isles to the dissemination of basic Christian knowledge through the ubiquitous catechisms, prayer books, metrical psalms and hosts of other devices helped lay the basic foundations upon which revivalists could later capitalize.[10] There would have been no Evangelical Revival without pre-existing strands of penitential Christianity nurtured by widespread cate-chizing and religious instruction. Evangelicals often criticized the spiritual and pastoral inadequacy of established churches in the eighteenth century, but they were partly the beneficiaries of their admittedly uneven attempts to spread rudimentary Christian knowledge, parish by parish.

As this brief attempt to dig up the root systems of the Evangelical Awakening has shown, the international revival of the eighteenth century had multiple and diverse origins. To what extent then is it possible to speak of the international revival beginning strongly in the 1730s as a unitary movement? In that decade, to highlight just a fraction of what was going on, Samuel Lutz (1674–1750) preached revival to the Reformed communities of the Bernese Oberland; the eccentric Lusatian Count Nikolaus Ludwig von Zinzendorf (1700–60) sent out the first Moravian missionaries to the Danish West Indies (1732); the Wesley brothers met up with Moravian migrants in the colony of Georgia (1736), thereby completing a religious triangle linking European Pietism, High Church Anglicanism and the American colonies; Howell Harris, Daniel Rowland, George Whitefield, Charles Wesley and John Wesley all experienced Evangelical conversions and began vibrant preaching ministries throughout the British Isles, and in Whitefield's case, colonial North America; Jonathan Edwards presided over a religious awakening in his church in Northampton, Massachusetts, and the Connecticut Valley (1734–35) and then published his famous account of it as *A Faithful Narrative of the Surprising Work of God* (1737), which became a widely circulating and influential testimony to the power of religious revivalism; and in the Netherlands in 1740 Willem Schortinghuis (1700–50) published his *Christianity Resting on Inward Experience* which became a clarion call for the revivalistic preaching of many Dutch pastors.

Though geographically disparate and denominationally diverse, the early Evangelicals, through transatlantic publishing networks, fraternal correspondence, personal encounters with one another, population migrations and extraordinarily mobile preachers, thought of themselves as a distinct and connected movement of the Spirit in their time.[11] There was a vast array of circulating literature that wafted around the international great awakening.[12] Letters, devotionals, journals, periodicals and prophetical squibs were ubiquitous, and the sheer scale of the enterprise was remarkable. The Pietist leader August Hermann Francke (1663–1727) had about 5,000 correspondents, and was in constant touch with 300–400. Similarly, in the new Abingdon edition of John Wesley's letters there are about 3,500 surviving letters by him and another 1,300 letters to him, while it is also possible to document a further 10,000 letters which passed between him and some 1,600 correspondents.[13] Some less well-known figures were equally prolific. The Baptist laywoman Anne Dutton (1692–1765) is reputed to have published some 25 volumes of letters during her own lifetime.[14] A veritable industry of Evangelical letter writing helped transform the form and function of the eighteenth-century letter, resulting in a more personal, more familiar and more spiritually directive genre. If one wanted to search for the essence of Evangelical spirituality in the eighteenth century, the ubiquitous letter, which can stand as a metaphor for sending and receiving, and experience and telling, is probably as good a place as any to start.[15]

In addition to the army of Evangelical correspondents, both the Moravians and the Methodists gathered frequently for 'letter days' on which letters were read aloud about the progress of religious revivals. The aim was to spread news, stimulate prayer and persuade the faithful that they were part of a worldwide movement of grace transforming the world in their own lifetimes. Not only were letters and print circulating at remarkable speed, but also revival groups borrowed from one another's liturgical forms, organizational structures and disciplining techniques. In short, the revived saw themselves as an expanding, communicating and connecting movement not confined to a particular locale or country. It is of course wise not to sugar coat this too much. These early Evangelicals were also sturdy individualists and were not without egos or disagreements. There were fierce fights between Calvinists and Arminians, between Moravian Quietists and Methodist activists, between Anglicans and dissenters, between Ulster-Scots Presbyterians and the rest, between those who believed in 'entire sanctification' (perfectionism) and those who thought it damnably heretical, and even between the Wesley brothers themselves on how new Methodism should relate to old Anglicanism.

In short, the Protestant Evangelical Awakening was an international and eclectic affair within which representatives of diverse, revived traditions were brought into cathartic contact with one another, either personally or through print, in unlikely places in both the Old and the New World. Although that explanatory framework is helpful, the nagging question remains why the 'religion of the heart' in the eighteenth century should have attracted such a diverse range of people from the Jansenists of Port Royal to the Old Believers in Russia, and from Hasidic Jews to English-speaking Evangelicals. How much of this can be explained by an appeal to the *Zeitgeist*, however that is to be formulated, and how much depends upon historical contingencies and demonstrable personal influences is a question without a clear answer. One of the most intriguing aspects of the international awakening, however, is that it was largely a generational movement of young people. Although influenced by an older generation, it was the young who spread Evangelicalism. Moreover, although the well-known leaders of the Evangelical Revival, with the possible exception of the Countess of Huntingdon (1707–91) and a sprinkling of Methodist women preachers, were male, most surveys have shown that the majority of the rank-and-file was female. There was also a powerful tradition of female prophets in both Pietism and in the environs of early Evangelicalism. One does not have to burrow very deeply into the archives of Evangelical awakenings to detect the ubiquitous influence of 'pious women' over siblings, husbands, children, parents and friends. Female piety was the lubricant of revival.

In summary, the roots of the Protestant Evangelical Awakening are to be found among continental European Pietists, networks of Reformed churches and communities, Anglican High Churchmen and pockets of religious enthusiasm in the Celtic fringes of the British state (in Wales, Scotland and Ireland). What brought a measure of cohesion to these disparate movements was a shared anxiety about the state of religion and society in their respective locations and a set of connections based upon circulating print and correspondence, personal connections and population migrations. Connecting tissue was also supplied by a renewed and experiential emphasis on the Reformation doctrine of justification by grace through faith (the New Birth), female piety, anti-Catholicism, millennialism and youthful energy. Once under way, a domino effect helped persuade Protestant populations across the north Atlantic region that they were experiencing a powerful visitation of the Spirit in their times. That was the message brought to them by a remarkable array of preachers and revivalists who plied their trade along the developing communication routes of the eighteenth century.

Dramatis personae

Who, then, were the most important leaders of the Protestant Evangelical Awakening as it emerged in the 1730s, and what was their most distinctive contribution to the Evangelical tradition? Working chronologically from the date of their entrance on to the stage, pride of place should go to the enigmatic Count Zinzendorf (1700–60). As the godson of Spener, a student at Francke's Halle, the aristocratic patron of the hugely influential Moravian settlement at Herrnhut on his Berthelsdorf estate, the driving force behind the rise of Moravian missions, and as a relentless Evangelical networker, Zinzendorf was an important bridge between the late seventeenth-century Pietists and the eighteenth-century revivalists. In particular, he had a decisive impact on John Wesley's religious development, both positively through the events surrounding Wesley's spiritual awakening and in the allure of Moravian communal life, and negatively as a result of the controversy that led to their parting of ways. What Zinzendorf most contributed to the Evangelical tradition was his radical ecumenicity (the children of God are one in Christ across all ethnic, national and denominational boundaries), his emphasis on the creation of living communities of revived Christians (the exportable Moravian paradigm of communal Christianity which so intrigued early Evangelicals), his exuberant and sometimes very strange Christocentrism (including the infamous 'blood and wounds' theology that absorbed Moravians in the 1740s), his distrust of scholarship and theological systems (as opposed to religious experience and the religion of the heart), and his repudiation of the rationalism of the early Enlightenment. So vast and eclectic are Zinzendorf's writings, and so colourful are some of the episodes of his life and thought, that he has been a subject of interest for students of Freud on the one hand, and for a distinguished array of twentieth-century theologians including Karl Barth, Jürgen Moltmann and Friedrich Schleiermacher on the other. Perhaps even more important is the way in which Zinzendorf's Moravian communities modelled important ecclesiastical innovations, such as love feasts, yearly prayer cycles, ritual foot-washing and celebratory music. From new liturgies to the casting of lots for decisions, and from a renewed affirmation of human sexuality to the raising of money in capital markets, there is much in Zinzendorf that intrigued, inspired and infuriated his Evangelical contemporaries and their successors.[16]

Jonathan Edwards (1703–58) was an exact contemporary of Zinzendorf. Both were the products of fading aristocracies, one landed and the other ministerial, both made vital contributions to the rise of Christian missions, both nurtured revived Christian communities and both were indebted to the heart religion of Pietism. But their characters and contributions to the Evangelical Awakening could hardly have been more different. Whereas Zinzendorf's inheritance line runs through the Austrian Protestant nobility and Lutheran Pietism, Edwards's line runs through Calvinism, English Puritanism and American Congregationalism. Edwards, as the grandson of Solomon Stoddard (1643–1728), was in the bloodline of one of New England's greatest clerical dynasties, and through his parents had close connections with the Mathers, another powerful clerical dynasty. Edwards was a pious and precocious youth who underwent one of those intense and protracted Puritan conversions while a student at Yale. But his connection to the Evangelical Awakening really starts with his pastorate in North-ampton, Massachusetts. Although congregational revivals were neither new to New England nor to Northampton prior to the 1730s, an unusually intense revival broke out in Northampton in 1734–35. The catalyst seems to have been growing tensions within Congregational belief and prac-tice, an economically unsettled youth culture, psychological anxiety in the community produced by a premature death, Edwards's affective preaching and the growth of small group meetings of young people characterized by spiritual intensity. Perhaps even more significant than the congregational revival that swept over Northampton in the spring of 1735 was Edwards's decision to publish an account of it. His *Faithful Narrative of the Surprising Work of God* was published in Europe and America and had a major influ-ence on English Methodists and Scottish Presbyterians. Revealingly, John Wesley later edited a version of it for his Methodist followers, albeit with the offending Calvinist language carefully edited out.

Although the Northampton revival, as with many before and since, petered out as quickly as it arrived, Edwards, through the *Faithful Narra-tive* and also through his close association with George Whitefield's colo-nial preaching tour, became a major figure in the early awakening. His most famous sermon 'Sinners in the Hands of an Angry God', preached in Enfield, Connecticut, in 1741 produced the kind of frightening and ecstatic phenomena that came to be sought after by exponents of revival and repu-diated as the grossest enthusiasm by its opponents. Edwards was, however, too cerebral and had too much integrity to become an uncritical peddler of religious enthusiasm, some of which unsettled him as much as it shocked its critics. His most enduring contribution to the Evangelical tradition came in the form of his brilliant contributions to philosophical theology. His overarching appeal to divine sovereignty, his aesthetic of nature, his work on religious affections and his resistance to the secularizing dynam-ics of Enlightenment thought have been appropriated by Evangelicals, especially Reformed Evangelicals, right down to the present. In terms of his significance for eighteenth-century America, Marsden has concluded that Edwards was 'a towering figure among the founding fathers of the first American revolution, the spiritual revolution of the awakening', which preceded political revolution by almost half a century. Perhaps the most important result of the Great Awakening in the American colonies for the future direction of American Christianity is the fact that 'the most vigorous of American churches were built on a popular voluntary principle, rather than on state control or inherited authority'.[17] Several centuries later, that still remains the case.

In the autumn of 1740 Jonathan Edwards was paid a visit to his home in

Northampton by the rising young star of the Evangelical Revival George Whitefield (1714–70), whose remarkable preaching tour of the American colonies in 1739–40, reported assiduously by Benjamin Franklin (1706–90), is one of the great religious events of the eighteenth century. Whitefield, an ordained Anglican, had been associated with the Wesley brothers in the Oxford Holy Club, but his Evangelical conversion preceded theirs, and he had already created something of a sensation by preaching to large outdoor crowds in London and Bristol before his second visit to the American colonies in 1739. Whitefield's grand tour of the American colonies was noteworthy for the ground he covered (from Savannah to Boston), the number of sermons he preached (averaging two to three a day), the size of the crowds he attracted (many thousands), the number of colonial religious leaders he influenced, the publicity he generated, the correspondence he sustained, and, above all, for the remarkable proportion of the colonial population he reached. Whitefield, as even those who disagreed with him conceded, was a preaching sensation. A combination of voice, gesture, dramatic training and profoundly affective content had audiences hanging on his every word.

While Whitefield was a preaching phenomenon, he was more than that. In a remarkable way he joined up the great coastal cities of the transatlantic world in the eighteenth century (London, Bristol, Glasgow, Philadelphia, New York and Boston), and he both exploited and revived the networks of Reformed Protestants whose Calvinistic theology he shared. He has been variously portrayed as a consummate religious salesman in the age of the consumer revolution, as a pioneer in taking religion out into the public sphere, as a theatrical genius who paid close attention to the techniques of audience manipulation and as an American cultural hero, 'the first in a long line of celebrities who through the sheer force of personality compelled the attention – and adoration – of an emerging nation'.[18] Whitefield's career is also replete with irony and unintended consequences. An ordained Anglican, he offended Anglican sensibilities in the American colonies and had his greatest success among Congregationalists, Presbyterians and dissenters. As someone ordained to parish ministry, he probably did more than anyone to erode the parochial foundations of early modern Christendom and supplied a major boost to voluntaristic, associational and para-church religion. Largely non-political in orientation, his style, rhetoric and influence are regarded by many historians as important preconditions for the American Revolution. A Calvinist with a strong belief in divine sovereignty and predestination, he preached the general invitation of the Gospel more directly than most Arminians. A willing preacher to slaves, and an earnest critic of the cruelties of American slavery, he became a slave-owner himself and put his to work in his Georgia orphanage.

The Bethesda orphanage later became the focal point of a bitter controversy between Whitefield and the Archbishop of Canterbury, Thomas
Secker (1693–1768), when Whitefield proposed to establish a college for
preachers on the same site. Sensing that the Great Awakening boded ill
for the future discipline and control of the Anglican Church, Secker was
determined that the proposed college should have an Anglican head, an
Anglican liturgy and no extempore prayers. Clearly he wanted neither
Evangelical Methodists nor dissenters to be the beneficiaries. Moreover,
Secker used his superior connections in the corridors of power in London
to outmanoeuvre Whitefield, who was forced to withdraw his proposal.
Whitefield then published the addled correspondence between himself and
Secker, which was reprinted in many of the American colonial newspapers
as yet another example of the crude exercise of British arbitrary power over
the beleaguered colonies. As a result, the Bethesda affair was an almost
perfect religious symbol for the growing conflict between Britain and her
American colonies, and helped radicalize the colonies by building a bridge
between Calvinist theology and republican ideology. Hence the curious
dynamics of the Evangelical Revival set one Anglican priest against his
archbishop, and in the process helped undermine the Anglican foundations
and political control of the American colonies of the British Empire.[19]

If George Whitefield's Calvinistic Methodism represents one pole of
the rise of Methodism, Charles Wesley's Arminian version is another.
Charles Wesley, so often overshadowed by his older brother John, is slowly
being rehabilitated as a more important figure in the rise of English Methodism than was once thought. In terms of churchmanship, he was the more
conservative of the two, often speaking up at critical moments to protest
against his brother's radical departure from the established practices of the
Church of England, from which he had no desire to separate. In terms of
personality, Charles was the more agreeable of the two. Unlike John, Charles
was a loving husband and father, which also had the effect of abbreviating
his career as an itinerant preacher. He was subject to greater mood swings
and could sink into melancholia, but he was also less prickly and autocratic.
He was more private and less egocentric than his brother, and less eager
to bask in the limelight. Charles also had a superior capacity for friendship, including a tender relationship with George Whitefield, with whom
he also disagreed vehemently over the theological issues of predestination
and perfection. As a man overshadowed by the sheer force of his brother's
personality, Charles has suffered from the neglect of those seduced by John
Wesley's self-propaganda, but that is a mistake. Charles Wesley was a brilliant religious poet, lyricist and hymn writer, who supplied in one biog-
rapher's words the 'soundtrack' of the Methodist revival.[20] It is estimated

that he composed some 9,000 hymns and sacred poems, some of which are classics of devotional literature while most others are undistinguished and easily forgettable. But wherever the hymn-singing tradition of Christianity survives, regardless of denomination, Charles Wesley's best-known hymns will continue to be sung. These include 'Love Divine, All Loves Excelling', 'And Can it be that I Should Gain?', 'O for a Thousand Tongues to Sing', 'Come, Thou Long-Expected Jesus', 'Christ the Lord is Risen Today' and 'Rejoice, the Lord is King'. The tercentenary of Charles Wesley's birth, which was celebrated in 2007, has brought forth a veritable industry of new publications and reassessments – and not before time. As the co-founder of Methodism, as the first of the brothers to experience an Evangelical conversion and as a much more significant figure in the formation of the Methodist movement than historians have recognized, Charles Wesley's importance to the Evangelical Revival should not be underestimated.

John Wesley and his younger brother Charles inherited a family tradition with deep roots in both Puritanism and High Church Anglicanism, grew up in a family where the strongest influences were female, and lived in a household poised uneasily between gentlemanly privileges and incipient poverty. These assorted shapers and tensions deeply affected John Wesley's life in his various capacities as son and brother, Anglican priest, itinerant evangelist, Methodist founder, authoritarian leader, unsuccessful husband, prickly controversialist, energetic educator, facilitator of female leadership and relentless activist and disciplinarian.[21] Of all the early leaders of the Evangelical Revival, John Wesley is the hardest to get a handle on. Paradoxes and ambiguities are everywhere, as even the titles of his many biographies make clear. He had brilliant organizational skills, but scarcely a single aspect of Methodism's organization was invented by him. He believed firmly in Original Sin, but was relentlessly critical of gloomy religion. He could raise himself to anti-Catholic vituperation but also to devotion inspired by Roman saints. His roots were deep within the Anglican High Church tradition, but as a priest he scandalously performed his own ordinations and repeatedly evaded Church discipline. He held a high Protestant doctrine of grace but married it to a stern Catholic insistence on holiness. He was obsessive about neatness, thrift and redeeming the time, but did not blame the poor for idleness or lethargy. He seems to some to be a gullible supernaturalist and counter-Enlightenment figure, and to others to be a devotee of the empiricism of Locke and Newton. To some, his theological ideas, including Christian perfection, are a hopeless mixture of inconsistency and incoherence, while others see him as a great folk theologian who preached a plain message for plain people.[22]

Whatever the nature of the disagreements about how to interpret

Wesley and his influence, one cannot deny that he founded one of the most dynamic movements in the history of Christianity. His ecclesiastical pragmatism and unquenchable energy, his determination to spread 'scriptural holiness' wherever he could reach, his remarkable capacity to bridge the gap between the elite culture of his educational background and the popular culture of the English poor, his deep concern for those beyond the gaze of church and state, and his relentless capacity to exhort, examine, expound and experiment all mark him out as a remarkable figure, a kind of Ignatius Loyola of the Protestant tradition. What then of the Methodist tradition he founded and moulded for over 50 years?

The rise of Methodism

By the end of the eighteenth century there were around 100,000 members of Methodist societies in Great Britain, around 20,000 in Ireland and about 65,000 in the United States. Half a century later there were over half a million Methodist members in Britain and well over a million in the United States. By then Methodism was the largest non-Anglican religious tradition in Britain and the largest religious denomination in the United States. By the beginning of the twentieth century there were just under 10 million Methodist church members spread over six continents. Given that historians conventionally multiply Methodist membership figures (the more deeply committed) by a multiple of at least three to estimate the numbers of worshippers coming under regular Methodist ministry, one can see that a formidable religious revolution had emerged out of the desultory Methodist societies formed in the 1730s and 1740s. What drove this expansion, and what were the chief characteristics of the Methodist movement?

Early Methodist expansion was spotty, eclectic and messy. Wesley's much vaunted genius for organization turns out upon closer inspection to have been a ragbag of pragmatic innovations borrowed from Moravians, Quakers and others, or suggested to him by other free market itinerant evangelists, most of whom he later fought with.[23] As research moves forward on Wesley's early contemporaries such as John Bennet (1714–59), Benjamin Ingham (1712–72) and David Taylor, it becomes clearer that Wesley was not the lonesome genius of Methodist legend. He often reaped where others had sown and borrowed ideas others had generated. What gave him his preponderance were energy, mobility, perseverance and sheer force of will. What gave Methodism its preponderance over many other evangelistic associations was its ability to bestow an element of organizational coherence and order on the disparate and sometimes bizarre religiosity it encountered. The surviving diaries of Methodist leaders in the 1740s reveal passionate attempts to impose a degree of religious discipline amid the psychological disturbance, sexual repression, millennial speculation and immediate prov-identialism that wafted around early Methodist spirituality. Both men and women felt anxiety, shed tears, prayed fervently, saw visions, encountered scoffers and slowly bowed the knee to Wesley's iron will and charismatic leadership. Bands and classes, hymns and love feasts, and rules and disci-pline supplied the requisite structures and rituals for reconstituted lives. In short, Methodism evolved with a theology and a structure that enabled it to meet the essential demands of individual assurance and communal disci-pline in a world order on the brink of very substantial changes. Put another way, Methodism survived as the fittest of the various brands of Evangelical piety on offer in the first half of the eighteenth century. The scale and scope of its future growth, however, depended largely on how well it would fit in with other major changes in the eighteenth century.

The changes from which Methodism stood to gain, or lose, show up in the standard histories of the later eighteenth century. They include rapid demographic expansion; population mobility, whether compulsory or voluntary, especially to the New World; the emergence of proto-industrial-ization, industrialization and social class; the rise of domestic and interna-tional markets; the growth of consumerism; the spread of the British Empire and of Anglicanism; the beginnings of revolutionary political movements; and the transplanting of old European religious conflicts into new soil in different parts of the world. These relatively concrete changes, which can be counted and reproduced in maps and graphs, were accompanied by less utilitarian but equally important changes in thought and culture. How did Methodism relate to these wider changes in the world order? In particular, what was the Methodist message, how was it transmitted and how was it heard and appropriated among the diverse transatlantic populations of the eighteenth century? One problem in getting to the heart of the Methodist message arises from the fact that Methodism was largely an oral movement, but its history has been constructed mostly from written sources. Of course sermons were printed, hymn books published, denominational magazines distributed and letters exchanged, but the living voices of an oral culture are not easily extracted from such materials. Moreover, religious insiders and outsiders heard noise differently. The phrase 'all nonsense and noise' was a favourite of critics of Methodist revival meetings, but for those enraptured attendees at love feasts or camp meetings there was nothing nonsensical about the noise. Itinerants preached the message of salvation, exhorters exhorted, class members confessed, hymns were sung, prayers were spoken, testimonies were offered and revival meetings throbbed with exclamatory noise.

If Methodism was a noisy and enthusiastic movement, it also had a distinctive spirituality based upon its remorseless emphasis on Scriptural holiness and on the need for human beings to take control of their spiritual destinies, not as passive respondents to the iron will of God but as active agents in working out one's own salvation, or what one scholar has aptly called 'responsible grace'.[24] The whole ecclesiastical superstructure of Methodism, its itinerant and local preachers, its bands and classes, its love feasts and camp meetings and its hymns and publications were all designed to promote Scriptural holiness and guard against laxity or levity. The activism and agency explicit in the message were explicit also in the mediums of transmission. Methodism was restless and energetic, introspective and expansionist, emotional and earnest. It was an unsettling movement led by unsettled people. But how was it appropriated? How did the populations of the north Atlantic world in the eighteenth and nineteenth centuries consume it?

In my recent book on Methodism's *Empire of the Spirit* I suggested that one way of capturing Methodism's essence is to construct two trinities, the first dealing with birth, life and death within the Methodist movement and the second dealing with hymns, sermons and meetings as means of transmission.[25] Birth, life and death, or, to Methodize these natural processes, conversion, sanctification and holy dying, were at the heart of Methodist spirituality. The preaching careers of most early Methodist itinerant and local preachers, as with the spiritual lives of most members of Methodist societies, began with keenly remembered conversion experiences. Indeed, the conversion narrative is a common Methodist genre in which is stressed the drama of the second birth as a means of escaping a world of sin and licentiousness and of entering a world of faith and godly discipline. Conversion was accompanied by an awareness of sensible experience, a desire for assurance, a quest for a subsequent blessing of entire sanctification, a fear of backsliding and a desire to become a useful instrument of God's grace in the world. Out of the drama of Methodist conversion experiences comes the remarkable energy of the movement. Whether regarded as the products of social anomie, psychosexual repression, economic dislocation or religious fervour (by no means exclusive categories), no history of Methodist expansion can afford to ignore them. Usually conversion came early, in the teenage years, and was often vivid and somewhat frightening. The subsequent struggle for entire sanctification (freedom from wilful sinning) was usually protracted and rarely resulted in the perfect peace that was unrealistically anticipated. Close experiences of suffering or death persuaded the believer of the transience of earthly life and the vanity of its fleeting pleasures. Converted Methodists were reinforced in their faith and kept on track by bands, classes, sermons, love feasts and camp meetings.

If conversion started the Methodist pilgrimage, and the pursuit of entire sanctification moved it along, death was its consummation. Much insight into the distinctive nature of Methodist spirituality can be gleaned from the attitudes to death portrayed in Methodist print and in the recorded experience of individual Methodists. The approach of death, that twilight zone between life and eternity, was the final testing point of Methodist spirituality. To die a good and holy death, free from anguish and uncertainty, was the aspiration placed before the Methodist faithful in the pages of the *Arminian Magazine*, a periodical read by as many as 100,000 people by the end of the eighteenth century. Like conversion narratives, accounts of deathbed scenes have a defined pattern and increasingly moved from edited description to even more edited prescription over the years. As with conversion narratives, the experience of death is recounted in language replete with metaphors, this time of slumber, surrender, flight, departure and rest in the arms of Jesus. Also present is resistance to Satan and his evil legions. In death evil is resisted and defeated, eternity is welcomed and embraced. Women, as well as men, had their experiences recounted, but for them metaphors of a heavenly embrace were more common than the surrender of the will in men. Children also had their stories told in pious laments, as the testimony of pious infants facing death was thought to have particular power of emotional persuasion. The deathbed scenes of the Methodist faithful popularized through print were melodramatic, ritualistic and paradigmatic. Above all they were meant to show to the immediate family, the wider Methodist community and thousands of readers that the faith of the Methodists worked unto death itself. Here were stories of earthly renunciation and heavenly anticipation in which lives well spent in disciplined holiness were given the ultimate reward of triumphant glory.

How then was this message of conversion, sanctification and holy dying transmitted to others? It has long been recognized that the most distinctive, characteristic and ubiquitous feature of the Methodist message, indeed of the entire Methodist revival, was its transmission by means of hymns and hymn-singing. If one were to choose one single artefact of Methodism to preserve in a time capsule for posterity as somehow capturing its essence for future generations, perhaps the most defensible choice would be the 1780 *Collection of Hymns for the Use of the People called Methodists*. For a movement that attracted far more literary abuse than praise, the *Collection of Hymns* has commanded almost universal admiration. It has been described as 'a work of supreme devotional art by a religious genius', 'a liturgical miracle', 'a Methodist manifesto ... a splendid summary of Methodist devotion' and as a beautiful piece of 'lyrical theology'.[26]

John Wesley was an inveterate collector and publisher of hymns begin-

ning with *A Collection of Psalms and Hymns*, published in 1737 for the use of
the infant colony in Georgia. Wesley had been influenced by his mother's
psalm-singing, his father's parish choir, the hymns of Isaac Watts and the
Moravians' *Singstunde* (singing hour). Over the next 50 years the Wesley
brothers issued some 30 hymn books: some with tunes, some without; some
intended for special occasions, some for more general consumption; and
some intended for all 'real Christians', some only for Methodists. John was
the selector, organizer, editor and publisher; Charles was the prolific poet,
writer and lyricist. The point is that well before the 1780 *Collection of Hymns*
Methodism was a movement distinguished by its devotion to sacred songs.
Why was there such a mania for singing? What was sung? Where were
hymns sung and by whom? How were they sung and what effects did they
have on the singers?

The 1780 *Collection of Hymns* offers a way into these questions. John
Wesley's preface is instructive. After carefully delineating the market
objectives for the new volume ('a collection neither too large, that it may
be cheap and portable, nor too small, that it may contain a sufficient variety for all ordinary occasions'), Wesley stated that the volume contained
'all the important truths of our most holy religion, whether speculative or
practical; yea to illustrate them all, and to prove them both by Scripture
and reason. And this is done in a regular order. The hymns are not care-
lessly jumbled together, but carefully ranged under proper heads according
to the experience of real Christians. So that this book is in effect a little
body of experimental and practical divinity.' [27] In Wesley's words poetry
was to be 'the handmaid of piety' in quickening devotion, confirming faith,
enlivening hope and kindling or increasing the Christian's love of God and
humankind.

As the contents page shows, Wesley was correct to state that the volume
was not casually organized. Part one was an exhortation to return to God by
describing the pleasantness of religion, the goodness of God, death, judgement, heaven and hell. Although the last four sections seem superficially
morose and threatening, many of these hymns strike more of a wooing than
a threatening note. The dominant themes are invitational ('Come sinners to
the Gospel feast; / Let every soul be Jesu's guest' [2]); celebratory ('Happy
the man that finds the grace, / The blessing of God's chosen race, / The
wisdom coming from above, / The faith that sweetly works by love.' [14]);
and anticipatory ('I long to behold him arrayed / With glory and light from
above, / The King in his beauty displayed, / His beauty of holiest love.' [68]).
In these hymns the reality of death, judgement and hell are all declared,
sometimes in strikingly morbid tones, but the main focus is on the 'pleasantness of religion' and the 'goodness of God'. These are expressed not with

cloying sentimentality or with banal platitudes, but with a poetic love of the invited life of faith in a harsh world. What is most striking about the hymns as a body is their concentration instead on the Christian life as a pilgrimage, a journey from earthly despair to heavenly blessing. They are filled with personal pronouns, active verbs and intense struggles. They aim to persuade, to convince and to plead; they are more winning than threatening, more appealing than damning.

How then was Wesleyan hymnody consumed by Methodists? Hymns played an important part in all the additional means of grace developed by the Methodist societies, including bands, classes, love feasts, watchnights, prayer meetings, covenant services, outdoor preaching services and camp meetings.[28] Almost every Methodist gathering began and ended with a hymn. Sometimes participants wanted to sing more often than Wesley deemed prudent, and he said so. The hymns designated for society meetings and love feasts in part five of the 1780 *Collection* resonate with themes of mutuality, partnership, and encouragement. 'Help us to help each other, Lord / Each other's cross to bear; / Let each his friendly aid afford, /And feel his brother's care. / Help us build each other up, / Our little stocks improve; / Increase our faith, confirm our hope, / And perfect us in love' (489). Hymns were not only sung on public occasions but were sung privately or memorized. Wherever one looks in Methodist archives, from the recorded experiences of itinerant preachers to the diaries of the Methodist faithful, hymns are used for expression, consolation, anticipation and interpretation. Methodists absorbed their faith through the words of their hymns and sacred verse.

The Wesley brothers – Charles as composer and poetic genius, John as collector and editor – were keenly aware of the power of hymns in achieving manifold objectives: they transmitted complex theological ideas in accessible language; they reached deep into the will and the emotions of believers through metre, rhyme and melody; they made connections with the wider culture through the appropriation of popular tunes; they were easily memorized (more so than the biblical verses that inspired them) and used by individual believers in the crisis moments of their lives; they helped build communal solidarity and collective devotion; they enlivened meetings of all kinds that otherwise would have run into the ground of emotional sterility; they inspired the imagination, mediated biblical metaphors and helped build a system of symbols; they defined for Methodism a religious content and style of a more vibrant and populist kind than was available through confessions of faith or chanted liturgies; in short, they supplied a poetic music of the heart for a religion of the heart. Hymnody was therefore somewhere near the heart and centre of Methodist popular religion. Hymn-singing was an expression of individual and corporate affirmation, an aid to memory, a trigger of religious emotion and a creator of spiritual identity. It was the message in poetry and music.

Sermons were equally ubiquitous. A veritable army of itinerant and local preachers and exhorters, of both sexes, preached millions of sermons in different kinds of social spaces throughout the north Atlantic world in the eighteenth and early nineteenth centuries. Most Methodist sermons were based on a selected biblical text; most were delivered extemporarily or from a loose structure of notes; most were preached many times and were refined on the move according to reception; most were designed to evoke a response, whether of conversion, sanctification or a warmed-up spirituality; most were delivered in plain language and enlivened by illustration, anecdote or humour; most operated within the accepted 'canon' of Wesleyan theology, sometimes guaranteed by use of Wesley's notes on the New Testament or by other established sources of connectional orthodoxy; most were delivered in a particular kind of social space which shaped content and style of delivery; most were measured by fruitfulness, however determined, not by eloquence; most were attempts at communication from the heart and to the heart, not bypassing the mind, but not aimed directly at it; most accepted the authority of Scripture at face value; most assumed that what was being declared was the plain truth untainted by sophisticated apologetics or hermeneutics; most were preached by preachers of a roughly similar social status to their listeners. Only a fraction of Methodist sermons were ever published, especially in the early days, before anniversary, funeral and special occasion sermons were printed for more general consumption.

What is most striking about Methodist hymns and sermons, taken together, is the close fit they exhibit between theology, practice and style. The communication media, the communicators and the content of the message displayed a harmony of values well adapted to Methodism's mobile mission to the common people. The respective emphases on invitation to a new life, freedom of choice and the journey to holiness, combined with the fusion of preached word and sung verse, offered an obvious appeal to populations breaking free from the more static and emotionally restrained religious styles of Established Churchmen, Calvinists and deists.

How then were those touched by the Methodist message organized into communities of faith capable of expansion and translation to other places? The Methodist ecclesiological structure of bands, classes, societies, circuits and conferences, what Wigger has helpfully called 'the social principle', was a riot of association in the age of associations. The basic unit was the class, which commenced in Bristol in the early 1740s initially as a financial expedient to support the ministry and relieve the poor. Originally classes were groups of about 12 meeting in a particular geographical area under a specified leader. Entry was based on a desire to 'flee from the wrath to come' and the aim was to nurture godly language, temperance, honesty, plainness, seriousness, frugality, diligence, charity and economic loyalty within the connection. The issue of the much prized quarterly membership tickets cultivated a sense of membership and identity. For those who were decidedly Christian believers pursuing sanctification, the smaller bands, divided by gender and marital status, were places of confession, or 'mutual inquisition' as Southey described it. The aims of these little Methodist associations were to finance the movement's expansion, exercise spiritual discipline (unrepentant backsliders were ejected), pursue Scriptural holiness, nurture fellowship and train future leaders. Opponents of Methodism criticized classes as popish (for their confessional element) and divisive (for raising the bar of spiritual devotion). Almost all membership surveys of Methodist classes show a preponderance of women on a ratio of almost three to two.[29] The early records of American Methodism show that classes were the most important building blocks of the movement. Generally speaking, over time classes grew in size to around 25–35, and displayed various patterns of gender and colour separation or integration according to time and place. Although classes also varied in terms of emotional intensity and noisiness, their sheer ubiquity in the surviving records of Methodism show them to be places where members were assimilated, voices were found, spiritual experiences were shared and communities of faith were built. Much would obviously depend on the personalities and diligence of class leaders and members, but at their best they were the building blocks of the Methodist movement.

If bands, classes and societies exemplify the principle of association within Methodism, love feasts, quarterly meetings and camp meetings demonstrated a principle of celebration. Love feasts, initially revived by the Moravians, were simple fellowship meals for the Methodist faithful; quarterly meetings transacted Methodist business, enforced discipline and spilt over into celebration; and camp meetings were prolonged outdoor revivalistic extravaganzas. Each had a different theatrical style and contributed something distinctive. Love feasts, admittance to which was by ticket only, built up notions of separation (from a hostile world), cohesion (the shared meal) and adoration (the offered praise of a loving community). Quarterly meetings brought church administration and ecclesiastical discipline (typically for Sabbath breaking, sexual immorality, drunkenness or debt) out of the closet of private bureaucracy, where many churches had confined it, into a more public arena, and by doing so nurtured a sense of participation and collective responsibility. Revealingly, in Britain quarterly meetings gradually became the law courts of Methodism, in which preachers with inflated views of their pastoral office laid down the law for the connection, whereas in America quarterly meetings often ran over into 'seasons of blessing' when routines shaded into revivals.[30] That major difference alone partly explains the faster growth rates of American Methodism in the nineteenth century.

In England camp meetings were resisted by the main branch of Methodism, becoming the grounds of secession for the Primitive Methodists, whereas in America they became a normal part of the Methodist experience, as much on the eastern seaboard as on the expanding frontier.[31] Camp meetings, described variously as Christian versions of the old Jewish feast of the Tabernacles, as modern equivalents of medieval pilgrimages and as religious embodiments of community fairs, were highly ritualized gatherings, which often resulted in large numbers of conversions or of commitments renewed. It is remarkable how often they show up in the reminiscences of the Methodist faithful as emotionally charged memories of life-changing encounters. Outdoor festivals organized around common collective purposes, and enriched by affecting music and ritualized behaviour, are literally sensory and sensible experiences for those in search of sociability, entertainment and community.

How then should one account for the emergence of Methodism as the fastest-growing religious movement in the transatlantic world at the turn of the eighteenth and nineteenth centuries? The first point to note is that John Wesley's evangelistic strategy, if such it can be described, varied with time and geographical location. Until the early 1750s his declared aim was to 'reform the nation, more particularly the Church; to spread scriptural holiness over the land'. To achieve this he allied himself with a clutch of country Tories and Jacobites who hoped to propel themselves into positions of national influence through the reversionary politics of the Prince of Wales at Leicester House. They hoped to reform the Established Church from above and within by having input into episcopal appointments. That strategy collapsed with the death of the Prince, but what was the alternative? In England Wesley set about creating an institution from his mission to the poor that could survive outside the episcopal discipline of the Established Church without necessarily attacking it or separating from it. In Scotland he flirted with the General Assembly of the Church of Scotland, routinely ridiculed Calvinists and got nowhere very fast. In Ireland he tagged alongside the Protestant Ascendancy, appealed to European Protestant minorities, endorsed the cultural superiority of Protestant Ulster over the rest of the country and not surprisingly made little headway among the nation's majority Catholic population. In America something more creative was accomplished largely without Wesley's input, though the sending of

Francis Asbury turned out to be an inspired choice.[32] But there is more to it than that. American Methodism 'inherited the "language of Canaan", that common language of European Pietism, which in America had been made a folk idiom by the First Great Awakening in the 'forties. It was natural to them to talk of the Spirit "falling" upon a meeting, for people to have "melting experiences", and to "find great freedom", to be knit together in "love", to call each other "brother", and "rejoice in the prosperity of Zion".'[33]

In recent times creative attempts have been made to come to terms with the relationship between the internal drama of Methodist experience and the external characteristics of Methodist expansion. In America, Methodism offered a plain Gospel to a plain people who, in the mass, were unwilling to embrace either the grim selectivity of Calvinism or the more inclusive but less emotionally compelling varieties of Unitarian Universalism. By offering a powerful religious alternative to republican civic culture, Methodism harnessed and organized the energies of a restless American people. One historian writing of southern Methodism shows that out of the 'marrow of the Methodist self' emerged a Methodist style of emotionalism, mysticism, asceticism, enthusiasm and evangelism.[34] So powerful was it that it temporarily broke the dams holding in place the white male honour codes of the South based on greed, gratification and slavery. Women and African Americans flocked into Methodism in great numbers, but ultimately Methodism made an unhappy peace with its surroundings and opened the way later for a tawdry reconciliation between Methodism and the culture of slavery.

Similar tales of how 'the making of the Methodist self' resulted in vigorous challenges to surrounding cultures have been told in the British Isles. Rural Methodists in turn-of-the-century England set themselves against the culture of Anglican paternalism and landowner dependency. Urban Methodists in northern manufacturing towns set themselves against the whole political structure of class hegemony, at least until Methodist leaders told them that neither their radical politics nor their methods would be tolerated within the connection. Methodists in Wales organized in liberal hordes against the Established Church, landowners and other forms of unwelcome Anglicization. Irish Methodists with enthusiastic zeal tried to occupy the narrow ground of opposition to Roman Catholicism, Ulster-Scots Presbyterianism and Anglican elitism. Immigration and assimilation eventually tempered the zeal. What is striking about each of these examples is that reconstituted Methodist selves had to live and bear witness in different cultural settings and in the process their message was shaped by those settings.[35]

By the second decade of the nineteenth century, Methodism's 'empire

of the spirit' had spread to surprisingly large parts of the world. Methodist expansion was the result not of an evangelistic strategy concocted by
elites, but was carried primarily by a mobile laity. Some moved along the
trading routes established by the British Empire, others were in military
regiments that patrolled it; many, including the migratory Irish and the
Cornish tinners,[36] moved in search of a better life in various parts of the
New World; others, like southern American blacks and English convicts,
moved because they were forced to; some moved out of a self-conscious
desire to spread Scriptural holiness, others discovered a holiness tradition
after they moved. The point is that all this took place long *before* the formation of official missionary societies. Methodism had a mobile laity before it
had missionaries, it had missionaries before it had a missionary society and
it had locally based missionary societies before it had a national missionary
society.[37] When the first great Methodist missionary society was formed
in Britain in 1816, the Methodists already had over 100 missionaries working in India, West and South Africa, the West Indies, the Canadas and
the Canadian Maritimes. More importantly, Methodism had established
self-sustaining and rapidly growing churches in the British Isles and North
America, the two most expansionist cultures of the nineteenth and twentieth centuries.

What kind of a religious empire were the Methodists building? David
Martin has asked a similar question of Pentecostalism, a religious movement that grew directly out of Methodism, and many of his answers, with
suitable refinement, apply equally to Methodism.[38] Methodism, like Pentecostalism, was a cultural revolution from below, not a political or ecclesiastical programme imposed from above. It grew without external sponsorship
and thrived among youthful and mobile populations exploiting the opportunities of new global markets. It was essentially a movement of women
who formed a clear majority of society members almost everywhere Methodism took root.[39] It was also a movement in search of a voice, which is why
it was so noisy and so devoted to singing.[40] It became first a transatlantic
and then a global phenomenon, but through acculturation and indigenization it adapted to local cultures and changed its character from place to
place. It was a movement that emphasized personal experience, but also
was infused with a set of personal and communal disciplines as means and
ways to a better life. Methodism thrived on the margins and frontiers of
race and class, continental expansion and empire. It was a world-affirming
movement, relatively free from the millenarian fantasies of other populist
religious strains, but it also set up clear boundaries of dress, speech and
behaviour, marking off the church from the world.

But there are also significant differences between Methodism and

Pentecostalism (maybe only so far), quite apart from those associated with Pentecostalism's emphasis on the baptism of the spirit. Methodism grew out of a religious establishment and never shrugged off some of its autocratic and establishmentarian inclinations. In England it cosied up to governments, expelled radicals and built its gothic chapels, often more out of a quest for social acceptance and respectability than for any more noble purpose. In America it first renounced slavery and then accommodated it, liberated women and then controlled them. Everywhere, Methodists began as cultural outsiders, but through work discipline and an unquenchable passion for education, they remorselessly moved to the centre, sometimes with remarkable speed. Ironically, the closer Methodism came to the centre of national cultures, the less able it was to promote growth on anything like the rates it achieved in the eighteenth and nineteenth centuries. Of course, it is impossible to grow faster than population growth forever (in that case there would be more Methodists than people!), but by the beginning of the twentieth century the growth of Anglo-American Methodism, if not that of the rest of the world, no longer kept up with the growth in population.

The impact of Evangelicalism

What then was the impact of the Protestant Evangelical Awakening? Five things stand out. First, it not only gave rise to a new religious tradition but also deeply affected pre-existing traditions. Anglicans, Presbyterians, Congregationalists, Baptists and dissenters of all stripes had their religious traditions at least modified by, if not transformed by, growing cohorts of Evangelicals within their ranks. Second, Evangelicalism sank particularly strong roots in the United States and among African Americans. Populist Evangelical groups such as the Baptists and the Methodists became the fastest-growing churches in the United States in the first half of the nineteenth century, and, according to some polls, around a third of the American population self-identify as Evangelicals. Similarly, although a majority of African Americans did not become Christians, Evangelical Christianity became the dominant faith tradition of those who did. Third, Evangelicalism supplied the backbone of the English-speaking missionary movement which emerged at the turn of the eighteenth and nineteenth centuries, and which has had an almost incalculable effect on the patterns of global religious and political affiliations in the modern world. Fourth, Evangelicalism made its strongest gains outside the portals of established churches and inexorably eroded the foundations of the Christendom model upon which the parish-based model of European Christianity was based. Methodism was but one of literally hundreds of voluntary associations founded by Anglo-American Evangelicals to improve, instruct and reform in the nineteenth century. The reforming voluntary association became one of the most conspicuous public expressions of lay Christianity in the modern era. Every imaginable social issue, from slavery to temperance and from urban vice to Sabbath observance had an Evangelical voluntary association devoted to it.[41] Finally, Evangelicalism made a profound impression on the personal and social mores of the populations within which it took root.

Evangelicalism helped shape culture, and as a result occasioned much controversy.[42] While many have appreciated its contribution to the ending of the British slave trade and its commitment to religious education, others have protested about its anti-intellectualism, its lack of artistic sensibility or its 'Victorian' narrowness of spirit. Even those writing from within the Evangelical tradition have castigated Evangelicals for their lack of depth in thinking about culture, their capacity for 'self-centred, egotistic and narcissistic spirituality', their obsessive introspection to the extent that social evils are often ignored, their persistent and narrow-minded sectarianism and their shoddy record over anti-Catholicism. Even their noble campaigns against human slavery led by Wilberforce, Wesley and others capitulated eventually to economic self-interest and racism among Evangelicals in the American South. More virulently, some outside the tradition have regarded the whole movement as a disease of the human spirit that has made the world worse not better.[43] However the balance sheet is to be totted up, there is no question that the international Evangelical Awakening of the eighteenth century gave a renewed boost to the flagging Protestantism of the Reformation and converted many millions to a Gospel message that claimed to transform lives, communities and cultures. Its impact on individuals, families, nations and the wider world should not be undervalued or underestimated. Many of the great shapers of Victorian civilization in both Britain and America were raised in the fierce disciplines and tender pieties of Evangelical households, even if some of them abandoned the faith of their fathers and mothers.[44]

CHAPTER 6

God and Caesar: Churches, States and Revolutions

The public social spaces most familiar to eighteenth-century Europeans were the cathedrals, parish churches and graveyards of established churches, whether Orthodox, Roman Catholic, Lutheran, Reformed/Presbyterian or Anglican. Churches dominated skylines, chaperoned the rites of passage, rang their bells on significant occasions, organized processions and festivals, supplied most of the available education, dispensed welfare, charity and poor relief, owned considerable amounts of property and were an important component of economic life.[1] In addition, European states relied upon established churches as their chief devices for Christianizing native populations and for controlling religious deviance and immorality. Established churches were regarded as simply indispensable to the theory and practice of governing, and they supplied divine sanction to the social order.

In exchange for extensive financial, administrative and legal privileges, including the running of their own courts, established churches were expected to be the state's record keepers of births, deaths and marriages, to add religious sanction to the theory and practice of governing and to help the state maintain social cohesion and reinforce stability. They were expected to baptize, catechize, confirm, ordain, pastor, bury, register, celebrate, regulate and educate. Adherents of non-established churches were variously expected to convert, conform, migrate or keep a low profile. Whatever niche they found, other religious traditions were assuredly not equals and were not treated as such. For much of the eighteenth century, established churches were not so much expected to do things as to be things. Within certain limits, the social salience of established churches depended less upon their rigorous performance of religious duties than upon their perceived centrality to the religious life of the nation. Established churches were as much bound up with local and national identities as they were agents of religious and spiritual transmission.[2] The purpose of this chapter is to look at how established churches functioned in different parts of Europe in the eighteenth century and to understand how they were affected by the major political revolutions of the late eighteenth century. That is, of course, a big topic, so I have chosen to concentrate on three different confessional traditions in three different locations: the Protestant established churches in the British Isles, the Roman Catholic established churches in Western and Central Europe, and the Orthodox established church in Russia. The chapter concludes with an evaluation of the religious components of revolution and the indelible imprint revolution left on churches.

Protestant churches in Britain and Ireland

Few subjects have attracted quite as much disagreement as evaluations of the function, performance and pastoral effectiveness of British established churches in the eighteenth century, particularly the Church of England.[3] Until relatively recently, much of the writing about established churches in all parts of the British Isles was critical of their moral, pastoral and structural deficiencies. Much of recent scholarship, while not denying the existence of abuses and anomalies, has presented a much more optimistic picture of the strength of established church religiosity, however that is to be measured. This work concludes that established churches were deeply embedded in the religious, political and social life of their countries and did a reasonable job within the parameters of what could be expected of large institutions operating under eighteenth-century conditions.[4] Even the Irish and Welsh churches, for so long regarded as the sharp edge of establishment malpractice, now have sophisticated modern defences of their achievements. What put established churches under increasing pressure in the later eighteenth and early nineteenth centuries, however, were not so much old shortcomings as new circumstances. These circumstances included rapid population growth, the virtual collapse of ecclesiastical coercion, the erosion of traditional deference and the rise of new religious alternatives. In addition, a subtle intellectual shift, itself the product of the Enlightenment, slowly began to subject established churches to rational audits of ecclesiastical performance, social utility and national acceptance. By the 1820s and 1830s, for example, it seemed that the Church of Ireland, which ministered to only a small minority of the Irish population, was in danger of failing that audit, with consequences that seemed to threaten all established churches in the British Isles. The Oxford Movement within the Church of England in the 1830s arose in part from the realization that politicians and intellectual elites, not church traditions, would in future set the terms under which established churches must exist.

Just as the impact of the Enlightenment was played out in different ways in different parts of the British Isles, the same is true of the fate of religious establishments. In England, the Toleration Act of 1689 partly undermined the legal basis for the enforcement of religious uniformity and moral discipline. Although the Anglican Church courts did not wither away as quickly as once was assumed, the combined effects of a decline in the enforceability of Christian morality and the expansion of the population and the economy contributed to their steady decline. By the end of the eighteenth century, many churchmen were more disposed to use persuasion than coercion, and more inclined to work for diocesan reform and renewal than to rest on existing privileges. It is true that the French Revolution and the rapid spread of itinerant preaching in England during the French wars reawakened old neuroses about the fate of church and state, but the attempt to restrain itinerant preaching failed miserably in 1811, and it was quickly followed by an extension of religious toleration in 1812.

The decline of its coercive power was not necessarily a bad thing for the Church of England, which had generally valued parochial loyalty to the Book of Common Prayer's rites and ordinances more highly than the fruits of inquisitorial zeal, but it did point up a subtle shift in the relations between church and people over the course of the long eighteenth century. Attendance at church services, participation in catechizing and the practice of communion all became more dependent on the inclination of parishioners than on the insistence of the clergy. This alteration in the balance of power between the producers and consumers of Anglicanism was perhaps the most important consequence of a century of increased religious toleration and the growth of religious alternatives to Anglicanism.

Nevertheless, the picture of the Church of England that has emerged from the large number of local studies and printed visitation returns of the past two decades is of an institution reasonably well adjusted to the prevailing social and political conditions of the eighteenth century, at least up to the 1770s and 1780s when those conditions rapidly began to change.[5] The Church retained significant legal powers and privileges, but was not unduly inquisitorial or persecuting. It was supported by property owners, and was in turn preoccupied, indeed almost obsessed, by the defence and enhancement of property rights and of its own properties including tithes, parsonages and pew rents. Its clergy, in the main, were neither unusually devoted nor scandalously negligent, but were generally dutiful if rather unambitious pastors. The clerical profession was a generally well-educated, hard-working, pastorally engaged, community-oriented, serious-minded and well-respected group, probably superior in most respects to most other eighteenth-century professions. Anti-clericalism was relatively muted, tithes were generally paid without conspicuous protest and the clergy acted as pillars of the community in their service as justices of the peace, dispensers of charity and purveyors of education.[6] Although pluralism and non-residence were rife, few parishes were pastorally neglected and few pluralists were consumed by greed. Its parish churches, much more even than its clergy, were focal points of a genuinely popular Anglicanism, which valued tradition, community rituals and religious harmony. The Church's performance of its basic duties of administering the rites of passage, conducting services and catechizing the people was overall more impressive than its critics alleged.

By the 1760s, therefore, it seemed that the Church had successfully weathered a century of intense religious conflict. Some of the Old Dissenting denominations were palpably waning. The deists had been refuted. The Whig proscription of Anglican Tory office-holders seemed to be a thing of the past. The old High Church party was on the verge of a remarkable intellectual and ecclesiastical revival. The growing Evangelical movement within the Church was pastorally innovative, but scarcely ecclesiastically radical. The perceived threat from Roman Catholicism was much diminished after the failure of the Jacobite uprisings. Methodism seemed nothing more than a relatively small coterie of deluded enthusiasts. Church parties were more united on essentials than divided on peripherals. The Church had profited enormously from the enclosure movement and the general prosperity of the British economy, and, above all, the Church of England was regarded as supplying the ideological underpinning of the fairest and most enlightened constitution in Europe. All was subsumed under a Protestant providentialism that viewed the English Church as a divinely blessed *via media* between the excesses of Rome and Geneva. England's successful wars against the French, its growing overseas empire, its social stability and its mercantile hegemony were all interpreted as the blessings of a beneficent providence on a Protestant people.[7] In short, by the 1760s the Church seemed to be functioning as well as an estimable *ancien régime* establishment could be expected to function.[8] Not all was rosy, however.

The Church's much vaunted connection with the state was more impressive in theory than in practice. During the eighteenth century the successive pet plans of bishops and archbishops such as William Wake (1657–1737), Edmund Gibson (1669–1748) and Thomas Secker (1693–1768), including appointing bishops for the colonies, were all entertained and then ignored by their political masters, a trend that became ever more alarming to churchmen in the early nineteenth century. The meagre resources of Queen Anne's Bounty could not adequately address the internal structural problems of the Church, which seriously hampered its pastoral efficiency.[9] More seriously, the Church's claim to be the church of the English nation suffered under the stresses and strains accompanying the American and French Revolutions and the wars they generated. By the early nineteenth century, rising population, the growing numbers of dissenters, Methodists and Roman Catholics, political disaffection in town and country and the establishmentarian neurosis of the Church itself all combined to give fresh credence to the old slogan, 'the Church in Danger'. Although in the nineteenth century the Church, sometimes aided by the state, displayed remarkable powers of survival, reform and even renewal, including a much better record of church building and pastoral supervision than it is sometimes given credit for, it never again emerged as the uncontested church of the English.

Understanding the fate of Anglicanism outside England poses special problems, because in both Ireland and Wales the churches were later disestablished, essentially for failing to attract enough support within their host populations to satisfy utilitarian calculations or to mitigate old cultural animosities. Once lack of success is defined by a terminal destination, especially a destination arrived at by a long history of bitter conflict, historians are inclined to concentrate on looking for the seeds of subsequent decline. The conventional picture of Anglicanism in Wales, therefore, is of a church of spectacular weaknesses and abuses, fully deserving of its disastrous fate in the nineteenth century, when Evangelical Nonconformity swept over the country like a tidal wave. That the Welsh Church was indeed riddled with defects, most of them occasioned by crippling administrative and financial problems inherited from the sixteenth and seventeenth centuries, is not in serious dispute. Some of the most quotable cases of ecclesiastical absenteeism, corruption and neglect in the entire eighteenth century are to be found in Wales. But such quotations draw attention away from other salient features of Welsh Anglicanism. The northern dioceses of Bangor and St Asaph were better off and attracted more ecclesiastical talent, sometimes of an unusually high order, than the southern dioceses of St David's and Llandaff. Moreover, for all its perceived weaknesses, the established church was not faced by rapidly growing alternatives. In Wales there were significant and energetic pockets of Roman Catholicism and, more commonly, dissent, but together they served probably less than ten per cent of the population before 1780. Most impressively of all, the Welsh Church, aided by a remarkable commitment to elementary education and to the dissemination of religious literature in Welsh, succeeded in nurturing a strong popular devotion to Protestant Christianity cloaked chiefly in Anglican garb. Seen from that perspective, the striking gains made by Methodists and other Evangelical Nonconformists later in the century were as much a result of pre-existing Anglican devotion as they were of Anglican pastoral neglect.[10]

If the Welsh Church has suffered from a bad historical press, it is as nothing compared to that endured by the episcopal established church in Ireland. The conventional picture of the Church of Ireland is of a minority religious establishment imposed ineffectually from above and buttressed by a draconian set of penal laws against Roman Catholics and the sacramental test against predominantly northern Presbyterians. Such a foundation, it is alleged, militated against the prosecution of the Church's pastoral mission. Criticized for preferring to rely upon coercion and political influence among the elite rather than pastoral efficiency among the many, the Irish Church had the appearance of an upper-class sect seeking to impose itself on an unwilling Catholic nation. Looked at from a different perspective, however, the Irish Church was not quite as bad as it was painted. Once the point is conceded that the Irish Church, whatever the stated aspirations of some of its more extreme High Churchmen, was not in reality a national establishment at all, but rather a church with a limited constituency, then its apparent lack of resources, manpower and national coverage become less critical. Shrill calls for internal reform from the likes of William King (1650–1729), Archbishop of Dublin, and the disappointed expectations of newly arrived English clergymen, who had a vested interest in exposing deficiencies, should not detract from the achievements of a church that in truth was embarked upon an unachievable mission in a country where neither Reformation nor Counter Reformation had taken much of a hold over the peasantry.

The Irish Church was neither fabulously wealthy nor, by eighteenth-century standards, unusually ineffectual in its pastoral conduct; it was simply a rather threadbare established church creaking under the weight of unrealistic expectations, not unlike many of its European counterparts.[11] Its main strength, partly owing to its patronage connections with the Church of England, was in supplying a religion ideally suited to the Irish landed classes. Its main weakness as an established church was that its rituals, symbols and celebrations could not operate as socially binding mechanisms on anything like the same terms as in England, for the Protestant historical victories it celebrated were interpreted as defeats by the majority Roman Catholic population it could neither convert nor coerce. The Church of Ireland was not without its reforming movements in the eighteenth century, most notably its commitment to elementary education in the early part of the century and its surprisingly vigorous Evangelical movement centred from the 1780s on Dublin, but it was hard for it to escape the logic of its own history as a church imposed from above and without. The Act of Union with Britain in 1800, far from helping to secure its position, merely reduced the influence of its bishops, brought it within the sphere of an increasingly unfriendly political culture and rendered it the softest target of all the established churches in the British Isles. Unsurprisingly, it was the first to be disestablished.

Arguably, the most successful of the established churches, at least in terms of popular allegiance, the exercise of moral discipline and the weakness of non-Reformed alternatives, was the Presbyterian Church of Scotland. Although the Act of Union of 1707 delivered favourable terms, the Church still had to work hard to clear out episcopal ministers from its parishes, redeem the Highlands from Catholicism and episcopalianism, and impose the Kirk's discipline on a rapidly changing society. Its Achilles heel was the issue of church patronage, which agitated the Church relentlessly for 150 years, resulting eventually in the creation of a Presbyterian dissenting population almost twice as large as that of the Church itself. The apparently simple question at issue in the bitter patronage disputes of the eighteenth century was who had the rightful authority to appoint ministers to parishes. But the issue was addled by serious disagreements about the proper role of the Church in Scottish society, social conflicts amounting almost to primitive class-consciousness in the Scottish countryside and the brokering of political power both within Scotland and between England and Scotland.

The genesis of the conflict was the Patronage Act of 1712, passed in contravention of the Act of Union of 1707 by an English Tory government, which left church patronage in the hands of the crown and the aristocracy. For some time after 1712, patrons were slow to exercise their right of presentation in the face of popular hostility, but the situation changed in the second quarter of the eighteenth century when Robert Walpole's (1676–1745) Scottish agents used patronage as a device to encourage political loyalty, social stability and religious moderation. Given the relatively open and democratic nature of the Kirk's ecclesiastical structure, patronage disputes had both local salience and national resonance. The predictable consequence was a string of Presbyterian secessions, not essentially over doctrine but over different styles of Presbyterianism. The rise of religious pluralism in Scotland, albeit on a rather modest scale before 1800, was therefore a predominantly Presbyterian phenomenon.

Concentration upon patronage disputes and the nuances of ecclesiastical politics can sometimes deflect attention away from the profound impact of Scottish Presbyterianism on Scottish life and culture.[12] Perhaps more than anywhere else in the British Isles, the Scottish Established Church was a vital instrument of civil, moral and judicial authority that affected the lives and behaviour of most of the Scottish people. Church courts there were able to conduct a more sustained campaign against fornication and other moral 'evils' than anywhere else in the British Isles. Conventional religious observance as measured by attendance at church and communion was probably not very high, but there was general acceptance of the Kirk's centrality to the life of the local community, at least until the end of the eighteenth century, when rapid social and economic transformation created new pressures and social divisions.

Local studies from around the British Isles have drawn attention to both the extent and the limits of the religious influence of established churches over their parishioners. Their almost universal control over the rites of passage, their surprisingly high levels of commitment to catechizing and their centrality to the ritualistic and celebratory rhythms of life in the countryside all testify to their significance. Eighteenth-century parishes, regardless of the state of their pastoral supervision, celebrated important events in national history such as Guy Fawkes Day, Oak Apple Day, the martyrdom of Charles I and the accession of the reigning monarch. They were also at the heart of a much wider range of celebrations associated with the Christian and agrarian calendars, the precise balance of which varied according to inherited local custom from parish to parish. But even these statements fail to convey the central importance of religious rites and customs in early modern Britain. Partly legitimized by the Book of Common Prayer and the Books of Homilies, and partly guided by ancient custom, parochial rituals helped shape the mental frameworks of rural dwellers. For example, the annual Rogation week celebrations following the fifth Sunday after Easter were designed to emphasize the beneficence of God as provider of all good things and as regulator of the social order. The custom of perambulating the parish was not only designed to inculcate a sense of spatial boundaries but was also a way of reinforcing a primitive social consensus about the ownership and utilization of land. Often associated with degrees of bawdiness and drunkenness, the purpose of these perambulations was to reinforce the mental maps of parishioners, including the boundaries of territory, the legitimacy of the social order, the management of change (associated with enclosures), the resolution of conflict and the right of access to rudimentary welfare provision. Even the aural culture of parishes, with their rough music and customary bell ringing, was inexorably linked to parochial celebrations of one kind or another.[13]

The days when the eighteenth-century Church of England was berated by a formidable phalanx of Evangelicals, High Churchmen, utilitarians and liberal and Marxist historians for its pastoral mediocrity, erastian bondage and structural weaknesses seem like a thing of the past (at least for a while), but as always there is a danger in going much too far. By the turn of the century a complex of social tensions caused by population growth, subsistence crises and the commercialization of agriculture, and further exacerbated by prolonged warfare, sharpened class conflict and undermined the old denominational order. The rising social status of the Anglican clergy and their unprecedented representation on the bench of magistrates in the English localities cemented the squire and parson alliance at the very time that establishment ideals in English society were beginning to come under attack. In such circumstances, the Church of England was in no position to resist a dramatic upsurge in undenominational itinerant preaching and cottage-based religion (especially from the 1790s on) that even the various Methodist connections struggled hard to keep under control.[14] That, along with the influx of Roman Catholic migrants from Ireland in the first half of the nineteenth century, ensured that by the time of the 1851 Census of Public Worship around half of public worshipers in England and Wales were non Anglicans, a situation far removed from a century earlier. On the other side, the established churches of England and Scotland, despite intense fears to the contrary, survived campaigns for disestablishment and remain established churches to this day. The establishment principle in Britain outside its Celtic fringes has proved remarkably durable, even if church attendance has withered dramatically since the 1960s.

Roman Catholic Europe

Roman Catholicism was the dominant Christian communion in eighteenth-century Europe. The post-Reformation expansion of Protestantism had been effectively checked, even partially reversed, and the Islamic threat from the Ottoman Empire was seriously diminished. In the majority of European states, 'Ireland, France, the kingdoms of Spain, Portugal, the Italian principalities, about one-third of the Holy Roman Empire, most of the Habsburg hereditary lands, Bavaria, Poland', and many of the German states and principalities Catholics comprised the great majority of the population.[15] Never an equal partnership, despite some clerical propaganda to the contrary, the nature of the relationship between churches and states in Catholic Europe varied enormously from fusion, as in the Catholic prince bishoprics of Cologne, Mainz and Trier, to the position of Catholicism as a small and barely tolerated minority in England. More commonly, the pattern varied from a close, if often vigorously contested relationship between church and state in France, Spain and the Habsburg lands, to the existence of a large majority Catholic population under foreign domination as in Ireland and Poland. Whatever the pattern, or indeed the nature of the confessional tradition, the general trend in the eighteenth century was for states to increase their control over churches, including increased administrative interference, seizure of church and monastic wealth and greater independence from papal and clerical authority. There were, however, limits beyond which it was prudent for rulers not to go, for states could ill afford to undermine the traditional religious legitimization of governance or so to alienate the ubiquitous clergy that they became leaders of popular opposition rather than facilitators of change. For that reason, relations between rulers and their established churches in the eighteenth century need to be approached with a certain delicacy.

In most of Catholic Europe the idea of the 'confessional state' survived mostly intact until the more radical phases of the French Revolution introduced a more voluntarist approach to religious adherence in France by the mid-1790s. In practice, what that meant was that states continued to rely on churches, with their formidable nationwide patchwork of parishes and established administrative systems, for pulpit propaganda, reliable registrations and widespread welfare and educational provision. Even when states wanted to reform the church, as was the case with Joseph II's enlightened reforms in the Habsburg lands in the 1780s, they often had little alternative but to rely on the administrative machinery of the church to implement state-directed changes. In return, monarchs were treated to elaborate religious consecrations at their coronations and were regarded as divine-right rulers, not appointees of social or clerical elites, still less of the people. The whole coronation theatre of sacred oils, holy water, medieval oaths, religious symbols, unctions, Masses and elaborate costumes was designed to invest monarchy with religious mystery, sacred tradition and divine empowerment.[16] It was in the interests of both church and state to cooperate in this elaborate pageantry.

However ceremonially united as twin pillars of God's rule on earth, states and churches were not without their tensions. Most obvious were the contests between monarchs and popes over power, authority and jurisdiction. The second half of the eighteenth century witnessed a serious decline in papal authority throughout Europe.[17] From the regalian policies of Charles III of Spain to the structural reforms of Joseph II, and from the suppression of the Society of Jesus to the blows from the French Revolutionaries, it seemed that the papacy in its dealings with European rulers was at a low ebb. On the other hand, papal diplomacy still counted for something, and as threats to Catholic autonomy mounted throughout Europe, conservative clerics began to rally round the papacy as the best guardian of the authority and privileges of the church. For example, some see the roots of a vigorous Ultramontanism (across the mountains to Rome), which flourished in the nineteenth century, in the reaction provoked by Jansenist-inspired appeals to lay public opinion in eighteenth-century France. Conservative ecclesiastics viewed these Jansenist tactics as seriously undermining the spiritual authority of the church. Ultimately, however, internal conflict within the church over its relations with the state rarely produced good results for churchmen. For example, 'the paradox of judicial Jansenism's exaltation of the monarchy in relation to its clerical subjects, the better to undermine it with respect to its lay subjects' helps explain both the internecine feuds that rocked the French Church on the eve of the Revolution and possibly even the Revolution itself.[18] In reality churches and rulers, despite their different agendas and competing self-interests, needed and depended upon one another in the eighteenth century, so much so in fact that periods of conflict between the two, whatever the short-term gains for either, generally boded ill for both. So much then for the generalities of church–state relations in Catholic Europe, but how did these relations play out in specific national contexts? We are fortunate to have access to particularly thorough treatments of one such established church, the French Catholic Church, and its relations with the crown in the century before the Revolution.[19]

The interdependence of church and state, so spectacularly displayed at coronation, was routinely ritualized in French parishes and dioceses to mark significant events in the lives of the royal family, to celebrate military victories or mourn defeats and to commemorate special religious occasions. Ubiquitous rituals and celebrations were partly propaganda devices for placing the church–state connection at the centre of local and national identities. But the connection was not merely ceremonial. By the Concordat of 1516 the crown appointed all bishops (except Strasbourg), heads of the great abbeys (some 800) and many other recipients of ecclesiastical patronage which oiled the wheels of governance, service and reward: 'The Church was rich, and there were sinecures and pensions enough to placate the lukewarm, vocationless, or useless sons of the aristocracy, to support government business, promote learning and gratify local worthies.'[20] To modern eyes, and to the Church's anti-clerical opponents, all this looked like a great pot of corruption, but patronage systems can ill afford to ignore conspicuous talent, destabilizing conflicts or political realities.

In terms of the practical workings of the church–state connection, ecclesiastics offered advice (three first ministers of the French crown in the eighteenth century were in religious orders), kept the registers (somewhat imperfectly), policed morality (with predictably ambiguous results), enforced laws through their ecclesiastical courts (mostly by threatening ecclesiastical penalties), collected tithes and feudal payments (scarcely a popular task), managed property (land, feudal obligations and extensive urban holdings), and even determined the location of graveyards. The clergy also had the privilege of voting taxation to the crown in their own elected assemblies. In all of these areas there was sufficient clerical wealth and malpractice to give anti-clericals and Jansenist reformers ammunition for a more wide-ranging attack on clerical abuses and corruption, whether deserved or not. Ironically, according to recent calculations, the Church was bearing a much fairer burden of the state's finances at the end of the eighteenth century when it was most under threat than it was at the beginning of the century when its role was largely accepted.[21] Thus clerical intransigence in the face of lay criticism in the decades before the French Revolution was designed more to protect clerical independence and exemption from paying secular taxation than necessarily to evade its share of the national budget.

However, given the changes of climate in the long eighteenth century about the social acceptability of institutions which combined 'immense material wealth and lofty spiritual ideals', the French Catholic Church was in an increasingly vulnerable position. As one historian has it, 'While the skepticism of the Enlightenment did not endanger the Church in the short term – it was a spectacular firework display on the horizon – the earthly realities of anticlerical feeling accumulated over questions of taxa-tion, tithe, church fees and rates, leasehold and feudal dues – envy was intensified by oppressiveness.'[22] To speak thus is not to deny some of the real achievements of the French Church in terms of episcopal reform, progress towards an educated priesthood, increased frequency of services and liturgical observances, and dedicated service of the sick, the poor and the ignorant. With pardonable indulgence, John McManners concludes that by the time of the Revolution the French Church was in 'the mellow autumn season adorning the landscape with rich colours before the winter came and the leaves began to fall'. But what the more ardent defenders of the eighteenth century's established churches, whether contemporaries or historians, often fail to account for is that increasing performance of duties cannot adequately compensate for the erosion of the social acceptability of ecclesiastical privileges – social, financial and legal. Nor, in the face of wider structural changes in politics and society, was the Church fully in control of its own destiny. In the case of France, the royal government was grinding towards bankruptcy at the same time as the Gallican Church was enmeshed in the inefficiencies of an archaic administrative system. This deadly combination, as it turned out, was not a happy one for either church or state: 'a new order was coming in by stealth and osmosis, then, finally, in a brutal cataclysm'.[23]

Elsewhere in Catholic Europe, different patterns of church–state relations produced quite different results. In Poland, for example, an unusual combi-nation of post-Tridentine reforms combined to produce a largely Catholic commonwealth. These include the achievements of baroque Catholicism, the folk missions of the religious orders, the experience of subjection to

military occupation, the decline of Orthodoxy and the growth (and Latini-
zation) of the Uniate Greek-Catholic Church, the reforms of a distinctively
Catholic enlightenment, the reinvigoration of parochial Catholicism and
the growing weakness of other Christian traditions (Protestant and Orthodox). In 1772, out of a population of some 12 million, around 10½ million
were Catholics, whether of the Latin, Greek or Armenian versions.[24] There
were, however, some tough times ahead for Polish Catholicism during the
Partitions of 1772–95 when much of the former Polish Commonwealth was
parcelled out to Catholic Austria, Protestant Prussia and Orthodox Russia.
At the same time, the religious orders were restricted or dissolved. The
harsh reality of partition was followed by complex changes in ecclesiastical control by the three partitionist powers and by the Age of the Uprisings (1830–64), when Poland experienced the grim rhythms of rebellion
and repression. But repression produced unexpected benefits to the Catholic Church in terms of greater solidarity between priests and people and,
despite the condemnations of the papacy, the emergence of a distinctive
kind of Polish Catholic nationalism which helped build one of the most
enduring Catholic cultures in modern Europe. Polish Catholicism thrived
on adversity.

The Polish story has some parallels with Irish Catholicism. In the eighteenth century a combination of penal laws (however loosely enforced),
economic and political disadvantage and Anglo-Irish Protestant ascendancy helped forge a closer relationship between priests and people, and set
the scene for the emergence of a primitive kind of Catholic democratic
nationalism led by Daniel O'Connell in the 1820s. However, not all was
plain sailing for the Church in the early nineteenth century. A rapidly
growing and largely peasant population, lack of resources, the persistence of
an ecclesiastically resistant brand of folk Catholicism, inadequacies within
the priesthood and the relative absence of religious orders all made it difficult for the Church to impose reforms on the wider population, especially
in the impoverished west of the country. Ultimately, the Church was helped
by circumstances, however grim, beyond its immediate control. Structural
changes, such as the rise of a market economy and the rapid population
decline caused by the devastating effects of the Irish famine, ultimately
helped Catholic bishops and clergy produce what amounted to a 'devotional
revolution' in Catholic practices in the middle decades of the nineteenth
century. By then mass attendance in Irish towns and cities was well on its
way to the kind of extraordinarily high percentages that seemed inconceiv-
able in the long eighteenth century.[25] In both Ireland and Poland, therefore,
the national project, namely the solidification of a national identity around
the Roman Catholic Church as the one institution strong enough to attract

the loyalty of the people against external 'oppressors', helped produce religious cultures of surprising strength and durability in the nineteenth and twentieth centuries.

A different pattern took shape in Joseph II's Habsburg Empire. In an attempt to create a national church freed from papal control and available to help modernize the state, Joseph instigated wide-ranging reforms in the 1780s. These included the dissolution of many monasteries, a massive cull of the regular clergy (they were outside state control) and the reduction in the number of feast days, pilgrimages, processions and fraternities. Through widespread reform of parishes and ecclesiastical welfare provision, the aim was to produce a more contemplative and streamlined form of pastoral Catholicism shorn of some of its baroque pretentiousness. In particular, the mendicant orders were slowly eradicated, clerical wealth redistributed and new parishes created. This more 'rational' and state-directed form of Catholicism, however well intentioned, was scarcely popular at the time and may have contributed to the demise of Roman Catholicism in late nineteenth-century cities, when new demographic and political pressures could not be contained by any amount of parochial reform and there was less popular Catholicism to fall back on.[26]

As the preceding discussions have shown, the relationship between churches and states in early modern Europe needs to be rooted in the particular historical contingencies of national contexts. But given the fact that the most important faith traditions in this period were also international in reach and scope (especially Roman Catholicism), it is not surprising to find that some conflicts were not easily confined to tidy geographical and political boundaries. That was certainly true of the long-lasting disputes between Jansenists and Jesuits which reached back to Tridentine disagreements over the Catholic doctrine of justification. While distancing themselves from Martin Luther's Reformation doctrine of justification by grace through faith alone, Jansenists embraced a more rigorously Augustinian view of the operation of divine grace in salvation than was characteristic of Jesuit theology, with its stronger sense of human agency in the salvation process. In the stereotyping that followed, Jesuits portrayed Jansenists as closet Catholic Calvinists plotting to overthrow the Church from within, while Jansenists portrayed Jesuits as heretical Pelagians seeking to dominate the Church. But as with most theological conflicts in the history of Christianity there was more at stake than theology alone. The parsing out of Augustinian propositions was undeniably important to both parties, but Jansenists also became alarmed by the increasing power and influence of the Jesuit Order over Catholic education, the confessional and missions.[27]

In France the conflict revved up in the early eighteenth century as the

Bourbon monarchy, with Jesuit advisers to the fore, pressed the papacy for action against the Jansenists culminating in the papal bull *Unigenitus* (1713), four years after the destruction of the Jansenist enclave of Port Royal (1709). As the century wore on, however, Jansenism strengthened its appeal both to the laity in northern French cities and to those wishing to defend the liberties of the Gallican church against papal encroachment. By the middle of the century the Jansenist cause was gaining ground within the Paris *parlement* and among lawyers and publishers. Meanwhile, throughout Europe and beyond, a storm tide was gathering against the Jesuits, once the heralds of the Counter Reformation, who by the mid-eighteenth century had seemed to become too powerful for their own good. From the Jesuit reductions in Paraguay to the bankruptcy of the Jesuits' mission in the French West Indies, and from the reforming energies of 'enlightened' administrators in Portugal and Spain to a series of legal feuds in the Paris *parlement*, the Jesuits seemed to be on the receiving end of remorselessly bad news, all the more serious because it could neither be contained within a single country nor confined to a single issue. Beginning in Portugal with the expulsion of the Jesuits from the metropolitan mainland and the Asian and South American colonies in 1759, the dominoes of the demise of the Jesuit Order tumbled with inexorable rapidity. In 1764 the Society was dissolved in France; in 1767, following the infamous Hat and Cloak Riots of a year earlier, Charles III of Spain followed the Portuguese model by expelling the Jesuits from Spain and its colonies; Naples and Parma followed suit the same year; and in 1773 Clement XIV, under irresistible pressure from the Bourbon powers, formally dissolved the society with the bull *Dominus ac Redemptor*. The papal dissolution naturally spelt the end of the Jesuits among the Catholic German states, within the domains of the Austrian Habsburgs and in missions everywhere.

The Jansenist international had secured its objective but at the price of polarizing Catholic Europe, undermining the authority of the papacy, emboldening lay anti-clericalism and prizing open divisions within the French Church, which came home to roost before and during the French Revolution, when the Civil Constitution of the Clergy literally split the French clergy in two. The rage once directed at the Jesuits, in the heat of Revolution, came to be directed against the Church itself. By then the arch supported by the twin pillars of church and state became a pile of dust.[28] There is of course an important postscript to this story. Not only did Jesuit influence, however mutilated, survive suppression, but in 1814 the Society was restored by an official act of Pius VII and grew steadily throughout the nineteenth century, returning eventually to almost all of its former territories.[29]

The Orthodox Church in Russia[30]

In some respects the trajectory of the eastern Orthodox churches in the seventeenth century closely mirrored that of Counter Reformation Catholicism. There were similar attempts to impose hierarchical control of the clergy, improve educational standards, purify public worship and liturgies, revitalize parish life and purge popular beliefs and practices of their superstitious elements. But reform came at a price. The central figure in the ensuing storm of controversy was Nikon (1605–81), the Patriarch of Moscow, who had risen to power in the church under the patronage of Tsar Aleksei Mikhailovich (1645–76). Nikon and other church reformers at court became persuaded, erroneously as it happens, that the Greek Church's liturgies were purer and of more ancient provenance than those of the Russian Church. Based on that assumption, the ruthlessness with which Nikon's liturgical reforms were carried out inevitably provoked a counter-reaction among the traditional Orthodox or Old Believers as they came to be called. Although Nikon and the tsar came to a parting of the ways, Aleksei and his reforming advisers continued the policy of rigorous liturgical reform with unfortunate consequences. A dangerous cocktail of conservatism, millennialism, rebellion, martyrdom and even mass suicides rocked the Russian Orthodox Church in the closing decades of the seventeenth century. Assailed Old Believers established conservative communities far away from the reaches of imperial persecution, but church and state in close partnership continued their attempts to reform the Church and suppress unofficial saints' cults and other unacceptable expressions of folk religiosity.[31]

When Peter I (1682–1725) became tsar he presided over an empire of considerable ethnic and religious diversity, but the Orthodox Church was the established church, membership of which was a virtual precondition for political influence, social advance, financial exemptions and legal privileges. Although authorized to proselytize and expected to be an agent for the disciplining of Russian subjects, the Orthodox Church faced formidable difficulties in pursuing its holy mission. In the first place, Peter sought to reduce the Church's political power, exploit its material wealth and gain more control over its administrative structures. When Patriarch Adrian died in 1700, Peter appointed a Ukrainian as *locum tenens* of the patriarchal throne and in 1721 the Church was placed under the control of the Most Holy Governing Synod. This change from patriarchal to collegial governance did not lead to the degree of secular political control over the Church that was once thought, but it did make clear that the Church was both politically subservient and spiritually responsible for the vast domains under its authority.[32] How did it measure up to the task?

With a larger and more divided leadership and with weak institutional instruments of policy implementation in the localities, the Holy Synod's influence was not felt until the middle of the century when diocesan administration and clerical education were slowly improved. Though even here the Russian Church experienced the same kinds of problems as did predominantly Catholic countries with strong traditions of folk Catholicism; namely the more austere and enlightened the piety the less likely it was to have mass popular appeal.[33] In the reign of Catherine II (1762–96) some bishops introduced enlightened reform to their dioceses, appointed controversial 'upholders of good order' (*blagochinnye*) and expanded access to theological seminaries. By the end of the century, 'though brutalized by their teachers, isolated from their flock by a curriculum steeped in Latinity, and impoverished by their lowly social status, Russia's parish priests were now more professionally prepared than ever'.[34] On the other hand, the Church as an institution was less respected by social elites and suffered from the secularization of considerable amounts of its land and property. The European-wide phenomenon of secular rulers appropriating ecclesiastical land and wealth for secular purposes, while expecting the church to deliver a superior service, was one of the chief characteristics of the Enlightenment era, and Russia was no exception.

Despite the Western-inspired reforming energies of Peter and Catherine, the Russian Church remained something of a ramshackle institution throughout the century, but as in many other parts of Europe it is important not to equate church performance with popular piety. For millions of Russian peasants the Orthodox tradition with its simple icons, calendrical rhythms of fasts and feasts, rites of passage (baptism, marriage and death), remembered prayers, control of the spirits of home and nature, appeals to saints for healing and protection, visits to shrines and pilgrimages, construction of sacred and mythical stories, and rudimentary commitment to the Eucharist and the liturgies, brought together religious meaning with a deep sense of local and national identity.[35] In that respect, as in others, the Orthodox tradition was both distinctively and profoundly Russian in nature, but also shared many of the same devotional and ecclesiastical characteristics as other European countries in the eighteenth century, including a discrepancy between what reforming elites considered were acceptable religious practices and what had been sanctified by long usage in popular culture.

But Russia was not only a European country facing west in the eighteenth century; it was also an enormous empire of uncertain geographical boundaries extending from the Black Sea to the Arctic Ocean, and from the Baltic Sea to the Pacific Ocean. Its territory was huge, covering one-sixth of the earth's land mass, and it contained an enormous variety of ethnicities, languages and religious traditions. Research into how the Russian Orthodox Church conceived of its mission to this sprawling empire, and even more how that mission was received by diverse populations, is still at an early stage, but it is nevertheless possible to sketch the most salient characteristics. Perhaps most important of all is how the Orthodox mission, after the middle of the sixteenth century, became a major part of the growing Russian Empire's sense of imperial destiny. Another point of interest is how treatment of the Old Believers, as a heretical Orthodox community, set a paradigm for the approach to non-Christians and Christians alike in the late seventeenth and eighteenth centuries. Buffering the population against Old Believers became a major goal of church and state, even to the extent of the Church using pagans as examples of laudable behaviour in comparison to Orthodox backsliding and Old Believer heresy. Moreover, in some areas, as in Archbishop Afanasii's newly created diocese of Kholmogory in northern Russia, the Old Believers acted as a cadre of itinerant preachers who forced the Orthodox Church to work even harder to promote its own version of Orthodoxy. In this way the challenge from Old Believers both distracted the Church from evangelizing non-Christian communities and made the point that diversity was better tolerated among non-Orthodox believers than within Orthodoxy itself.[36]

The Russian time line of missions to those outside the Orthodox fold altogether is well summarized by Michael Khodarkovsky, who states that the 'intensity of state and church efforts to convert non-Christians varied from brutal campaigns under Ivan IV to benign neglect in the seventeenth century, from unambiguous discrimination under Peter I to systematic coercion during the middle of the eighteenth century, and finally, to toleration under Catherine II. At all times, however, religious conversion remained one of the most important tools of Russia's imperial policies.'[37] Under Peter I the missionary imperative grew stronger in importance owing to a combination of factors including competition with the missionary exploits of European Catholic empires, the perceived need for imperial coherence and a growing sense of political and religious struggle with Islam in the southern and eastern parts of the empire. The essayist and economist Ivan Pososhkov (1652–1726), who was a close supporter of Peter I, wrote in 1719 that 'The Catholics are sending their missionaries to China, India, and America' while we, despite having the right faith, cannot convert our own peoples. 'Our pagans are like children without a written language, without a law, and they do not live far away, but within the Russian empire, along the Volga and the Kama rivers; and they are not sovereign, but the subjects of Russia.'[38]

Missionary strategy under Peter I was largely based on a combination of financial incentives, draconian laws and rigorous discrimination against non-Christians. It soon became clear to the Russians, however, as it had earlier to the Spanish and Portuguese, that social incentives and legislative discrimination did not make for very inspiring converts, and some efforts were made to understand and persuade rather than to coerce and constrain. However, these efforts largely foundered on the rocks of inadequate language preparation, lack of resources and widespread corruption among local officials who manipulated the elaborate code of financial and military exemptions for their own interests. Moreover, the disturbing news that growing numbers of non-Russians were converting to Islam led to some enforced resettlement and rough handling, which left a deep and enduring scar on Muslims in the Kazan and Azov provinces.

An even more determined and ultimately more brutal mission policy began in the 1740s with the establishment of a new Agency of Convert Affairs which concentrated much of its attention on the Muslim and pagan populations of the Kazan region in the south. The old carrot-and-stick approach returned with a vengeance. In 1743 the government ordered the demolition of 418 out of 536 mosques (yet more were demolished in Astrakhan province and Siberia), tolerated forced conversions and offered criminal pardons and exemption from military service to potential converts. In this phase of missionary zeal the Russian state and church had to strike a balance between exerting sufficient force to maintain the stream of converts, but not so much that it provoked revolts and political instability. In the middle decades of the eighteenth century, the reports of conversions by the Agency of Convert Affairs were impressive in number and unimpressive in quality, which was a persistent refrain in reports from the regions to the centre. Christian missions were obviously in trouble when state and church had to implement policies to punish those who converted multiple times merely to secure the bribes and inducements that were on offer.

The reign of Catherine II, as befitted her enlightened credentials, was marked by a return to a policy of pragmatic religious toleration and a more educative and persuasive kind of Christian mission. The Agency of Convert Affairs was abolished and much more pragmatic policies were put in place for dealing with the insupportable inducements that had been offered to converts. Partly out of imperial exigencies, and partly out of a growing sense that bribed or forced religious conversion was both ineffectual and counter-productive, both state and church relaxed the intemperate zeal of the middle decades of the century.

What then is the balance sheet of a century of Orthodox missions to the imperial populations of Russia? Most striking is the degree of collaboration between state and church in trying to extend the sway of Orthodox

Christianity over the non-Christian peoples of the empire. This was seen as part imperial necessity, part religious obligation and part civilizing mission. Religious conversion, and the change of identity that inevitably accompanied it, seems to have operated most successfully among those individuals who had expressly something to gain from it, especially propertied elites and those at the very bottom of the social pyramid. Even in these cases, however, active Christianization was much more difficult to produce than mere baptism or the standard signed petition of a new religious affiliation. In addition, conversions by Muslims, outside periods of serious coercion, were more difficult to secure than from other non-Christian subjects, largely because they were already beneficiaries of an established religious system with its clergy, mosques, inherited tradition and literary culture. Perhaps even more so than with the Roman Catholic missions to the Americas, and certainly more than with the British and Dutch Protestant missions, Russian Orthodox missions were viewed as an essential part of the state's colonization process. That was both their strength and weakness.

A rather different, almost Jesuitical pattern of mission emerged among early nineteenth-century Orthodox missionaries to the Aleut population of Alaska and the Chukchi and Altaians in Siberia. Although there was an earlier mission to Alaska from the Valaam monastery in the 1790s, the most important figure in the Orthodox penetration of Alaska was Fr Ivan (Ioann) Popov (Veniaminov) (1797–1871), who while not encouraging pre-Christian native practices nevertheless displayed a more flexible and tolerant attitude to native culture than his predecessors. Although well read in Enlightenment literature, Veniaminov contrasted the corruption of Europeans with the moral simplicity and purity of the Aleut people. A similar, if an even more spiritually rigorous, approach was taken by Makarii Glukharev (1792–1847), the founder and head of the Altai mission. At the centre of their approaches was 'an optimistic belief in upgrading all of the indigenous peoples of the empire through gentle persuasion'.[39] Relatively free from imperial control and expectation, and shaped by Orthodox monastic disciplines of self-abnegation and physical labour, Orthodox missionaries to the borderlands of the Russian Empire in the nineteenth century were far removed in style and substance from those owing obedience to the Agency of Convert Affairs in the mid-eighteenth century. Greater sensitivity to indigenous religion, combined with more rigorous standards of what was expected of converts to Orthodox Christianity, was pioneered more on the fringes of the Russian Empire than in its heartlands. Thus the Orthodox missions to the imperial populations of Russia from the mid-sixteenth to the mid-nineteenth century were determined as much by the nature of their connection to the imperial project as to their Orthodox theology.[40]

What drove the Orthodox mission to the non-Christian inhabitants of the Russian Empire in the eighteenth century was the idea that conversion to Orthodox Christianity was 'a way of consolidating the society into a single political and religious identity under one tsar and one God'.[41] The rest was a matter of tactics.

Revolutions

The revolutions that swept across the North Atlantic world in the later eighteenth century had complex origins and very different characteristics. Hence their ramifications for Christianity, in both the short and the long term, varied considerably from place to place. The roots of the Atlantic revolutions have been variously located in imperial competition, especially between Great Britain and France, international warfare, increased financial pressures on states (largely caused by wars), the impact of Enlightenment critiques of established institutions, changing economic and social structures and the fraying of *ancien régime* established churches. Since Christianity, albeit of different stripes, was deeply embedded in eighteenth-century states, religion was a significant component of the causes and consequences of revolutionary energy. At the most basic level, revolutions divided Christians between supporters of a divinely sanctioned established order and supporters of new movements designed to sweep away corruption and establish purer and less tyrannical forms of government. Within those broad camps there were of course many variations and shifts over time as fast-changing events radicalized revolutionaries and hardened reactionaries. Few aspects of revolutionary situations remained stable for long.

Moreover, the meaning of revolution differed from place to place. In America, revolutionaries were protesting about arbitrary government, unfair taxation, colonial exploitation and infringements on liberty. When revolution came, established churches, especially Anglican, did not fare well, but Christianity itself if anything became more revivalistic and even more popular. In France, the revolutionary dynamic was more corrosive of all established institutions, including the monarchy, the nobility and the church, and the result was a more wide-ranging attack on Christianity itself, especially during the most radical phase of the revolution when a thoroughgoing de-Christianization was in vogue. Perhaps the best way of penetrating to the heart of what was at stake for the history of Christianity in the age of revolution is to compare and contrast the two most momentous revolutions, the American and the French. The first took place among the relatively small but overwhelmingly Protestant population of the American colonies, the second occurred in the much larger and overwhelmingly Roman Catholic population of Bourbon France.

In the same way that historians of France draw attention to the Jansenist campaign against the Jesuits as helping to form a revolutionary discourse of much wider application, American colonial historians emphasize the importance of the Great Awakening – as the first great inter-colonial movement – in shaping a discourse of liberty from sin, millennial expectancy (including a vigorous anti-Catholicism) and colonial identity. Whitefield's sermons in particular supplied the American colonists with 'a rhetoric of community' that successfully promoted 'a common conceptual system among the variegated colonial cultures', in which rough bridges were built connecting Calvinist theology and republican ideology.[42] By communicating with unprecedented numbers of people, both verbally and in print, Whitefield's rhetoric, though ostensibly non-political, contributed to the emergence of a shared American identity at a time of increasing stress and strain between the mother country and her colonies.

One of the main conundrums of the American Revolution from a European perspective, however, is how to explain the fact that Enlightenment deists, Evangelical Protestants and other diverse religious traditions could come together in a relatively unified (not forgetting the Empire loyalists) front to cast off British rule and institute a libertarian constitution. The most recent answer to this problem emphasizes five shared principles of religious freedom on which deists, Evangelicals and others could agree: the desirability of disestablishing state churches; the recognition of the natural rights of all humans as God's creatures; the danger (given the propensities of human sinfulness) of the consolidation of political power by rulers and governments; the importance of virtue and benevolence in securing the common good; and the belief that divine providence ordered the affairs of peoples and nations.[43] In particular, enlightened advocates of religious freedom such as Thomas Jefferson (1743–1826) and James Madison (1751–1836) shared with Evangelical Baptists such as Isaac Backus (1724–1806) and other dissenters a mutual dislike of the persecuting tendencies of established churches. It is important to state that these shared principles, important though they were, theoretically had as much capacity to divide as unite the broad spectrum of American religious traditions on the eve of the Revolution. There were, after all, *varieties* of positions on established churches, natural rights, political power, virtue and providence. What promoted a degree of colonial unity was British colonial policy, from unwelcome taxation to Anglican aspirations to have a resident American bishop, and from the Quebec Act's (1774) toleration of French Canadian Catholics (and a substantial grant of territory) to the insensitivities of royal government. As the decade of the 1770s unfolded, from the Boston Massacre of 1770 to the skirmishes in Concord and Lexington in 1775, Americans were radical-

ized by events, as well as by long-established political and religious convictions, into thinking that their liberties were under sustained attack and that
resistance was not only necessary but right. As the luxuriant literature on
the outbreak of the American Revolutionary War makes clear, there was
an abundance of revolutionary motives on display, including economic and
political self-interest, but in the words of Martin Marty, 'it did not hurt
and in the end helped immensely that so many believers made "the sacred
cause of liberty" their own by claiming that a Provident God would bless
their efforts, ennoble their sacrifices, and bless their beginnings as a new
nation'.[44]

With the war won and independence secured, not surprisingly old
religious disagreements and animosities revived between those in New
England who wanted to retain their established churches and those
who wanted rid of them, between enlightened (and militant) deists and
Evangelical populists, and between old-style Calvinists and vociferous
new Arminians (especially the fast-growing Methodists). Once the dust
of constitution making subsided, it seemed that the American constitution was more of an Enlightenment document than anything else, with
its famous First Amendment declaring that 'Congress shall make no law
respecting an establishment of religion nor prohibiting the free exercise
thereof'. Individual states within the federal union could of course retain
their religious establishments, and some did, for a while at least, but the
nineteenth century belonged not so much to religious establishments, nor
to the deists who had helped abolish them, but to the Evangelical populists
– Methodists, Baptists, and others – who stood to gain most from their
demise. These were the fastest-growing religious movements of the first
half of the nineteenth century. Only the great influx of European Catholics
(with an entirely different view of religion and liberty) from the middle
decades onwards threatened their numerical supremacy in the new republic.
Whether forming new churches in the expanding south and west, or new
organizations to promote religious causes or resist vice, American religiosity increasingly seemed to be in the hands of voluntary associations and
seemed to thrive on it. Not all was sweet progress, however. White men
more than women determined events, if not the inner functioning of religious communities; African Americans embraced Methodist and Baptist
forms of Christianity in surprising numbers, but most remained slaves or
economically impoverished; Native Americans embraced Christianity in
fewer numbers and were remorselessly pushed westwards; and Evangelical
populism for all its religious and humanitarian zeal had dark sides including support for slavery in its southern strongholds, ubiquitous anti-Catholicism and a propensity to fragment and give rise to new religious traditions

far removed from the 'enlightened' visions that people like Jefferson had for the new nation.

Ironically, the debts incurred by France during the American Revolutionary War helped set the scene for another revolution on the other side of the Atlantic. But revolutionary events in France, and their impact on the history of Christianity, played out very differently from those along the Atlantic seaboard of North America. Given the different demographic trajectories of France and the United States since the late eighteenth century, it is good to be reminded that the French Revolution occurred in a country of some 28 million people at the outset of the Revolution, compared with a population of fewer than 3 million in the new American republic. Not only in terms of scale, but also in terms of its immediate impact on the Western Christian psyche at the end of the eighteenth century, the French Revolution was for contemporaries an event of incalculably greater significance. Whether one takes an optimistic or pessimistic view of the performance and popularity of the eighteenth-century French Church – as we have already seen there are good grounds for both positions – almost no one alive in the early spring of 1789 could possibly have foreseen or predicted the scope and extent of religious transformation in France over the next decade. In that period the French Catholic Church experienced a deep schism, the complete separation of church and state, the religious toleration of Protestants and Jews, the loss of much of its landed property, tithes and feudal dues, the exile of its bishops and many of its clergy and the complete erosion of its legal privileges and its traditions of clerical self-governance. Moreover, as the French Revolution entered its most radical phase in 1793 and 1794, the attack on French Catholicism was followed by a fierce attack on Christianity itself, as anti-religious revolutionaries embarked on a concerted campaign of de-Christianization. Existing religious symbols, artefacts and practices were destroyed and new secular ones instituted, including the adoption of a new revolutionary calendar with ten-day weeks and the dating of time, not from the birth of Christ, but from the creation of the French Republic. How could all this happen in such a short space of time to a formidably wealthy and powerful church at the heart of Europe's *ancien régime*?

Taking a long view there is no doubt that the bitter internecine disputes between Jansenists and Jesuits, and Gallicans and Ultramontanists undermined the Church from within and supplied a rhetoric of ecclesiastical criticism which carried over into secular institutions. Similarly, the audacity of *philosophes'* critique of the Church, more radical and sustained than anywhere else in Europe, took a toll on the Church's ideological ramparts. Moreover, French historians have detected a decline in the social acceptability of the Church among urban elites from about the middle of the century as clerical recruitment declined, wills became more secular, anti-clericalism surfaced more regularly (especially in the French *parlements*) and Freemasonry experienced explosive growth. This was part of a European-wide pattern as Counter Reformation spirituality increasingly lost its appeal to professional and mercantile elites in towns and cities. In addition, the whole structure of ecclesiastical financial exactions, never the Church's most popular feature, came under more sustained pressure as the century wore on. As external pressures mounted, the Church was not without its internal dissensions. The suppression of the Jesuits forced a major restructuring of the Church's educational mission and there was a growing antagonism between the humble parish *curés* and the much wealthier upper and regular clergy.[45] In this way social class played out within the Church as it did in the wider society.

Important though this long view is, one needs to be careful not to exaggerate the difficulties faced by the Church on the eve of the Revolution or to neglect the evidence of a vigorous intellectual and spiritual life within the Church. That said, nothing prepared the Church for the trauma that was to come. As is well known, whatever its deeper structural causes, the French Revolution was precipitated by the virtual bankruptcy of the French state and the summoning of the deputies of the Estates General to advise the king in May 1789. Events moved fast from there: the surprisingly radical decrees of 4 August; the confiscation of clerical land in November; the extension of religious freedoms to Protestants and Jews in December 1789 and January 1790; the suppression of most of the religious orders in February 1790; the controversial failure of a motion to declare Catholicism the official 'state religion' in April; the adoption in July of the Civil Constitution of the Clergy, which reorganized French dioceses, abolished clerical positions without cure of souls and subjected clerical appointments to electoral assemblies; and the imposition of a clerical oath of allegiance to the new Constitution, which was hugely divisive, in November. By the spring of 1791, the French Catholic Church had split in two, had lost most of its wealth and privileges and was becoming the target of attack by an even more radical group of anti-clerical deists and atheists. During these two years, from the spring of 1789 to the spring of 1791, neither conservative nor papal resistance could stem the flow of attacks and forced concessions.

The Constitutional Church (as the Church conforming to the Civil Constitution became known) that emerged out of the first phase of the Revolution was not without its ardent clerical defenders, nor was it deficient in reforming zeal, but the agitated state of the country was scarcely an ideal setting for the re-establishment of clerical control and parochial discipline. The fate of the non-jurors was another matter. Subject to violent harassment, and ultimately forced into exile after the overthrow of the monarchy in the summer of 1792, many thousands of French émigré clergy streamed out of France into other parts of Europe. Conservative Catholic uprisings in northern and western France, though indicating that revolutionary changes to the Church were not supported everywhere, merely steeled the anti-clerical wing of the Revolution to even more draconian measures, including the de-Christianization that was to follow.[46] When the dust settled a little under Napoleon, a Concordat was signed with the papacy in 1801 and Organic Articles imposed on the Church in 1802. They merely confirmed what was already clear; there was no going back to the pre-1789 days. The state now called the shots.

This bare narration of the details cannot adequately convey the sense of shock and dismay the dismantlement of the French Catholic Church created among conservative ecclesiastics and established churchmen in revolutionary Europe. Moreover, the export of French revolutionary principles and practices with Napoleon's armies added considerably to the sense of religious calamity. Not all was lost to the Catholic cause, however. Napoleon's accession produced a new settlement in which Catholicism was re-established as the 'religion of the majority of the French', and French Catholicism participated in a Europe-wide confessional revival of unexpected intensity in the nineteenth century.[47] Even the papacy seemed to emerge from the ashes of the Revolution in a stronger position. Nevertheless, the seismic shock of what happened to the French Catholic Church altered forever the terms under which religious establishments operated, not only in France but throughout Europe and beyond, and the divisions between religious conservatives and the anti-clerical and potentially socialistic radicals persisted until well into the twentieth century. In short, the French Revolution not only dealt a body blow to Europe's most prestigious Church but helped define the terms for future religious and political alignments in post-revolutionary Europe.

The Atlantic revolutions at the end of the eighteenth century, in their different ways, established important conditions for the modern development of Christianity in the West. Europe's established churches were not crushed by the revolutions, but their bargaining power with states had been dealt a heavy blow. On the other hand, the American Revolution, which on the surface seemed to weaken the role of religion in national affairs, opened up the possibility of vigorous new forms of voluntary religious organizations outside the purview of state control. Christianity was nothing if not resilient.

Continuity and Change

The confessional geography of Europe that emerged from the long and bloody wars of religion known as the Thirty Years' War (1618–48) survived with only minor modifications throughout the long eighteenth century. There are of course examples of Protestant princely houses converting to Roman Catholicism, and there are any number of migrations of religious minorities in search of more tolerant air, but by the end of the eighteenth century, as at its beginning, Roman Catholicism was still in the ascendancy across much of Southern Europe and the western Mediterranean and Protestantism remained dominant throughout much of Northern and North-Central Europe. On the south-western fringes of Europe, Christianity of a predominantly Orthodox hue still confronted the Islamic Ottoman Empire in the Balkans, but the Ottoman Turks had lost some ground over the course of the century. Our period ends with the beginning of the Greek War of Independence against Ottoman rule in 1821, when confessional pogroms carried out by both Christians and Muslims were a shocking indication of the durability of confessional conflict in Turkey and the Balkans, and also a segue into the rise of nationalism in the nineteenth century.

In other respects also, continuity seemed to be the order of the day. European states, whether Catholic or Protestant, still employed established churches as the chief means of Christianizing their populations, and the seemingly eternal rhythms of parishes and graveyards, religious rites of passage and religious processions and festivals seemed to go on as before. Even what we know of the popular beliefs and practices of the urban and rural poor, still a much neglected topic of research, suggests that deferential submission to Christianity co-existed with a complex set of beliefs about the supernatural designed to bring good luck, to cure people and animals, to foretell the future and to cope with fear and death. There was also a subcultural world of witches and wise men, oracles and folk healers in which belief in the devil or other malevolent forces was at least as prevalent as adherence to the kind of Christianity taught by the ubiquitous catechisms. In short, the beliefs and practices of the European peasantry, whether living in states dominated by Catholicism, Protestantism or Orthodoxy, probably changed very little over the course of the eighteenth century.[1] Other continuities are also striking – from Western Christianity's complicity in the thriving slave trade to the unwillingness of most Christian states to grant religious toleration to their confessional minorities.

Moreover, the bitter confessional divisions between Catholics and Protestants bequeathed by the Reformation and Counter Reformations of the sixteenth century had still not run their course. Anti-Catholicism was a primary organizing principle of states and peoples throughout the Protestant and most of the Orthodox environs of Europe, North America and beyond. Protestants and Catholics organized themselves into rival secret societies in parts of Ireland, confronted one another in New South Wales in eastern Australia (mostly British and Irish convicts), and devised rival mission strategies in many other parts of the world.

An emphasis on historic continuities is an essential part of the story of the Christian church in the eighteenth century, but it is not sufficient. Tectonic shifts were also evident. Within Roman Catholicism the high water mark of Tridentine Catholic renewal with its Iberian empires, Jesuit colleges, lay confraternities, Marian sodalities, rural missions and popular pilgrimages was passing. 'Plagued by internal squabbles, attacked by Catholic monarchs, challenged by atheist and deist philosophies,' states Hsia, 'the Catholic Church on the eve of the French Revolution was everywhere under siege.'[2] Put another way, 'as the Counter Reformation ran into the sands, more new things were happening on a local basis in the Protestant world than the Catholic'. Pietism, Methodism, Evangelicalism and the rise of the Protestant missionary societies all threw up vital new communities of faith and helped lift the siege of Catholic gains made in the century after the Peace of Westphalia (1648).[3]

Other changes were just as dramatic. In one of the unlikeliest cultural transitions in the history of the Christian church, at precisely the time when the slave trade (in terms of numbers) reached its apogee in the second half of the eighteenth century, the foundations were being laid for the emergence of a vibrant black Christianity in the Caribbean islands, the American colonies and ultimately in Africa itself. This study makes no apology for devoting large amounts of space to telling that remarkable story. On a less optimistic note for the future of Christianity, this period also witnessed a series of intellectual challenges from which Christianity, at least among educated elites, has never fully recovered. Whereas in the seventeenth century most educated Westerners presumed Christianity was true unless these were very good reasons for doubt, something like the reverse is the case in the early twenty-first century. The roots of this shift go back to the complex of intellectual changes we designate as the Enlightenment. As this study has shown the Enlightenment was not primarily an atheistic movement, nor was the rise of science a necessarily secularizing phenomenon, but it is the case that in the eighteenth century belief in supernatural and revealed religion encountered serious intellectual challenges that in some respects have never been fully answered. Equally seriously for the churches was the fact that over the course of the long eighteenth century there had been a substantial 'secularization' of church lands which inexorably reduced the economic and social power of Europe's established churches, and hence their political and cultural influence.

Another change of global significance for the history of Christianity was the slow decline of the Catholic Iberian empires of Spain and Portugal and the rise of the Protestant empires of Britain, the Netherlands and, in a provisional way, the United States. Missionary dynamics followed imperial realities, even if missionaries were rarely cast in the role of mere imperial lackeys. It seemed that by the end of the eighteenth century, even the oceans had deserted the Catholic cause as the volume of trade and shipping began to shift inexorably to the Protestant empires. As expelled Jesuits were returning home, new Protestant missions were beginning to pick up steam, pioneered by Moravians, Methodists and Evangelicals. At the end of our period the first Protestant missionaries had reached China, Australia and New Zealand, and Protestantism swept through some of the Pacific islands such as Tonga, Tahiti and Samoa like a tidal wave. Meanwhile, the demise of the Catholic empires was accompanied by independence movements within Latin America, within which Catholic Christianity played a predictably ambiguous role. With pardonable simplification, most of the bishops and many of the religious were *peninsulares* and royalists, many of the upper-class creole priests essentially wanted a 'creole Church for a creole state', while many of the lower-class priests were more sympathetic to the victims of imperial rule.[4] The fissions produced by these different ecclesiastical points on the imperial compass go a long way towards explaining the complex history of religion within the independence movements of Latin America throughout the nineteenth century.

Other tectonic shifts were also affecting Christianity by the early nineteenth century. Phenomenal population increase, proto-industrialization and rapid urbanization was affecting religious expression, especially in England where Anglicanism, especially after 1790, confronted a surging Evangelical Nonconformity (principally Methodist) in areas where its parochial organization was least able to cope. In other parts of Europe, Catholic Christianity had partly weathered the storm of revolutionary iconoclasm and Napoleonic subjugation to emerge with dreams of revival and restoration in post-1815 Europe. The next 30 years would show that while Catholic Christianity showed remarkable signs of religious life (even the Jesuit Order was restored), it had taken a fearful pounding. The Church waged a long, and not entirely unsuccessful, war against liberals and socialists throughout the nineteenth century, but in places like France the indices of religious belief and practice were not moving in the Church's direction.

Perhaps the most important change of all over the course of the long eighteenth century was the indisputable fact that by the early nineteenth century the Christian West had emerged as the economic powerhouse of the world. The predominantly Islamic societies of the Middle East, including the Arab countries, Iran, Turkey and the Balkans, had fallen behind. This shift in the economic balance of power underpinning religious traditions was the product of 'a long divergence' going back centuries, but it was not until the beginning of the nineteenth century that its effects became obvious. What were its causes and consequences?

Economic historians suggest that it was not so much the religious content of Islam as much as the legal system that grew up around it that lies at the root of Middle Eastern economic underperformance. The alleged 'culprits' are inheritance laws, polygamy, the relative absence of corporations and merchant organizations and the particular characteristics of courts and social welfare systems. Collectively these led to a lack of property and capital accumulation, which placed the Middle East at a competitive disadvantage with Western Europe long before the consequences of Western colonialism took their toll. Technical legal regulations on the inheritance of property or on the formation and dissolution of partnerships had dramatic long-term consequences for economic activity. For example, the Islamic inheritance system dispersed wealth to a wide class of family members, including women, which was superficially fair but economically disastrous, in that the descendants of prosperous Ottoman families in the early modern period rarely remained wealthy for more than a couple of generations. Hence, it was more difficult for established aristocracies to develop in the Middle East than in Europe, just as the inflexibility of Islamic partnership law made it more difficult for larger corporations to emerge.

Moreover, systems and regulations that worked tolerably well in the early Middle Ages were found wanting in the different economic circumstances of a later period. Hence, the first predominantly owned joint-stock company of the Ottoman Empire, a marine transportation company, was not founded until 1851, long after the formation of similar companies in Western Europe. Similarly, the first two successful banks of the Middle East, the Bank of Egypt and the Ottoman Bank, were also founded in the 1850s, long after it became clear that Islamic economies were seriously underperforming those in the West. One does not have to resort to 'essentialist' religious arguments about Protestantism and the rise of capitalism or Islam and economic underperformance to conclude that by the beginning of the nineteenth century a powerful combination of historical contingencies and the outworking of religious cultures had produced an economic disequilibrium that boded ill for future relations between Christians and Muslims.[5]

In conclusion, it is difficult to sum up over a century's worth of persistent continuity and dynamic change in a short statement. Perhaps the editors of the *New Cambridge History* came close when they entitled their eighteenth-century volume *Enlightenment, Awakening and Revolution*. Irreversible changes in patterns of thought, ubiquitous examples of renewal and revival throughout the world (not just Europe) and the shock of revolutions in Europe, the Americas and beyond were the most important shapers of global Christianity in the eighteenth century. On the other hand, the three words 'Enlightenment', 'Awakening' and 'Revolution' betray more of a European than a wider world version of Christianity's eighteenth-century trinity. From a vantage point outside Europe, different trinities might apply, such as imperial power, colonial encounters and native resistance, or, alternatively, mission, hybridism and indigenization. In the eighteenth century, Christianity was not only transformed within the confines of Europe but also at the margins of European overseas empires. Perhaps the most important message of this study is not to conflate European Christendom with the full extent of world Christianity, even if the former played a major role in the shaping of the latter.

Finally, Christianity, for all its associations with imperialism, slavery and other unpleasant realities, was unmistakably a missionary religion, capable of translating its texts, symbols and idioms into manifold new spaces throughout the world. Naturally, translation, when associated with differentials of power, could produce regrettable results, but it also lay at the heart of Christianity's capacity to transcend cultural specificities to become a genuinely global religious tradition. Christianity's worldwide expansion was not without its cruelties and cultural impositions, but neither was it devoid of heroism and humanitarianism, sacrifice and service.

Chronology

1680	The Pueblo Revolt against Spanish colonization in New Mexico.
1685	The revocation of the Edict of Nantes by Louis XIV.
1689	The Act of Toleration passed by the English Parliament.
1699	The Treaty of Karlowitz concluded between the Ottoman Empire and Austria, Venice and Poland, which ceded territory permanently to Christian powers.
1701	The Society for the Propagation of the Gospel in Foreign Parts (SPG) is founded in London.
1702	The outbreak of the Revolt of the Camisards in the Cévennes region of France.
1704	The beginning of the Antonian Movement in the Kongo under the leadership of Dona Beatriz.
1706	Bartholomäus Ziegenbalg and Heinrich Plütschau establish a Protestant mission in the Danish colony of Tranquebar in India.
1711	Christopher Wren completes the construction of St Paul's Cathedral in London.
1715	Clement XI issues papal bull *Ex illa Die* officially condemning the Chinese Rites.
1721	Peter the Great abolishes the Moscow patriarchate and places the Russian Orthodox Church under the government-controlled 'Holy Synod'.
1722	The settlement of the Moravians on Count Zinzendorf's Berthelsdorf Estate and the founding of Herrnhut.
1723	Johann Sebastian Bach appointed cantor at St Thomas's Church in Leipzig.

1730	The beginning of Oxford Methodism under the leadership of John and Charles Wesley.
1735	The Northampton (Massachusetts) revival inspired by the preaching of Jonathan Edwards. Also regarded as the beginning of the 'Great Awakening' in the American colonies.
1737–38	George Whitefield launches his preaching career in England and America.
1739	The first Methodist Societies are formed in London and Bristol.
1742	G.F. Handel's oratorio *Messiah* has its premier in Dublin.
1750	The Treaty of Madrid defines the boundaries between Spanish and Portuguese colonies in South America.
1755	The Lisbon earthquake kills at least 30,000 people.
1756	The War of the Seven Reductions between the Guaraní Indians and the Portuguese and Spanish in South America.
1773	Clement XIV issues papal bull *Dominus ac redemptor* suppressing the Society of Jesus (Jesuits).
1775	The outbreak of the American War of Independence (1775–83).
1779	John Newton and William Cowper publish *Olney Hymns* which includes the classic hymn 'Amazing Grace'.
1780	Túpac Amaru II leads an indigenous rebellion against Spanish rule in Peru.
1783	Joseph II reorganizes diocesan boundaries in the Habsburg Empire.
1784	Immanuel Kant publishes *What is Enlightenment?*
1789	The beginning of the French Revolution.
1790	Civil Constitution of the Clergy passed in France.
1791	The Bill of Rights (amendments 1–10 of the US Constitution) is ratified.
1792	Mary Wollstonecraft publishes *A Vindication of the Rights of Woman*.
	The formation of the Particular Baptist Society for the Propagation of the Gospel Amongst the Heathen (Baptist Missionary Society).
	The Sierra Leone Company arranges for the relocation of African Americans to Freetown in Sierra Leone (West Africa).

1795	The formation of the London Missionary Society.
1798	The Rebellion of the United Irishmen.
1801	Concord between France and the Vatican.
1804	Coronation of Napoleon in Notre Dame Cathedral in Paris.
1807	The slave trade (but not slavery) is abolished throughout the British Empire.
	Robert Morrison, the first Protestant missionary, arrives in China.
1810	The formation of the American Board of Commissioners for Foreign Missions.
1814	Jesuits universally restored by the Bull *Sollicitudo omnium ecclesiarum*.
1821	The outbreak of the Greek War of Independence.

Notes

Introduction

1. W.R. Ward, *Christianity under the Ancien Régime 1648–1789* (Cambridge, 1999), preface.
2. I do not mean to imply by this that single-volume and single-authored histories of Christianity in the early modern period are no longer produced. See, for example, Meic Pearse, *The Age of Reason: From the Wars of Religion to the French Revolution* (Grand Rapids, MI, 2006).
3. For a superb account of the shift in Christianity's centre of gravity in the twentieth century see Todd M. Johnson and Kenneth R. Ross (eds), *Atlas of Global Christianity* (Edinburgh, 2009).
4. See John McManners (ed), *The Oxford Illustrated History of Christianity* (Oxford, 1990); Stewart J. Brown and Timothy Tackett (eds), *The Cambridge History of Christianity*, vol. VII, *Enlightenment, Reawakening and Revolution* (Cambridge, 2006); and Adrian Hastings (ed), *A World History of Christianity* (London, 1999).

Chapter 1. Surveying the Contours: Maps, Travels and Empires

1. Andrew F. Walls, *The Missionary Movement in Christian History: Studies in the Transmission of Faith* (Maryknoll, NY, 1996), p 3.
2. W.R. Ward, *Christianity under the Ancien Régime 1648–1789* (Cambridge, 1999), pp 74–82.
3. *Ibid.*, p 68. The best introduction to early modern Roman Catholicism is R. Po-Chia Hsia, *The World of Catholic Renewal, 1540–1770* (Cambridge, 2005). For the period under discussion see pp 217–32.
4. Nigel Aston, *Art and Religion in Eighteenth-Century Europe* (London, 2009), pp 7–8. Much of the preceding paragraph is based on Aston's authoritative survey.
5. Bars'kyj's untitled travel journal survives in an autograph manuscript of over 500 folios and around 240,000 words. See Alexander Grishin, 'Bars'kyj and the Orthodox Community', in Michael Angold (ed), *The Cambridge History of Christianity*, vol. 5, *Eastern Christianity* (Cambridge, 2006), pp 210–28.
6. For a good treatment of Orthodox Christians within the Ottoman Empire see Barbara Jelavich, *The History of the Balkans: The Eighteenth and Nineteenth*

Centuries (Cambridge, 1983), vol. 1, pp 39–126.

7. For an excellent account of the Antonian Movement see John K. Thornton, *The Kongolese Saint Anthony: Don Beatriz Kimpa Vita and the Antonian Movement, 1684–1706* (Cambridge, 1998).

8. This is the argument presented by Adrian Hastings, *The Church in Africa 1450–1950* (Oxford, 1994), p 129.

9. *Ibid.*, pp 167–8.

10. For the geography of Christian settlements and mission activity in North America see Bret E. Carroll, *The Routledge Historical Atlas of Religion in America* (New York, 2000).

11. Ondina E. González and Justo L. González, *Christianity in Latin America* (New York, 2008), p 102.

12. See James D. Riley, 'Christianity in Iberian America', in Stewart J. Brown and Timothy Tackett (eds), *The Cambridge History of Christianity*, vol. VII, *Enlightenment, Reawakening and Revolution 1660–1815* (Cambridge, 2006), pp 373–91.

13. David Brion Davis, *Inhuman Bondage: The Rise and Fall of Slavery in the New World* (New York, 2006), p 1.

14. Samuel Hugh Moffett, *A History of Christianity in Asia*, vol. II, *1500–1900* (New York, 2005), p 167.

15. *Ibid.*, p 167.

16. *Ibid.*, pp 193–209.

17. For good introductions to the complexity of Middle Eastern Christianity, past and present, see Anthony O'Mahoney and Emma Loosley (eds), *Eastern Christianity in the Modern Middle East* (London, 2010); and Philip Jenkins, *The Lost History of Christianity* (New York, 2008).

18. I am grateful to my research assistant Sonia Hazard for introducing me to Latin American baroque. For more extensive and authoritative treatments see Gauvin Alexander Bailey, *Art of Colonial America* (New York, 2005); Kelly Donahue-Wallace, *Art and Architecture of Viceregal Latin America, 1521–1821* (Albuquerque, NM, 2008); George Kubler and Martin Soria, *Art and Architecture in Spain and Portugal and Their American Dominions, 1500 to 1800* (Baltimore, 1969); and the chapters by Damián Bayón and J.B. Bury in the *Cambridge History of Latin America*, vol. II (Cambridge, 1984), pp 709–69.

19. John McManners (ed), *The Oxford Illustrated History of Christianity* (Oxford, 1990), p 301.

20. C.A. Bayly, *The Birth of the Modern World 1780–1914: Global Connections and Comparisons* (London, 2004), p 64. For a more sustained analysis of Europe's relations with the wider world see his second chapter, 'Passages from the Old Regimes to Modernity'.

21. For more information on how Europeans constructed views of the 'other' see Anthony Pagden, *European Encounters with the New World, from Renaissance to Romanticism* (New Haven, 1993); and P.J. Marshall and Glyndwr Williams, *The Great Map of Mankind: British Perceptions of the World in the*

Age of Enlightenment (London, 1982). See also Roger M. Downs and David Stea, *Maps in Mind: Reflections on Cognitive Mapping* (New York, 1977); Peter R. Gould and Rodney White, *Mental Maps*, 2nd ed. (Boston, 1986); and David Buisseret, *The Mapmaker's Quest: Depicting New Worlds in Renaissance Europe* (Oxford, 2003). For an insightful survey of the relationship between missions and science see David N. Livingstone, 'Scientific Inquiry and the Missionary Enterprise', in Ruth H. Finnegan (ed), *Participating in the Knowledge Society: Researchers Beyond the University Walls* (New York, 2005).

22. Marshall and Williams, *The Great Map of Mankind*, p 294.

23. Pagden, *European Encounters*, p 150. See also Anthony Pagden, *The Fall of Natural Man: The American Indian and the Origins of Comparative Ethnology* (Cambridge, 1982).

24. For an authoritative discussion of race in the eighteenth century see Colin Kidd, *The Forging of Races: Race and Scripture in the Protestant Atlantic World, 1600–2000* (Cambridge, 2006), pp 79–120.

25. Marshall and Williams, *The Great Map of Mankind*, p 102.

26. Andrew C. Ross, 'Christian Encounters with Other World Religions', in Stewart J. Brown and Timothy Tackett (eds), *The Cambridge History of Christianity*, vol. VII, *Enlightenment, Reawakening and Revolution 1660–1815* (Cambridge, 2006), pp 475–94.

27. Jean Pierre Purry, *Mémoire sur le Pais des Cafres, et la Terre de Nuyts. Par raport à l'utilité que la Compagnie des Indes Orientales en pourroit retirer pour son commerce* (Amsterdam, 1718). There is a modern edition of this pamphlet along with a second memoir and other writings by Purry, with an excellent editorial introduction by Arlin C. Migliazzo, *Lands of True and Certain Bounty: The Geographical Theories and Colonization Strategies of Jean Pierre Purry* (London, 2002).

28. Migliazzo (ed), *Lands of True and Certain Bounty*, p 40.

29. This is the point made by Carlo Ginzburg, which also acts as his defence of the discipline of microhistory. I first learned about Jean Pierre Purry as a result of a lecture given by Ginzburg at Boston University. The text of the lecture is posted on the web under the title 'Latitude, Slaves and the Bible: An Experiment in Microhistory'. The lecture was delivered before the publication of Migliazzo's English edition of Purry's memoirs.

30. Migliazzo (ed), *Lands of True and Certain Bounty*, p 105.

31. C.R. Boxer, *The Church Militant and Iberian Expansion 1440–1770* (Baltimore, 1978), p 39.

32. Boyd Stanley Schlenther, 'Religious Faith and Commercial Empire', in P.J. Marshall (ed), *The Oxford History of the British Empire: The Eighteenth Century* (Oxford, 1998), pp 128–50.

33. Carla Gardina Pestana, *Protestant Empire: Religion and the Making of the British Atlantic World* (Philadelphia, 2009).

34. See, for example, Andrew Porter, *Religion Versus Empire? British Protestant Missionaries and Overseas Expansion, 1700–1914* (Manchester, 2004).

35. *Ibid.*, p 116.
36. The most influential advocates of this view are Jean and John Comaroff. Although their research base is southern Africa, their conclusions are more widely applicable to other areas. For the theoretical underpinning of their views see 'Christianity and Colonialism in South Africa', *American Ethnologist*, vol. 13, no. 1 (February 1986), pp 1–22.
37. For an explanation of this view see Ryan Dunch, 'Beyond Cultural Imperialism: Cultural Theory, Christian Missions, and Global Modernity', *History and Theory*, vol. 41, no. 3 (October 2002), pp 301–25.

Chapter 2. Heart Religion and the Rise of Global Christianity: New Selves and New Places

1. I am greatly indebted to my colleague Michelle Molina and to my research assistants Dana Logan and Matt Dougherty for many suggestions and references, and for their willingness to discuss and help form the ideas in this chapter. I am also grateful to Mark Teasdale and others at Southern Methodist University for their helpful responses to an earlier version of this chapter.
2. The importance of millennialism is still an underappreciated aspect of the globalization of Christianity. See J.A. De Jong, *As the Waters Cover the Sea: Millennial Expectations in the Rise of Anglo-American Missions 1640–1810* (Kampen, 1970); Ruth H. Bloch, *Visionary Republic: American Thought, 1756–1800* (Cambridge, 1985); and Andrew Porter, *Religion Versus Empire? British Protestant Missionaries and Overseas Expansion, 1700–1914* (Manchester, 2004).
3. Stephen Neill, *A History of Christian Missions* (New York, 1986).
4. See J.W. O'Malley, G.A. Bailey, S.J. Harris and T.F. Kennedy (eds), *The Jesuits: Cultures, Sciences, and the Arts, 1540–1773* (Toronto, 1999); and *The Jesuits II: Cultures, Sciences, and the Arts, 1540–1773* (Toronto, 2006).
5. Andrew C. Ross, *A Vision Betrayed: The Jesuits in Japan and China, 1542–1742* (Maryknoll, NY, 1994).
6. J. Michelle Molina, 'A Heart-Shaped World: Jesuit Consolation Culture in a Globalizing World, 1500–1800', an unpublished paper delivered at Harvard Divinity School in spring 2008. I am very grateful to Dr Molina for discussing her ideas with me.
7. Arnold I. Davidson, 'Ethics as Ascetics: Foucault, the History of Ethics, and Ancient Thought', in Jan Goldstein (ed), *Foucault and the Writing of History* (Oxford, 1994). See also Mark R. Leary, *The Curse of the Self: Self Awareness, Egotism, and the Quality of Human Life* (New York, 2004).
8. George E. Ganss, SJ (ed), *The Spiritual Exercises of Saint Ignatius* (Chicago, 1992). See especially paragraphs 102–7.
9. *Jesuit Relations* is the common abbreviation of the *Relations des Jésuites de la Nouvelle France*, which were annual reports issued by the superior of the Jesuit missions in New France to the Jesuit overseer in France in the

seventeenth century.

10. For an excellent treatment of this subject see Eric Jager, 'The Book of the Heart: Reading and Writing the Medieval Subject', *Speculum* 71 (1996), pp 1–26. See also David Brakke, Michael L. Satlow and Steven Weitzman (eds), *Religion and the Self in Antiquity* (Bloomington, IN, 2005).

11. Quoted by J. Michelle Molina in 'A Heart-Shaped World', p 22.

12. Natalie Zemon Davis, *Women on the Margins: Three Seventeenth-Century Lives* (Cambridge, MA, 1995).

13. *Ibid.*, p 78.

14. *Ibid.*, p 79.

15. *Ibid.*, p 102.

16. *Ibid.*, p 130.

17. *Ibid.*, p 82.

18. I am grateful to Dana Logan for this insight.

19. Davis, *Women on the Margins*, p 98.

20. D. Bruce Hindmarsh, *The Evangelical Conversion Narrative: Spiritual Autobiography in Early Modern England* (Oxford, 2005), p 32.

21. This is the approach taken by Phyllis Mack, *Heart Religion in the British Enlightenment: Gender and Emotion in Early Methodism* (Cambridge, 2008).

22. For a helpful recent interpretation of Pietism see Hartmut Lehmann, 'Continental Protestant Europe', in Stewart J. Brown and Timothy Tackett (eds), *The Cambridge History of Christianity*, vol. VII, *Enlightenment, Reawakenings and Revolution 1660–1815* (Cambridge, 2006), pp 33–53.

23. Carter Lindberg (ed), *The Pietist Theologians* (Oxford, 2005), p 4.

24. For a brief but well-informed review of the issues at stake in defining Pietism see W.R. Ward, 'German Pietism, 1670–1750', *Journal of Ecclesiastical History*, 44, no. 3 (1993), pp 476–506.

25. See W.R. Ward, *The Protestant Evangelical Awakening* (Cambridge, 1992) and *Christianity under the Ancien Régime, 1648–1789* (Cambridge, 1999).

26. For the roots of an earlier tradition of Reformed Pietist missions see James Tanis, 'Reformed Pietism and Protestant Missions', *Harvard Theological Review* 67 (1974), pp 65–73.

27. J.C.S. Mason, *The Moravian Church and the Missionary Awakening in England 1760–1800* (London, 2001).

28. See Norman Nagel, 'Luther and the Priesthood of All Believers', *Concordia Theological Quarterly* 61, no. 4 (1997), pp 276–98; and Anthony La Volpa, 'Vocations, Careers, and Talent: Lutheran Pietism and Sponsored Mobility in Eighteenth-Century Germany', *Comparative Studies in Society and History* 28, no. 2 (1986), pp 255–86.

29. Philipp Jakob Spener, *Pia Desideria* (1675), in Peter C. Erb (ed), *Pietists: Selected Writings* (London, 1983), p 48.

30. *Ibid.*, pp 34–5.

31. *Ibid.*, pp 37–9.

32. The original version of this painting (smaller copies were also produced) was

painted at Herrnhaag in 1747 but was later moved to the Moravian settlement at Zeist in the Netherlands where it is now located. It is hard to forget the impression this huge canvass has on the observer, located as it is in a white and gold chapel almost devoid of any other colour or ornamentation.

33. Hindmarsh, *The Evangelical Conversion Narrative*, p 99.

34. For much of what follows I am indebted to Douglas D. Tzan for allowing me to read his unpublished Boston University doctoral seminar paper, 'Mental Maps and Missions'.

35. See Roger M. Downs and David Stea, *Maps in Mind: Reflections on Cognitive Mapping* (New York, 1977); Peter R. Gould, and Rodney White, *Mental Maps*, 2nd ed. (Boston, MA, 1986); Peter J. Marshall and Glyndwr Williams, *The Great Map of Mankind: Perceptions of New Worlds in the Age of Enlightenment* (Cambridge, MA, 1982); and David Buisseret, *The Mapmaker's Quest: Depicting New Worlds in Renaissance Europe* (Oxford, 2003).

36. For an insightful survey of the relationship between missions and science see David N. Livingstone, 'Scientific Inquiry and the Missionary Enterprise', in Ruth H. Finnegan (ed), *Participating in the Knowledge Society: Researchers Beyond the University Walls* (New York, 2005).

37. William Carey, *An Enquiry into the Obligations of Christians, to Use Means for the Conversion of the Heathen. In which the Religious State of the Different Nations of the World, the Success of Former Undertakings, and the Practicability of Further Undertakings, are Considered* (Leicester, 1792).

38. Eustace Carey, *Memoir of William Carey, D. D., Late Missionary to Bengal; Professor of Oriental Languages in the College of Fort William, Calcutta* (Boston, MA, 1836); Brian Stanley, *The History of the Baptist Missionary Society, 1792–1992* (Edinburgh, 1992); and David A. Schattschneider, 'William Carey, Modern Missions, and the Moravian Influence', *International Bulletin of Missionary Research* 22 (1998).

39. George Smith, *The Life of William Carey* (New York, 1935), p 22. I owe this reference to Doug Tzan.

40. Carey, *Enquiry*, pp 19–20.

41. John Vickers, *Thomas Coke: Apostle of Methodism* (London, 1969).

42. John A. Vickers (ed), *The Journals of Dr. Thomas Coke* (Nashville, 2005).

43. *Ibid.*, p 26.

44. *Ibid.*, pp 26–7.

45. *Ibid.*, pp 27–8.

46. *Ibid.*, p 85.

47. *Ibid.*, p 188.

48. *Ibid.*, p 108.

49. *Ibid.*, p 98.

50. *Ibid.*, p 255.

51. *Ibid.*, p 140.

52. *Ibid.*, pp 70, 177.

53. *Ibid.*, p 30.

54. *Ibid.*, p 158.
55. *Ibid.*, p 136.
56. *Ibid.*, p 172.
57. *Ibid.*, p 206.
58. *Ibid.*, p 220.
59. Davis, *Women on the Margins*, p 98.
60. Vickers (ed), *The Journals of Dr. Thomas Coke*, p 76.
61. Dana L. Robert, *Christian Mission: How Christianity Became a World Religion* (Chichester, 2009).
62. Davis, *Women on the Margins*, p 120.
63. J. Michelle Molina, 'Technologies of the Self: The Letters of Eighteenth-Century Mexican Jesuit Spiritual Daughters', *History of Religions* 47, no. 4 (May 2008), p 303.

Chapter 3. Encountering the Other: Stories and their Meanings

1. Barbara Ganson, *The Guaraní under Spanish Rule in the Río de la Plata* (Stanford, CA, 2003), p 192. This is now the standard work on the Jesuit mission to the Guaraní and is the foundation for what follows. See also Branislava Susnik, *El Rol de las Indigenas en la Formación y en la Vivencia del Paraguay*, 2 vols. (Asunción, Paraguay, 1982–83); and José Cardiel, *Las Misiones del Paraguay* (Madrid, Historia 16, 1988), especially the introduction by Héctor Sáinz Ollero. Also worth reading, both despite and because of its ideological thrust, is Graham R.B. Cunningham, *A Vanished Arcadia, Being Some Account of the Jesuits in Paraguay, 1607–1767* (London, 1924). I am also grateful to Matthew Dougherty for his help in researching this section.
2. This phrase, and the idea it represents, is taken from Anthony Pagden, *European Encounters with the New World* (London, 1993), pp 17–49.
3. See Asunción Lavrin, 'Female Religious', in Louisa S. Hoberman and Susan M. Socolow (eds), *Cities and Societies in Latin America* (Albuquerque, NM, 1986); and Dot Tuer, 'Old Bones and Beautiful Words: The Spiritual Contestation between Shama and Jesuit in the Guaraní Missions', in Allan Greer and Jodi Blinkoff (eds), *Colonial Saints: Discovering the Holy in the Americas, 1500–1800* (New York, 2003).
4. Philip Caraman, *The Lost Paradise: The Jesuit Republic in South America* (London, 1975), p 232. See also Ganson, *The Guaraní*, pp 68–71.
5. Ganson, *The Guaraní*, pp 164–87. The quotation is from p 187.
6. The trial is recounted by Kenneth Mills, *Idolatry and its Enemies: Colonial Andean Religion and Extirpation* (Princeton, 1997), pp 259–62.
7. Kenneth Mills, 'The Limits of Religious Coercion in Mid-Colonial Peru', *Past and Present* 145 (1994), p 89.
8. Nicholas Griffiths, *The Cross and the Serpent: Religious Representation and Resurgence in Colonial Peru* (Norman, OK, 1996), p 8. See also Sabine MacCormack, *Religion in the Andes: Vision and Imagination in Early Colonial Peru* (Princeton, 1991).

9. *Ibid.*, p 114. See also Mills, *Idolatry and its Enemies*, p 3.
10. See Thierry Saignes, 'The Colonial Condition in the Quecha-Aymara Heartland 1570–1780', in Frank Salomon and Stuart B. Schwartz (eds), *The Cambridge History of the Native Peoples of the Americas*, vol. III, *South America, part 2* (Cambridge, 1999), pp 59–137.
11. For a good account of these developments and their impact on Latin America see Ondina E. González and Justo L. González, *Christianity in Latin America: A History* (New York, 2008), pp 104–30.
12. De Tournon's legatorial mission is best followed in Andrew C. Ross, *A Vision Betrayed: The Jesuits in Japan and China, 1542–1742* (New York, 1994), pp 190–9; Samuel H. Moffett, *A History of Christianity in Asia*, vol. II, *1500–1800* (New York, 2005), pp 126–33; and D.E. Mungello, *The Great Encounter of China and the West, 1500–1800*, 3rd ed. (Lanham, MD, 2009), pp 28–32.
13. For a fine example of how the Jesuits used European science and technology as a way of attracting the attention of Chinese elites see Catherine Pagani, 'Clockwork and the Jesuit Mission in China', in J.W. O'Malley, G.A. Bailey, S.J. Harris and T.F. Kennedy (eds), *The Jesuits II: Cultures, Sciences, and the Arts, 1540–1773* (Toronto, 2006), pp 658–77. Clocks in particular resonated with European notions of order in the state and nature which appealed to the Chinese literati.
14. D.E. Mungello (ed), *The Chinese Rites Controversy: Its History and Meaning* (Nettetal, 1994), p 3.
15. Klaus Koschorke, Frieder Ludwig and Mariano Delgado (eds), in cooperation with Roland Spliesgart, *A History of Christianity in Asia, Africa, and Latin America, 1450–1990: A Documentary Sourcebook* (Grand Rapids, MI, 2007), pp 39–41.
16. Mungello (ed), *The Chinese Rites Controversy.*
17. Ronnie Po-Chia Hsia, 'Twilight in the Imperial City: The Jesuit Mission in China, 1748–1760', in O'Malley et al (eds), *The Jesuits II*, p 735.
18. *Ibid.*, pp 725–37, and P.J. Marshall and Glyndwr Williams, *The Great Map of Mankind: British Perceptions of the World in the Age of Enlightenment* (London, 1982), pp 20–3, 80–6.
19. Mungello, *The Great Encounter of China and the West*, pp 26–7, 65.
20. Robert E. Entenmann, 'Catholics and Society in Eighteenth-Century Sichuan', in Daniel H. Bays (ed), *Christianity in China: From the Eighteenth Century to the Present* (Stanford, 1996), p 23. For a recent attempt to capture the flavour of a more popular Chinese Christianity see Lars Peter Laamann, *Christian Heretics in Late Imperial China: Christian Inculturation and State Control, 1720–1850* (London, 2006).
21. R.G. Tiedemann, 'Christianity in East Asia', in Stewart J. Brown and Timothy Tackett (eds), *The Cambridge History of Christianity*, vol. VII, *Enlightenment, Reawakening and Revolution 1660–1815* (Cambridge, 2006), pp 451–74.
22. Robert E. Entenmann, 'Christian Virgins in Eighteenth-Century Sichuan',

in Daniel H. Bays (ed), *Christianity in China*, pp 180–93.

23. For a brilliant interpretation of the complex forces at work in the creation of a new world order at the end of the eighteenth century see C.A. Bayly, *The Birth of the Modern World 1780–1914: Global Connections and Comparisons* (Oxford, 2004).

24. Jonathan D. Spence, 'Claims and Counter Claims: The Kangxi Emperor and the Europeans (1661–1722)', in Mungello (ed), *The Chinese Rites Controversy*, pp 15–28.

25. Erik Zürcher, 'Jesuit Accommodation and the Chinese Cultural Imperative', in Mungello (ed), *The Chinese Rites Controversy*, p 64.

26. Lin Jinshui, 'Chinese Literati and the Rites Controversy', in Mungello (ed), *The Chinese Rites Controversy*, p 82.

27. Robert Eric Frykenberg, *Christianity in India: From Beginnings to the Present* (Oxford, 2008), pp 116–41.

28. Francis X. Clooney, *Fr. Bouchet's India: An 18th Century Jesuit's Encounter with Hinduism* (Chennai, 2005), p 7.

29. *Ibid.*, p 51.

30. *Ibid.*, pp 84–5.

31. D. Dennis Hudson, *Protestant Origins in India: Tamil Evangelical Christians, 1706–1835* (Grand Rapids, MI, 2000), p 38.

32. *Ibid.*, p 40.

33. *Ibid.*, p 180.

34. See, for example, the account of Rajanayakan, the pariah catechist, in Hudson, *Protestant Origins in India*, pp 42–8.

35. Frykenberg, *Christianity in India*, p 151.

36. See Daniel Jeyaraj, 'Mission Reports from South India and Their Impact on the Western Mind: The Tranquebar Mission of the Eighteenth Century', in Dana Robert (ed), *Converting Colonialism: Visions and Realities in Mission History, 1706–1914* (Grand Rapids, MI, 2008), pp 21–42.

37. The life of Rebecca Protten upon which this section depends is recorded with consummate skill by Jon F. Sensbach, *Rebecca's Revival: Creating Black Christianity in the Atlantic World* (Cambridge, MA, 2005). The quotation is from p 10.

38. J.C.S. Mason, *The Moravian Church and the Missionary Awakening in England, 1760–1800* (Woodbridge, Suffolk, 2001).

39. W.R. Ward, 'The Renewed Unity of the Brethren: Ancient Church, New Sect or Interconfessional Movement?', *Bulletin of the John Rylands University Library of Manchester* 70 (1988), pp 77–92.

40. Sensbach, *Rebecca's Revival*, p 70.

41. See Jon Sensbach, '"Don't Teach My Negroes to be Pietists": Pietism and the Roots of the Black Protestant Church', in Jonathan Strom, Hartmut Lehmann and James Van Horn Melton (eds), *Pietism in Germany and North America 1680–1820* (Farnham, Surrey, 2009), pp 183–98.

42. *Ibid.*, pp 191–2.

43. Sensbach, *Rebecca's Revival*, pp 188–9.

44. Haidt's painting of the 'First Fruits' and of the Protten family are reproduced and discussed in more detail by Sensbach, *Rebecca's Revival*, pp 189–201. The authority on Haidt's paintings is Vernon Nelson who published extensively on Haidt and has translated his *Lebenslauf* into English.

45. The story is well told by Lamin Sanneh, *Abolitionists Abroad: American Blacks and the Making of Modern West Africa* (Cambridge, MA, 1999), pp 41–3.

46. For the distinctive flavour of this Evangelicalism as preached by the likes of Henry Alline, William Black, and Freeborn Garrettson see George A. Rawlyk, *The Canada Fire: Radical Evangelicalism in British North America 1775–1812* (Kingston and Montreal, 1994).

47. Hindmarsh, *The Evangelical Conversion Narrative*, p 321. See also the account in Rawlyk, *The Canada Fire*, pp 33–43. For a modern edition of George's spiritual autobiography see Grant Gordon, *From Slavery to Freedom: The Life of David George, Pioneer Black Baptist Minister* (Hansport, Nova Scotia, 1992).

48. Alexander X. Byrd, *Captives and Voyagers: Black Migrants across the Eighteenth-Century British Atlantic World* (Baton Rouge, 2008), p 166.

49. Lamin Sanneh, *Disciples of All Nations: Pillars of World Christianity* (Oxford, 2008), pp 127–8.

50. *An Account of the Colony of Sierra Leone*, 2nd ed. (1795), p. 80, quoted by A.F. Walls, 'A Christian Experiment: The Early Sierra Leone Colony', *Studies in Church History* 6, in G.J. Cuming (ed), *The Mission of the Church and the Propagation of the Faith* (Cambridge, 1970), pp 107–29.

51. Rawlyk, *The Canada Fire*, pp 37–41.

52. A.F. Walls, 'A Colonial Concordat: Two Views of Christianity and Civilization', in Derek Baker (ed), *Church, Society and Politics* (Oxford, 1975), pp 293–302.

53. See W. Jowett, *Memoir of the Rev. W. A. B. Johnson* (London, 1852), p 94, quoted by Walls, 'A Colonial Concordat', pp 300–1.

54. Sanneh, *Disciples of All Nations*, p 173.

55. *Ibid.*, p 176.

56. For more sustained and far more expert analyses of how these processes operated see Andrew F. Walls, *The Missionary Movement in Christian History: Studies in the Transmission of Faith* (Maryknoll, NY, 1996); and Walls, *The Cross-Cultural Process in Christian History* (Maryknoll, NY, 2002).

57. *Ibid.*, p 128.

58. Sanneh, *Abolitionists Abroad*, p 125.

59. Berndt C. Peyer (ed), *American Indian Nonfiction: An Anthology of Writings, 1760s–1930s* (Norman, Oklahoma, 2007), pp 43–51.

60. W. DeLoss Love, *Samson Occom and the Christian Indians of New England* (Boston, 1899), p 123.

61. For a helpful critical reading of Occom's Narrative see Eileen Razzari Elrod '"I did not make myself so …": Samson Occom and American Religious

Autobiography', in John C. Hawley (ed), *Historicising Christian Encounters with the Other* (London, 1998), pp 135–49.

62. Hawley (ed), *Historicising Christian Encounters*, p 3.

63. Elrod, 'Samson Occom', p 146.

64. Peyer, *American Indian Nonfiction*, p 6. For an excellent new treatment of Occom's life in a much richer historical context than I have supplied see the forthcoming book by Linford D. Fisher, *The Great Indian Awakening: Religion and the Shaping of Native Cultures in Early America*.

65. Daniel K. Richter, *Facing East from Indian Country: A Native History of Early America* (Cambridge, MA, 2001). See also Emma Anderson, *The Betrayal of Faith: The Tragic Journey of a Colonial Native Convert* (Cambridge, MA, 2007); and Allan Greer, *Mohawk Saint: Catherine Tekakwitha and the Jesuits* (New York, 2005).

66. James Axtell, *Natives and Newcomers: The Cultural Origins of North America* (New York, 2001), pp 145–73. See also James Axtell, *The Invasion Within: The Contest of Cultures in Colonial North America* (New York, 1985).

67. Axtell, *Natives and Newcomers*, p 163.

68. Jane T. Merritt, 'Dreaming of the Savior's Blood: Moravians and the Indian Great Awakening in Pennsylvania', *The William and Mary Quarterly*, 3rd series, 44, no. 4 (October 1997), pp 723–46.

69. *Ibid.*, p 741.

70. Catherine L. Albanese, *A Republic of Mind and Spirit: A Cultural History of American Metaphysical Religion* (New Haven, 2007), pp 112–17.

71. See Thomas Kidd, *The Great Awakening: The Roots of Evangelical Christianity in Colonial America* (New Haven, 2007); and William S. Simmons, 'The Great Awakening and Indian Conversion in Southern New England', in William Cowan (ed), *Papers of the Tenth Algonquian Conference* (Ottawa, 1979).

72. Linford D. Fisher, '"Traditionary Religion": The Great Awakening and the Shaping of Native Cultures in Southern New England, 1736–1776', Harvard University Th.D thesis, 2008.

73. Fisher, 'Traditionary Religion', ch. 3. See Azariah Horton, 'First Journal of Mr. Azariah Horton, the Society's Missionary in Long-Island, near New York from August 5th 1741 to November 1st That Year', in Gaynell Stone (ed), *The History & Archaeology of the Montauk* (Stony Brook, NY, 1993).

74. D. Bruce Hindmarsh, *The Evangelical Conversion Narrative: Spiritual Autobiography in Early Modern England* (Oxford, 2005), pp 326–9.

75. Richard Fox Young, *Resistant Hinduism: Sanskrit Sources on Anti-Christian Apologetics in Early Nineteenth-Century India* (Vienna, 1991), pp 22–25. See also Daniel Jeyaraj, 'Colonialism and Mission in Tranquebar – Their Relationship to the "Hindus"', in George Oomen and Hans Raun Iversen (eds), *It Began in Copenhagen* (Delhi, 2005), pp 101–24; and Sigvard von Sicard, 'Ziegenbalg and the Muslims', in Oomen and Iversen (eds), *It Began in Copenhagen*, pp 125–55.

76. Douglas Lancashire, 'Anti-Christian Polemics in Seventeenth Century China', *Church History*, vol. 38, no. 2 (June 1969), pp 218–41.

77. Richard Fox Young, 'The Carpenter-Preta: An Eighteenth-Century Sinhala-Buddhist Folktale about Jesus', *Asian Folklore Studies*, vol. 54 (1995), pp 49–68.

78. For this section I am relying principally on Ramón A. Gutiérrez, *When Jesus Came, The Corn Mothers Went Away: Marriage, Sexuality, and Power in New Mexico, 1500–1846* (Stanford, 1991); Robert H. Jackson and Eric Langer (eds), *The New Latin American Mission History* (Lincoln, NE, 1995); and H. McKennie Goodpasture (ed), *Cross and Sword: An Eyewitness History of Christianity in Latin America* (Maryknoll, NY, 1989).

79. Gutiérrez, *When Jesus Came*, p 93.

80. *Ibid.*, pp 130–40.

81. For a superb treatment of the issues at stake in the choice of different metaphors and linguistic devices in dealing with European encounters with the rest of the world, and their place in the evolution of cultural history, see Peter Burke, *What is Cultural History?* (Cambridge, 2007).

Chapter 4. Enlightenment and Society: Glimpses of Modernity

1. Margaret C. Jacob, 'The Enlightenment Critique of Christianity', in Stewart J. Brown and Timothy Tackett (eds), *The Cambridge History of Christianity*, vol. VII, *Enlightenment, Reawakening and Revolution* (Cambridge, 2006), p 265.

2. Jonathan I. Israel, *Radical Enlightenment: Philosophy and the Making of Modernity 1650–1750* (Oxford, 2001), p v.

3. *Ibid.*, pp 3–22.

4. Jacob, 'The Enlightenment Critique of Christianity', p 280.

5. See Dorinda Outram, *The Enlightenment* (Cambridge, 1995), pp 31–46.

6. Knud Haakonssen (ed), *Enlightenment and Religion: Rational Dissent in Eighteenth-Century Britain* (Cambridge, 1996).

7. Richard B. Sher, *Church and University in the Scottish Enlightenment* (Princeton, 1985).

8. Ian R. McBride, *Scripture Politics: Ulster Presbyterians and Irish Radicalism in the Late Eighteenth Century* (Oxford, 1998).

9. Helena Rosenblatt, 'The Christian Enlightenment', in Brown and Tackett (eds), *The Cambridge History of Christianity*, vol. VII, *Enlightenment, Reawakening and Revolution*, pp 284–91.

10. *Ibid.*, pp 292–7.

11. David S. Katz, *God's Last Words: Reading the English Bible from the Reformation to Fundamentalism* (New Haven, 2004).

12. Roy Porter, 'Introduction', in Porter (ed), *The Cambridge History of Science*, vol. 4, *Eighteenth-Century Science* (Cambridge, 2008), p 6.

13. Peter Hanns Reill, 'The Legacy of the "Scientific Revolution": Science and the Enlightenment', in Porter (ed), *The Cambridge History of Science*, vol. 4,

Eighteenth-Century Science, p 23.

14. John Hedley Brooke, 'Science and Religion', in Porter (ed), *The Cambridge History of Science*, vol. 4, *Eighteenth-Century Science*, p 741.

15. Louis Châtelier, 'Christianity and the Rise of Science, 1660–1815', in Brown and Tackett (eds), *The Cambridge History of Christianity* vol. VII, *Enlightenment, Reawakening and Revolution 1660–1815*, p 254.

16. Brooke, 'Science and Religion', p 746.

17. Charles Taylor, *A Secular Age* (Cambridge, MA, 2007), pp 221–69.

18. Brooke, 'Science and Religion', p 751.

19. See Margaret C. Jacob, *The Radical Enlightenment: Pantheists, Freemasons and Republicans* (London, 1981).

20. Reill, 'The Legacy of the "Scientific Revolution"', p 41. See also Peter Hanns Reill, *Vitalizing Nature in the Enlightenment* (Berkeley, 2005).

21. For a suggestive treatment of the role of vitalism and Paracelsianism in Pietism and Evangelicalism see W.R. Ward, *Early Evangelicalism: A Global Intellectual History, 1670–1789* (Cambridge, 2006).

22. For the popularization of science see Jeffrey R. Wigelsworth, *Selling Science in the Age of Newton: Advertising and the Commoditization of Knowledge* (Farnham, 2010).

23. Benjamin J. Kaplan, *Divided by Faith: Religious Conflict and the Practice of Religious Toleration in Early Modern Europe* (Cambridge, MA, 2007), p 122.

24. *Ibid.*, p 156.

25. *Ibid.*, p 170.

26. C. Scott Dixon, Dagmar Freist and Mark Greengrass (eds), *Living with Religious Diversity in Early-Modern Europe* (Farnham, 2009), p 11.

27. *Ibid.*, pp 281–95.

28. See Perez Zagorin, *How the Idea of Religious Toleration Came to the West* (Princeton, 2003).

29. Linda Colley, *Britons: Forging the Nation, 1707–1837* (New Haven, 1992).

30. See James E. Bradley, 'Toleration and Movements of Christian Reunion, 1660–1789', in Brown and Tackett (eds), *The Cambridge History of Christianity*, vol. VII, *Enlightenment, Reawakening and Revolution 1660–1815*, pp 348–70.

31. Alf J. Mapp, Jr, *The Faiths of our Fathers: What America's Founders Really Believed* (New York, 2006), p 7.

32. Ole Peter Grell and Roy Porter (eds), *Toleration in Enlightenment Europe* (Cambridge, 2000), p 4.

33. David Brion Davis, *Inhuman Bondage: The Rise and Fall of Slavery in the New World* (New York, 2006), pp 80–91. See also his *The Problem of Slavery in Western Culture* (New York, 1966); and *Slavery and Human Progress* (New York, 1984).

34. Davis, *Inhuman Bondage*, p 100.

35. Some of the most important trajectories of interpretation may be found in the following books: Roger Anstey, *The Atlantic Slave Trade and British Abolition 1760–1810* (Atlantic Highlands, NJ, 1975), which has fine chapters

on the Evangelical worldview and Evangelical theology; Seymour Drescher, *Capitalism and Antislavery: British Mobilization in Comparative Perspective* (New York, 1987), which thoroughly examines the popular mobilization against slavery within its economic and social context; Clare Midgley, *Women Against Slavery: The British Campaigns 1780–1870* (London, 1992), which brings the contribution of women to centre stage for the first time; Christopher Leslie Brown, *Moral Capital: Foundations of Antislavery* (Chapel Hill, 2006), which is an insightful investigation into the roots of British anti-slavery with a special emphasis on the complex relationship between moral opinion and political action. For a useful survey of the longer historiography of anti-slavery see the essay by Roger Anstey, 'The Historical Debate on the Abolition of the British Slave Trade', in Roger Anstey and P.E.H. Hair (eds), *Liverpool, the African Slave Trade and Abolition*, Historic Society of Lancashire and Cheshire, occasional series, vol. 2 (1976), pp 157–66.

36. For a useful summary of these debates see Davis, *Inhuman Bondage*, pp 240–4. For more on the conflicting arguments about the economics of slavery see Eric Williams, *Capitalism and Slavery* (Chapel Hill, 1994); Seymour Drescher, *From Slavery to Freedom: Comparative Studies in the Rise and Fall of Atlantic Slavery* (London, 1999); Seymour Drescher, *Econocide: British Slavery in the Era of Abolition* (Chapel Hill, 2010); and David Eltis, *Economic Growth and the Ending of the Transatlantic Slave Trade* (New York, 1987).

37. See Brown, *Moral Capital*, pp 333–89.

38. See Midgley, *Women Against Slavery*, pp 9–40.

39. For a good recent survey of these debates and how they have changed over time see Peter Berger, Grace Davie and Effie Fokas, *Religious America, Secular Europe?* (Aldershot, 2008), and Peter Berger, 'Secularization Falsified', *First Things* (February 2008), pp 23–7.

40. Hugh McLeod, *The Religious Crisis of the 1960s* (Oxford, 2007).

41. Charles Taylor, *A Secular Age* (Cambridge, MA, 2007), pp 522–35.

42. For the most influential works in these historiographical traditions see Roger Finke and Rodney Stark, *The Churching of America, 1776–2005: Winners and Losers in our Religious Economy* (New Brunswick, NJ, 2005); Nathan O. Hatch, *The Democratization of American Christianity* (New Haven, 1989); Isaac Kramnick and R. Laurence Moore, *The Godless Constitution: The Case Against Religious Correctness* (New York, 1996); and Frank Lambert, *The Founding Fathers and the Place of Religion in America* (Princeton, 2003).

43. See David Hempton, *Methodism: Empire of the Spirit* (New Haven, 2005).

44. Research on the relationship between the strength of religious traditions and fertility rates is surprisingly sparse. Here I am relying mostly on Thomas Frejka and Charles F. Westoff, 'Religion, Religiousness, and Fertility in the U.S. and Europe', Max Planck Institute for Demographic Research Working Paper (2006).

Chapter 5. Renewal and Revival: Evangelicals and Methodists

1. W.R. Ward, *The Protestant Evangelical Awakening* (Cambridge, 1992); *Christianity under the Ancien Régime, 1648–1789* (Cambridge, 1999); and *Early Evangelicalism: A Global Intellectual History, 1670–1789* (Cambridge, 2006). See also his published collection of articles, *Faith and Faction* (London, 1993), which bear on these themes in a more concentrated way.

2. Ward, *Protestant Evangelical Awakening*, p 240.

3. Ward, *Early Evangelicalism*, p 4.

4. C. Scott Dixon, *Protestants: A History from Wittenberg to Pennsylvania 1517–1740* (Chichester, 2010), p 175.

5. *Ibid.*, pp 56–7. See also Mark Noll, *The Rise of Evangelicalism: The Age of Edwards, Whitefield and the Wesleys* (Leicester, 2004), pp 48–54. For a more extensive treatment of the Reformed tradition see Philip Benedict, *Christ's Churches Purely Reformed: A Social History of Calvinism* (New Haven, 2002).

6. See, for example, Michael A.G. Haykin and Kenneth J. Stewart, *The Advent of Evangelicalism: Exploring Historical Continuities* (Nashville, 2008). See especially the response by David Bebbington, pp 417–32.

7. John Walsh, '"Methodism" and the Origins of English-Speaking Evangelicalism', in Mark A. Noll, David W. Bebbington and George A. Rawlyk (eds), *Evangelicalism: Comparative Studies of Popular Protestantism in North America, the British Isles, and Beyond, 1700–1990* (New York, 1994), p 22.

8. *Ibid.*, p 27.

9. See D. Densil Morgan, 'Continuity, Novelty, and Evangelicalism in Wales, c. 1640–1850', in Haykin and Stewart, *The Advent of Evangelicalism*, p 99. See also David Hempton, *Religion and Political Culture in Britain and Ireland from the Glorious Revolution to the Decline of Empire* (Cambridge, 1996), pp 49–63.

10. I make this argument more extensively in 'Established Churches and the Growth of Religious Pluralism: A Case Study of Chrisianisation and Secularisation in England since 1700', in Hugh McLeod and Werner Ustorf (eds), *The Decline of Christendom in Western Europe, 1750–2000* (Cambridge, 2003), pp 81–98.

11. See, for example, Susan O'Brien, 'Eighteenth-Century Publishing Networks in the First Years of Transatlantic Evangelicalism', in Noll et al (eds), *Evangelicalism*, pp 38–57.

12. Susan O'Brien, 'A Transatlantic Community of Saints: The Great Awakening and the First Evangelical Network, 1735–1755', *American Historical Review* 91 (1986), pp 811–15.

13. F. Baker, Introduction to *The Works of John Wesley*, vol. 25, *Letters I: 1721–1739* (Oxford, 1980), p 82.

14. A modern edition of her works includes a volume of letters: *Selected Spiritual Writings of Anne Dutton: Eighteenth-Century British-Baptist, Woman Theologian*, ed. J.F. Watson (Macon, GA, 2003). I am indebted to Bruce

Hindmarsh for this reference.

15. Unpublished conference paper, Bruce Hindmarsh, 'The Medium is the Message: Spiritual Experience in the Personal Letters of the Early Evangelicals', delivered at Regent College, Vancouver, July 2005. See also D. Bruce Hindmarsh, *The Evangelical Conversion Narrative: Spiritual Autobiography in Early Modern England* (Oxford, 2005).

16. The best short introductions to Zinzendorf's life and thought are to be found in Peter Vogt, 'Nicholas Ludwig von Zinzendorf (1700–1760)', in Carter Lindberg (ed), *The Pietist Theologians* (Oxford, 2005), pp 207–23, and Ward, *Early Evangelicalism*, pp 99–118.

17. George Marsden, *A Short Life of Jonathan Edwards* (Grand Rapids, MI, 2008), pp 134–5.

18. Harry S. Stout, 'George Whitefield in Three Countries', in Noll et al (eds), *Evangelicalism*, pp 61–2. For a more extended biography of Whitefield see Stout, *The Divine Dramatist: George Whitefield and the Rise of Modern Evangelicalism* (Grand Rapids, MI, 1991).

19. For differing accounts of the Bethesda affair see Robert G. Ingram, *Religion, Reform and Modernity in the Eighteenth Century: Thomas Secker and the Church of England* (Woodbridge, 2007); and Jerome Dean Mahaffey, *Preaching Politics: The Religious Rhetoric of George Whitefield and the Founding of a New Nation* (Waco, TX, 2007).

20. John R. Tyson, *Assist Me to Proclaim: The Life and Hymns of Charles Wesley* (Grand Rapids, MI, 2007).

21. For an expert delineation of John Wesley's early life and the formation of Methodism see Richard P. Heitzenrater, *Wesley and the People Called Methodists* (Nashville, 1995). For his relationship with his brother Charles Wesley see Tyson, *Assist Me to Proclaim*.

22. The best short introduction to Wesley's life is John Walsh, *John Wesley 1703–1791: A Bicentennial Tribute* (London, 1993), published by the Dr Williams's Library.

23. Benjamin Ingham and Richard P. Heitzenrater, *Diary of an Oxford Methodist, Benjamin Ingham, 1733–1734* (Durham, NC, 1985); Simon Ross Valentine, *John Bennet and the Origins of Methodism and the Evangelical Revival in England* (Lanham, MD, 1997).

24. Randy L. Maddox, *Responsible Grace: John Wesley's Practical Theology* (Nashville, 1994).

25. David Hempton, *Methodism: Empire of the Spirit* (New Haven, 2005), pp 55–85.

26. The most authoritative volume on the content and practice of Methodist worship in the United States is Karen B. Westerfield Tucker, *American Methodist Worship* (New York, 2001). The best critical edition of Wesleyan hymns is now Franz Hildebrandt and Oliver A. Beckerlegge (eds), *A Collection of the Hymns for the Use of the People called Methodists*, in *The Works of John Wesley*, vol. 7 (Nashville, 1983).

27. Hildebrandt and Beckerlegge, *The Works of John Wesley*, vol. 7, pp 73–4.

28. *Ibid.*, p 63.

29. Dee E. Andrews, *The Methodists and Revolutionary America, 1760–1800: The Shaping of an Evangelical Culture* (Princeton, 2000), pp 247–54; John H. Wigger, *Taking Heaven by Storm: Methodism and the Rise of Popular Christianity in America* (New York, 1998), pp 84–5.

30. W.R. Ward, 'Was There a Methodist Evangelistic Strategy in the Eighteenth Century?', in Nicholas Tyacke (ed), *England's Long Reformation 1500–1800* (London, 1998).

31. Julia S. Werner, *The Primitive Methodist Connexion: Its Background and Early History* (Madison, WI, 1984); Bernard A. Weisberger, *They Gathered at the River* (Boston, 1958).

32. For Asbury's significance in the growth of American Methodism see John Wigger, *American Saint: Francis Asbury and the Methodists* (New York, 2009).

33. *Minutes of the Methodist Conference* (London, 1812–54), I, p 9; G.F. Nuttall, 'Howell Harris and the "Grand Table": A Note on Religion and Politics, 1744–50', *Journal of Ecclesiastical History* 39 (1988), pp 531–44. See also W.R. Ward, *The Protestant Evangelical Awakening* (Cambridge, 1992).

34. Andrews, *The Methodists and Revolutionary America*, pp 73–96; and Cynthia, Lynn Lyerly, *Methodism and the Southern Mind 1770–1810* (New York, 1998), pp 27–46.

35. James Obelkevich, *Religion and Rural Society: South Lindsey 1825–1875* (Oxford, 1976), pp 220–58; David Hempton, *Methodism and Politics in British Society 1750–1850* (Stanford, CA, 1984), pp 55–115; and David Hempton and Myrtle Hill, *Evangelical Protestantism in Ulster Society 1740–1890* (London, 1996).

36. Robert Moore, *Pit-Men, Preachers & Politics* (London, 1974).

37. W.J. Townsend, G. Eayrs and H.B. Workman, *A New History of Methodism*, (London, 1909), vol. 2, pp 283–360.

38. David Martin, *Pentecostalism: The World Their Parish* (Oxford, 2001).

39. See the gender proportions of Methodist societies in New York, Philadelphia and Baltimore in Andrews, *The Methodists and Revolutionary America*, pp 247–8. See also Clive D. Field, 'The Social Composition of English Methodism to 1830: A Membership Analysis', *The Bulletin of the John Rylands University Library of Manchester* 76, no. 1 (1994), pp 153–69. Based on a large sample of Methodist members, Field estimated a female mean of 57.7 per cent.

40. Dickson D. Bruce, Jr, *And They All Sang Hallelujah: Plain-Folk Camp-Meeting Religion, 1800–1845* (Knoxville, TN, 1974).

41. See, for example, the long list of Evangelical voluntary associations in Ford K. Brown, *Fathers of the Victorians: The Age of Wilberforce* (Cambridge, 1961).

42. These controversies are explored by Doreen Rosman, *Evangelicals and Culture* (London, 1984).

43. See, for example, the now infamous chapter on Methodism in E.P.

Thompson, *The Making of the English Working Class* (Harmondsworth, 1968), which has helped shape many subsequent interpretations of Methodism. For an explanation of why Thompson wrote this way see David Hempton and John Walsh, 'E. P. Thompson and Methodism', in Mark Noll (ed), *God and Mammon* (New York, 2002), pp 99–120.

44. See David Hempton, *Evangelical Disenchantment: Nine Portraits of Faith and Doubt* (New Haven, 2008).

Chapter 6. God and Caesar: Churches, States and Revolutions

1. Henry Chadwick and G.R. Evans (eds), *Atlas of the Christian Church* (Oxford, 1987).

2. David Hempton, *Religion and Political Culture in Britain and Ireland: From the Glorious Revolution to the Decline of Empire* (Cambridge, 1996).

3. For an excellent survey of the literature for and against the Church of England in the eighteenth century see Jeremy Gregory, 'The Long Eighteenth Century', in Randy L. Maddox and Jason E. Vickers (eds), *The Cambridge Companion to John Wesley* (Cambridge, 2010), pp 13–39.

4. The most intellectually coherent expression of this view is J.C.D. Clark, *English Society 1660–1832* (Cambridge, 2000). See also his 'England's Ancien Regime as a Confessional State', *Albion* (1989), pp 450–74, and 'The Eighteenth-Century Context', in William J. Abraham and James E. Kirby (eds), *The Oxford Handbook of Methodist Studies* (Oxford, 2009), pp 3–29.

5. See Gregory, 'The Long Eighteenth Century', n.86, for an up-to-date list of visitation returns and local studies. See also John Walsh, Colin Haydon and Stephen Taylor (eds), *The Church of England c.1689–1833: From Toleration to Tractarianism* (Cambridge, 1993).

6. W.M. Jacob, *The Clerical Profession in the Long Eighteenth Century, 1680–1840* (Oxford, 2007).

7. See Linda Colley, *Britons: Forging the Nation, 1707–1837* (New Haven, 1992).

8. For a recent statement of the optimistic case for the Church of England in this period see Robert G. Ingram, *Religion, Reform and Modernity in the Eighteenth Century: Thomas Secker and the Church of England* (Woodbridge, Suffolk, 2007).

9. See Ian Green, 'The First Years of Queen Anne's Bounty', in Rosemary O'Day and Felicity Heal (eds), *Princes and Paupers in the English Church 1500–1800* (Leicester, 1981). For a more extensive critique of the structural inadequacies of the English Church in the long eighteenth century, which still bear examination, see Peter Virgin, *The Church in an Age of Negligence: Ecclesiastical Structure and Problems of Church Reform 1700–1840* (Cambridge, 1989).

10. G.H. Jenkins, *The Foundations of Modern Wales 1642–1780* (Oxford, 1987).

11. S.J. Connolly, *Religion, Law and Power: The Making of Protestant Ireland 1660–1760* (Oxford, 1992).

12. Callum G. Brown, *Religion and Society in Scotland since 1707* (Edinburgh, 1997).

13. For an excellent treatment of Anglicanism and popular culture, still a much neglected topic, see Bob Bushaway, *By Rite: Custom, Ceremony and Community in England 1700–1880* (London, 1982).

14. The most articulate and persuasive voice for a less than euphoric estimation of the Church of England's popular appeal in this period is not supplied by Marxist historians, as is sometimes assumed, but by W.R. Ward, *Religion and Society in England, 1790–1850* (London, 1972).

15. Nigel Aston, *Christianity and Revolutionary Europe c.1750–1830* (Cambridge, 2002), pp 14–15.

16. *Ibid.*, pp 154–6. For a superb evocation of the coronation of Louis XVI at Rheims in 1775 see John McManners, *Church and Society in Eighteenth Century France*, vol. 1, *The Clerical Establishment and its Ramifications* (Oxford, 1998), pp 7–15.

17. See, for example, Olwen Hufton, *Europe: Privilege and Protest 1730–1789* (London, 1980), and William Doyle, *The Old European Order 1660–1800* (Oxford, 1992).

18. Dale Van Kley, *The Religious Origins of the French Revolution: From Calvin to the Civil Constitution, 1560–1791* (New Haven, 1996), pp 191–203.

19. John McManners, *Church and Society in Eighteenth-Century France*, vol. 2, *The Religion of the People and the Politics of Religion* (Oxford, 1998). For an excellent treatment of the French Church in the seventeenth and early eighteenth centuries see Joseph Bergin, *Church, Society and Religious Change in France, 1580–1730* (New Haven, 2009).

20. McManners, *Church and Society*, vol. 1, p 55.

21. *Ibid.*, pp 166–7.

22. *Ibid.*, p 3.

23. *Ibid.*, p 4.

24. Jerzy Kloczowski, *A History of Polish Christianity* (Cambridge, 2000), p 133.

25. See P.J. Corish, *The Irish Catholic Experience: A Historical Survey* (Dublin, 1985), and the excellent trilogy of books by S.J. Connolly, *Priests and People in Pre-Famine Ireland 1780–1845* (Dublin, 1982), *Religion and Society in Nineteenth-Century Ireland* (Dundalk, 1985) and *Religion, Law and Power: The Making of Protestant Ireland 1660–1760* (Oxford, 1992).

26. Derek Beales, *Joseph II* (New York, 1987–2009). See also T.C.W. Blanning, *Joseph II and Enlightened Despotism* (London, 1970).

27. See Dale K. Van Kley, 'Jansenism and the International Suppression of the Jesuits', in Stewart J. Brown and Timothy Tackett (eds), *The Cambridge History of Christianity*, vol. VII, *Enlightenment, Reawakening and Revolution 1660–1815* (Cambridge, 2006), pp 302–28. For a fuller account see also his *The Religious Origins of the French Revolution*.

28. For a fuller account of the suppression of the Jesuits see W.R. Ward, *Christianity under the Ancien Régime 1648–1789* (Cambridge, 1999).

29. For some fresh treatments of Jesuit suppression and restoration, from an admittedly friendly perspective, see chapters 31–7 in J.W. O'Malley, G.A.

Bailey, S.J. Harris and T.F. Kennedy (eds), *The Jesuits II: Cultures, Sciences, and the Arts, 1540–1773* (Toronto, 2006), pp 679–784.

30. This section deals with the Russian Orthodox Church and its relationship with a growing Russian Empire. For an introduction to the wider family of Orthodox churches which share much in common in terms of historical roots, monastic spirituality and liturgies see John Binns, *An Introduction to the Christian Orthodox Churches* (Cambridge, 2002); and John Anthony McGuckin, *The Orthodox Church: An Introduction to its History, Doctrine, and Spiritual Culture* (Oxford, 2008).

31. Robert O. Crummey, 'Eastern Orthodoxy in Russia and Ukraine in the Age of the Counter Reformation', in Michael Angold (ed), *The Cambridge History of Christianity*, vol. 5, *Eastern Christianity*, pp 302–24.

32. G.L. Freeze, 'Handmaiden of the State? The Church in Imperial Russia Reconsidered', *Journal of Ecclesiastical History* 36 no. 1 (1985), pp 82–102.

33. See John McManners, *The Clerical Establishment and its Social Ramifications*, vol. 1, *Church and Society in Eighteenth-Century France* (Oxford, 1998), p 3.

34. Simon Dixon, 'The Russian Orthodox Church in Imperial Russia 1721–1917', in Angold (ed), *Eastern Christianity*, p 328. See also G.L. Freeze, *The Russian Levites: Parish Clergy in the Eighteenth Century* (Cambridge, MA, 1977).

35. Chris Chulos, 'Russian Piety and Culture from Peter the Great to 1917', in Anglod (ed), *Eastern Christianity*, pp 348–70.

36. Georg Michels, 'Rescuing the Orthodox: The Church Policies of Archbishop Afanasii of Kholmogory, 1682–1702', in Robert P. Geraci and Michael Khodarkovsky (eds), *Of Religion and Empire: Missions, Conversion, and Tolerance in Tsarist Russia* (Ithaca, NY, 2001), pp 19–37.

37. Michael Khodarkovsky, 'The Conversion of Non-Christians in Early Modern Russia', in Geraci and Khodarkovsky (eds), *Of Religion and Empire*, p 116.

38. *Ibid.*, p 127.

39. Andrei A. Znamensky, *Shamanism and Christianity: Native Encounters with Russian Orthodox Missions in Siberia and Alaska, 1820–1917* (Westport, CT, 1999), p 59.

40. See Sergei Kan, 'Russian Orthodox Missionaries at Home and Abroad: The Case of Siberian and Alaskan Indigenous Peoples', in Geraci and Khodarkovsky (eds), *Of Religion and Empire*, pp 173–200.

41. Khodarkovsky, 'The Conversion of Non-Christians', p 117.

42. Jerome Dean Mahaffey, *Preaching Politics: The Religious Rhetoric of George Whitefield and the Founding of a New Nation* (Waco, TX, 2007).

43. Thomas S. Kidd, *God of Liberty: A Religious History of the American Revolution* (New York, 2010), pp 5–9. For fine treatments of American theology in the revolutionary era emphasizing conservative continuity as well as innovation see Mark Noll, *America's God* (New York, 2002), pp 114–57; and E. Brooks Holifield, *Theology in America* (New Haven, 2003).

44. Martin E. Marty, 'The American Revolution and Religion, 1765–1815', in

Brown and Tackett (eds), *The Cambridge History of Christianity* vol. VII, *Enlightenment, Reawakening and Revolution 1660–1815*, p 506.

45. See Timothy Tackett, 'The French Revolution and Religion to 1794', in Brown and Tackett (eds), *The Cambridge History of Christianity* vol. VII, *Enlightenment, Reawakening and Revolution 1660–1815*, pp 536–41.

46. Nigel Aston, *The French Revolution, 1789–1804: Authority, Liberty, and the Search for Stability* (London, 2004), pp 113–18.

47. See Suzanne Desan, 'The French Revolution and Religion, 1795–1815', in Brown and Tackett (eds), *The Cambridge History of Christianity* vol. VII, *Enlightenment, Reawakening and Revolution 1660–1815* pp 556–74. See also John McManners, *The French Revolution and the Church* (London, 1969).

Conclusion: Continuity and Change

1. For the content of rural popular religion in Protestant and Catholic countries see the still unsurpassed James Obelkevich, *Religion and Rural Society: South Lindsey, 1825–1875* (Oxford, 1976); and Sean J. Connolly, *Priests and People in Pre-Famine Ireland, 1780–1845* (Dublin, 2001).

2. R. Po-Chia Hsia, *The World of Catholic Renewal, 1540–1770* (Cambridge, 2005), p 233.

3. W.R. Ward, *Christianity under the Ancien Régime, 1648–1789* (Cambridge, 1999), p x.

4. Adrian Hastings (ed), *A World History of Christianity* (London, 1999), p 351.

5. This section draws on Timur Kuran, *The Long Divergence: How Islamic Law Held Back the Middle East* (Princeton, 2011). For an authoritative treatment of the relation between Protestantism and capitalism see Philip Benedict, *Christ's Churches Purely Reformed: A Social History of Calvinism* (New Haven, 2002), pp 533–46. Benedict largely rejects the Weberian causal connection between Calvinism and capitalism in favour of an emphasis on historical contingencies.

Bibliography

This represents only a selection of books likely to be most useful to students and general readers wishing to find out more about the most important events and themes of eighteenth-century world Christianity.

General histories

Angold, M. (ed), *The Cambridge History of Christianity*, vol. 5, *Eastern Christianity* (Cambridge, 2006)

Bayly, C.A., *The Birth of the Modern World 1780–1914* (Oxford, 2004)

Bayón, D. and Bury, J.B. (eds), *The Cambridge History of Latin America*, vol. II (Cambridge, 1984)

Brown, S.J. and Tackett, T. (eds), *The Cambridge History of Christianity*, vol. VII, *Enlightenment, Reawakening and Revolution* (Cambridge, 2006)

Buisseret, D., *The Mapmaker's Quest: Depicting New Worlds in Renaissance Europe* (Oxford, 2003)

Burke, P., *What is Cultural History?* (Cambridge, 2004)

Chadwick, H. and Evans, G.R. (eds), *Atlas of the Christian Church* (Oxford, 1987)

Hastings, A. (ed), *A World History of Christianity* (London, 1999)

Jenkins, P., *The Lost History of Christianity* (New York, 2008)

Kidd, C., *The Forging of Races: Race and Scripture in the Protestant Atlantic World, 1600–2000* (Cambridge, 2006)

MacCulloch, D., *A History of Christianity: The First Three Thousand Years* (London, 2009)

McManners, J. (ed), *The Oxford Illustrated History of Christianity* (Oxford, 1990)

Marshall, P.J. (ed), *The Oxford History of the British Empire: The Eighteenth Century* (Oxford, 1998)

___ and Williams, Glyndwr, *The Great Map of Mankind: British Perceptions of the World in the Age of Enlightenment* (London, 1982)

Pagden, Anthony, *European Encounters with the New World* (New Haven, 1993)

Pestana, C.G., *Protestant Empire: Religion and the Making of the British Atlantic World* (Philadelphia, 2009)

Salomon, F. and Schwartz, S.B. (eds), *The Cambridge History of the Native Peoples of the Americas*, vol. III, *South America, part 2* (Cambridge, 1999)

Europe

Aston, N., *Christianity and Revolutionary Europe c.1750–1830* (Cambridge, 2002)

___, *The French Revolution, 1789–1804: Authority, Liberty, and the Search for Stability* (London, 2004)

___, *Art and Religion in Eighteenth-Century Europe* (London, 2009)

Bergin, J., *Church, Society and Religious Change in France, 1580–1730* (New Haven, 2009)

Bradley, J.E. and Van Kley, D.K. (eds), *Religion and Politics in Enlightenment Europe* (Notre Dame, IN, 2001)

Brown, C.G., *Religion and Society in Scotland since 1707* (Edinburgh, 1997)

Clark, J.C.D., *English Society 1660–1832* (Cambridge, 2000)

Connolly, S.J., *Religion, Law and Power: The Making of Protestant Ireland 1660–1760* (Oxford, 1992)

Corish, P.J., *The Irish Catholic Experience: A Historical Survey* (Dublin, 1985)

Davis, N.Z., *Women on the Margins: Three Seventeenth-Century Lives* (Cambridge, MA, 1995)

Doyle, W., *The Old European Order 1660–1800* (Oxford, 1992)

Dixon, C.S., Freist, D. and Greengrass, M. (eds), *Living with Religious Diversity in Early-Modern Europe* (Farnham, Surrey, 2009)

Hempton, D., *Religion and Political Culture in Britain and Ireland: From the Glorious Revolution to the Decline of Empire* (Cambridge, 1996)

Hufton, O., *Europe: Privilege and Protest 1730–1789* (London, 1980)

Kaplan, B.J., *Divided by Faith: Religious Conflict and the Practice of Toleration in Early Modern Europe* (Cambridge, MA, 2007)

Kloczowski, J., *A History of Polish Christianity* (Cambridge, 2000)

McManners, J., *Church and Society in Eighteenth Century France*, vol. 1, *The Clerical Establishment and its Ramifications* (Oxford, 1998)

___, *Church and Society in Eighteenth-Century France*, vol. 2, *The Religion of the People and the Politics of Religion* (Oxford, 1998)

Van Kley, D.K., *The Religious Origins of the French Revolution: From Calvin to the Civil Constitution, 1560–1791* (New Haven, 1996)

Ward, W.R., *Christianity under the Ancien Régime, 1648–1789* (Cambridge, 1999)

Zagorin, P., *How the Idea of Religious Toleration Came to the West* (Princeton, 2003)

North America

Albanese, C.L., *A Republic of Mind and Spirit: A Cultural History of American Metaphysical Religion* (New Haven, 2007)

Anderson, E., *The Betrayal of Faith: The Tragic Journey of a Colonial Native Convert* (Cambridge, MA, 2007)

Axtell, J., *Natives and Newcomers: The Cultural Origins of North America* (New York, 2001)

Bloch, R.H., *Visionary Republic: American Thought, 1756–1800* (Cambridge, 1985)

Carroll, B.E., *The Routledge Historical Atlas of Religion in America* (New York, 2000)

Greer, A., *Mohawk Saint: Catherine Tekakwitha and the Jesuits* (New York, 2005)

Gutiérrez, R.A., *When Jesus Came, the Corn Mothers Went Away: Marriage, Sexuality, and Power in New Mexico, 1500–1846* (Stanford, 1991)

Holifield, E.B., *Theology in America: Christian Thought from the Age of the Puritans to the Civil War* (New Haven, 2003)

Kidd, T.S., *The Great Awakening: The Roots of Evangelical Christianity in Colonial America* (New Haven, 2007)

___, *God of Liberty: A Religious History of the American Revolution* (New York, 2010)

Lambert, F., *The Founding Fathers and the Place of Religion in America* (Princeton, 2003)

Mahaffey, J.D., *Preaching Politics: The Religious Rhetoric of George Whitefield and the Founding of a New Nation* (Waco, TX, 2007)

Marsden, G., *A Short Life of Jonathan Edwards* (Grand Rapids, MI, 2008)

Noll, M.A., *America's God* (New York, 2002)

Rawlyk, G.A., *The Canada Fire: Radical Evangelicalism in British North America 1775–1812* (Kingston and Montreal, 1994)

Richter, D.K., *Facing East from Indian Country: A Native History of Early America*, (Cambridge, MA, 2001)

Sensbach, J.F., *Rebecca's Revival: Creating Black Christianity in the Atlantic World* (Cambridge, MA, 2005)

South America

Bailey, G.A., *Art of Colonial America* (New York, 2005)

Boxer, C.R., *The Church Militant and Iberian Expansion 1440–1770* (Baltimore, 1978)

Caraman, P., *The Lost Paradise: The Jesuit Republic in South America* (London, 1975)

Donahue-Wallace, K., *Art and Architecture of Viceregal Latin America, 1521–1821* (Albuquerque, NM, 2008)

Ganson, B.A., *The Guaraní under Spanish Rule in the Río de la Plata* (Stanford, CA, 2003)

González, O.E. and González, J.L., *Christianity in Latin America: A History* (Cambridge, 2008)

Kubler, G. and Soria, M., *Art and Architecture in Spain and Portugal and Their American Dominions, 1500 to 1800* (Baltimore, 1969)

Mills, K., *Idolatry and its Enemies: Colonial Andean Religion and Extirpation* (Princeton, 1997)

Africa

Hastings, A., *The Church in Africa 1450–1950* (Oxford, 1994)

Sanneh, L., *Abolitionists Abroad: American Blacks and the Making of Modern West*

Africa (Cambridge, MA, 1999)

Thornton, J.K., *The Kongolese Saint Anthony: Don Beatriz Kimpa Vita and the Antonian Movement, 1684–1706* (Cambridge, 1998)

Asia

Bays, D.H. (ed), *Christianity in China: From the Eighteenth Century to the Present* (Stanford, CA, 1996)

Clooney, F.X., *Fr. Bouchet's India: An 18th Century Jesuit's Encounter with Hinduism* (Chennai, 2005)

Frykenberg, R.E., *Christianity in India: From Beginnings to the Present* (Oxford, 2008)

Hudson, D.D., *Protestant Origins in India: Tamil Evangelical Christians, 1706–1835* (Grand Rapids, MI, 2000)

Moffett, S.H., *A History of Christianity in Asia*, vol. II, *1500–1900* (New York, 2005)

Mungello, D.E. (ed), *The Chinese Rites Controversy: Its History and Meaning* (Nettetal, 1994)

___, *The Great Encounter of China and the West, 1500–1800*, 3rd ed. (Lanham, MD, 2009)

Ross, A.C., *A Vision Betrayed: The Jesuits in Japan and China, 1542, 1742* (New York, 1994)

Roman Catholicism

Châtellier, L., *The Europe of the Devout: The Catholic Reformation and the Formation of a New Society* (Cambridge, 1987)

Hsia, R.P.C., *The World of Catholic Renewal, 1540–1770* (Cambridge, 1999)

O'Malley, J.W., Bailey, G.A., Harris, S.J. and Kennedy, T.F. (eds), *The Jesuits II: Cultures, Sciences, and the Arts, 1540–1773* (Toronto, 2006)

Protestantism

Benedict, P., *Christ's Churches Purely Reformed: A Social History of Calvinism* (New Haven, 2002)

Dixon, C.S., *Protestants: A History from Wittenberg to Pennsylvania, 1517–1740* (Chichester, 2010)

Erb, P.C. (ed), *Pietists: Selected Writings* (London, 1983)

Heitzenrater, R.P., *Wesley and the People Called Methodists* (Nashville, 1995)

Hempton, D., *Methodism: Empire of the Spirit* (New Haven, 2005)

Hindmarsh, D.B., *The Evangelical Conversion Narrative: Spiritual Autobiography in Early Modern England* (Oxford, 2005)

Lindberg, C. (ed), *The Pietist Theologians* (Oxford, 2005)

Mack, P., *Heart Religion in the British Enlightenment: Gender and Emotion in Early Methodism* (Cambridge, 2008)

Noll, M.A., *The Rise of Evangelicalism: The Age of Edwards, Whitefield and the Wesleys* (Leicester, 2004)

___, Bebbington, D.W. and Rawlyk, G.A. (eds), *Evangelicalism: Comparative Studies of Popular Protestantism in North America, the British Isles, and Beyond, 1700–1990* (New York, 1994)

Strom, J., Lehmann, H. and Van Horn Melton, J. (eds), *Pietism in Germany and North America 1680–1820* (Farnham, Surrey, 2009)

Ward, W.R., *The Protestant Evangelical Awakening* (Cambridge, 1992)

___, *Early Evangelicalism: A Global Intellectual History, 1670–1789* (Cambridge, 2006)

Orthodoxy

Binns, J., *An Introduction to the Christian Orthodox Churches* (Cambridge, 2002)

Freeze, G.L., *The Russian Levites: Parish Clergy in the Eighteenth Century* (Cambridge, MA, 1977)

Geraci, R.P. and Khodarkovsky, M. (eds), *Of Religion and Empire: Missions, Conversion, and Tolerance in Tsarist Russia* (Ithaca, NY, 2001)

Jelavich, B., *History of the Balkans: Eighteenth and Nineteenth Centuries* (Cambridge, 1983)

McGuckin, J.A., *The Orthodox Church: An Introduction to its History, Doctrine, and Spiritual Culture* (Oxford, 2008)

O'Mahoney, A. and Loosley, E. (eds), *Eastern Christianities in the Modern Middle East* (New York, 2010)

Runciman, S., *The Great Church in Captivity* (London, 1968)

Missions

Carey, W., *An Enquiry into the Obligations of Christians, to Use Means for the Conversion of the Heathen. In which the Religious State of the Different Nations of the World, the Success of Former Undertakings, and the Practicability of Further Undertakings, are Considered* (Leicester, 1792)

Cox, J., *The British Missionary Enterprise since 1700* (New York, 2008)

De Jong, J.A., *As the Waters Cover the Sea: Millennial Expectations in the Rise of Anglo-American Missions 1640–1810* (Kampen, 1970)

Hawley, J. (ed), *Historicizing Christian Encounters with the Other* (London, 1998)

Mason, J.C.S., *The Moravian Church and the Missionary Awakening in England 1760–1800* (London, 2001)

Neill, S., *A History of Christian Missions* (New York, 1986)

Porter, A., *Religion Versus Empire? British Protestant Missionaries and Overseas Expansion, 1700–1914* (Manchester, 2004)

Robert, D.L., *Converting Colonialism: Visions and Realities in Missions History, 1706–1914* (Grand Rapids, MI, 2008)

___, *Christian Mission: How Christianity Became a World Religion* (Chichester, 2009)

Sanneh, L., *Disciples of All Nations: Pillars of World Christianity* (Oxford, 2008)

Stanley, B., *The History of the Baptist Missionary Society, 1792–1992* (Edinburgh, 1992)

Vickers, J.A. (ed), *The Journals of Dr. Thomas Coke* (Nashville, 2005)
Walls, A.F., *The Missionary Movement in Christian History* (New York, 1996)
___, *The Cross-Cultural Process in Christian History* (New York, 2002)

The Enlightenment

Grell, O.P. and Porter, R. (eds), *Toleration in Enlightenment Europe* (Cambridge, 2000)
Haakonssen, K. (ed), *Enlightenment and Religion: Rational Dissent in Eighteenth-Century Britain* (Cambridge, 1996)
Israel, J.I., *Radical Enlightenment: Philosophy and the Making of Modernity 1650–1750* (Oxford, 2001)
Jacob, M.C., *The Radical Enlightenment: Pantheists, Freemasons and Republicans* (London, 1981)
Outram, Dorinda, *The Enlightenment* (Cambridge, 1995)
Porter, R., *Enlightenment: Britain and the Creation of the Modern World* (London, 2000)
___ (ed), *The Cambridge History of Science*, vol. 4, *Eighteenth-Century Science* (Cambridge, 2008)
Reill, P.H., *Vitalizing Nature in the Enlightenment* (Berkeley, 2005)
Sher, R.B., *Church and University in the Scottish Enlightenment* (Princeton, 1985)
Taylor, C., *A Secular Age* (Cambridge, MA, 2007)

Slavery and anti-slavery

Anstey, R., *The Atlantic Slave Trade and British Abolition 1760–1810* (Atlantic Highlands, NJ, 1975)
Brown, C.L., *Moral Capital: Foundations of Antislavery* (Chapel Hill, 2006)
Byrd, A.X., *Captives and Voyagers: Black Migrants across the Eighteenth-Century British Atlantic World* (Baton Rouge, 2008)
Davis, D.B., *The Problem of Slavery in Western Culture* (New York, 1966)
___, *Slavery and Human Progress* (New York, 1984)
___, *Inhuman Bondage: The Rise and Fall of Slavery in the New World* (New York, 2006)

Index

'As all good general histories must, this volume offers a clear structure, expertly chosen details, authoritative judgments, and forcefully direct prose. Yet David Hempton's treatment of "the long eighteenth century" in the history of Christianity goes well beyond the usual requirements for a successful introduction. It is unusually sensitive to the most attractive as well as the most blameworthy aspects of its story; it blends large-scale political and imperial tectonics with telling biographical miniatures; it documents the deeds of women as well as men, the lowly as well as the exalted; and it exploits effortlessly a great range of scholarship. But above all, the book successfully combines fresh treatment of better-known European and American histories with probably the best general overview now available for the expansion of Christianity during the early-modern period from the Western to the non-Western world. In describing the complex transformations of western Christendom, Hempton is as illuminating as masters of this history like Hugh McLeod; in accounting for the even more complicated developments of the worldwide story — from central Russia to Sierra Leone, from Alaska to the Congo, from China to Brazil — he joins the rarefied company of Dana Robert, Andrew Walls, and only a few others. The result of this unusually adept combination is a terrific addition to I.B.Tauris' outstanding general series.'

Mark A. Noll, Francis A. McAnaney Professor of History, University of Notre Dame

'The social history of eighteenth-century Christianity is typically framed by pietism, Enlightenment, and revolution. David Hempton broadens and deepens the classic narrative by foregrounding the expansion of Christianity as a worldwide movement, including such themes as missions, European encounters with the "other", slavery, and Orthodoxy. He transforms old and new interpretations into an exciting and readable overview that makes sense in our contemporary global context. This fine book will remain an essential introduction to the subject for years to come.'

Dana L. Robert, Truman Collins Professor of World Christianity and History of Mission, Boston University